BENGAL DISTRICT GAZETTEERS

GAYA

BENGAL DISTRICT GAZETTEERS

Burdwan/ **J.C.K. Paterson**
Darjeeling/ **L.S.S. O'Malley**
Howrah/ **L.S.S. O'Malley**
Hooghly/ **L.S.S. O'Malley**
Santal Parganas/ **L.S.S. O'Malley**
Sambalpur/ **L.S.S. O'Malley**
Puri/ **L.S.S. O'Malley**
Gaya/ **L.S.S. O'Malley**

BIHAR AND ORISSA DISTRICT GAZETTEERS

Patna/ **L.S.S. O'Malley**
Shahabad/ **L.S.S. O'Malley**
Monghyr/ **L.S.S. O'Malley**
Saran/ **L.S.S. O'Malley**

BENGAL DISTRICT GAZETTEERS

GAYA

BY

L.S.S. O'MALLEY
Indian Civil Service

LOGOS PRESS
New Delhi-110 002

ISBN : 81-7268-137-2

First Published 1906

Reprinted 2007

Printed and Published by

LOGOS PRESS

Building No. 4788-90, Street No. 23, Ansari Road, Darya Ganj,
New Delhi-110 002 (India)

Phone : 23272187

PREFACE.

I desire to acknowledge my deep obligation to Mr. C. E. A. W. Oldham, I.C.S., Director of Agriculture, Bengal, and formerly Collector of Gaya, for the great assistance he has given in the preparation of this volume. I am indebted to him for placing at my disposal a collection of papers relating to Gaya, for revising the proofs, and for many valuable suggestions.

L. S. S. O'M.

PLAN OF CONTENTS.

TABLE OF CONTENTS.

CHAPTER I.

PHYSICAL ASPECTS.

CHAPTER II.

HISTORY.

CHAPTER III.

BUDDHA AND BODH GAYA.

CHAPTER IV.

THE GAYA PILGRIMAGE.

CHAPTER V.

POPULAR RELIGION.

CHAPTER VI.

THE PEOPLE.

CHAPTER VII.

PUBLIC HEALTH.

CHAPTER VIII.

AGRICULTURE.

CHAPTER IX.

NATURAL CALAMITIES.

CHAPTER X.

IRRIGATION.

CHAPTER XI.

SYSTEMS OF RENT PAYMENT.

CHAPTER XII.

RENTS, WAGES AND PRICES.

CHAPTER XIII.

OCCUPATIONS, MANUFACTURES AND TRADE.

CHAPTER XIV.

MEANS OF COMMUNICATION.

CHAPTER XV.

LAND REVENUE ADMINISTRATION.

CHAPTER XVI.

GENERAL ADMINISTRATION.

CHAPTER XVII.

LOCAL SELF-GOVERNMENT.

CHAPTER XVIII.

EDUCATION.

CHAPTER XIX.

GAZETTEER.

GAZETTEER

OF THE

GAYA DISTRICT.

CHAPTER I.

PHYSICAL ASPECTS.

THE district of Gayā, which forms the most southerly portion of the Patna Division, is situated between 24° 17′ and 25° 19′ north latitude and 84° 0′ and 86° 3′ east longitude. It extends over 4,712 square miles, and is bounded on the north by the Patna district, on the east by Monghyr and Hazāribāgh, on the south by the latter district and Palāmau, and on the west by Shāhābād, from which it is separated by the river Son. The chief town is Gayā, situated in 24° 49′ N. and 85° 1′ E., which is also the administrative head-quarters. GENERAL DESCRIPTION. Boundaries

The district includes the greater part of what was known as the district of Bihār until the year 1865, the tract to the south forming part of the district of Rāmgarh. When the Bihār subdivision was transferred to the Patna district in that year, it was felt that it was inappropriate that the district should be called Bihār any longer, and it was given the designation of Gayā from the name of its chief town. According to the Bhāgavata Purāna, Gayā was the name of a king who dwelt in the town in the Tretā-Yuga or silver age; but the more generally accepted legend is that contained in the Vāyu Purāna, according to which Gayā was the name of an Asura or demon of giant size, who by long and austere penance and devotion became so pure and holy that all who saw or touched him were admitted into heaven. Yama, the lord of hell, jealous of this intrusion on his prerogative, appealed to the gods, pleading that his post was becoming a sinecure. The gods conferred in council, and then visited Gayā, and persuaded the demon to grant his body as a place of sacrifice. To this Gayā assented, and lay down with his head resting where the old city of Gayā Origin of name.

now is. Yama then placed a sacred rock (Dharmasilā) on his head, but this was not sufficient to keep the monster quiet, and Brahmā sought Vishnu's aid. Then Vishnu in various forms, as well as many other gods, sat upon the demon to render him motionless, but to no effect. At length Vishnu plied his mighty mace, and quieted the monster for ever, but not until Gayā had obtained a promise that the ground covered by his body, some 10 miles in extent, should be the holiest spot on earth; that the gods should rest there, the locality being known as the Gayā-Kshetra; and that the ancestors of all who offered funeral ceremonies there should be translated straight to heaven.

General configuration.

Gayā is bounded on the south and south-east by the high lands of the Chotā Nāgpur plateau, from which numerous spurs project into it. Thence a wide alluvial plain stretches away to the north, broken here and there by groups and low ranges of hills or isolated peaks springing abruptly from the level country at their feet. These gradually disappear the further north one goes, and the Jahānābād subdivision is almost entirely a level plain. The whole of this tract is seamed by a number of rivers, which debouch from the southern hills and flow, in more or less parallel courses, towards the Ganges. During the rains they are subject to violent floods; and as the general slope of the country northwards is comparatively rapid, they flow swiftly when in flood, but in the dry season they dwindle into trickling streams or lines of pools in the midst of long expanses of sand.

Natural divisions.

The district is accordingly divided into two distinct divisions with different physical features. To the south is a region of broken undulating country merging into long ranges of hills, with a wide belt of brushwood jungle at their base. Much of this tract is high and barren, and incapable of cultivation; it is unprotected by irrigation; the soil yields poor and precarious crops, and the population is sparse. The greater part of the district, however, consists of the flat alluvial plain mentioned above, which comprises the whole of the Jahānābād subdivision and the northern portion of the head-quarters, Aurangābād and Nawāda subdivisions. This tract is protected from drought by a wonderful system of indigenous irrigation; it is comparatively densely populated; and, compared with the southern part of the district, it is a region of great fertility. The whole history of Gayā has been determined by the widely different characteristics of these two divisions. The northern portion, which is highly cultivated and extensively irrigated, was in very early times a civilized country and the home of Aryan races; it was part of Magadha, the nucleus of the first great empire in India and the centre of

Buddhism for many centuries; and in later years it was the arena of the conflicts of contending armies. The south was long the shelter of aboriginal tribes, and did not yield to the advance of civilization till a late period in the history of the district; it was untouched by Buddhism; it is still thinly peopled, and many of its hill and jungle fastnesses are even now untilled.

HILL SYSTEM. The whole of the southern edge of the district is cut up by a number of ridges and spurs projecting from the plateau of Chotā Nāgpur, which in a few places attain an altitude of nearly 1,800 feet above sea-level. Beyond these again semi-isolated ranges, outliers from the flanks of the plateau, stand out from the plains, and still further north separate ridges and wholly isolated rocky hills crop up here and there. The most remarkable of these long low outlying ranges is the Ganjās, Bhindās and Jethian range, which extends from near Bodh-Gayā north-eastwards for a distance of 40 miles with only two breaks, and rises at the Handia Hill to a height of 1,472 feet. The other ranges seldom exceed 1,000 feet, and few of the isolated peaks are of any great height, the highest being the Maher Hill, which rises to a height of 1,612 feet. In the southern range, however, the hills attain a greater altitude, the Durvāsārhi and Mahābar Hills in the south of the Nawāda subdivision being respectively 2,202 and 1,832 feet above sea-level: the former is the highest hill in the district. Of the other hills, the most noticeable are the Barābar Hills, lying partly in the head-quarters and partly in the Jahānābād subdivision; the Hasrā, Pahrā and Chirkī Hills, the Brahmajuni Hill, which rises some 400 feet above Gayā town, the precipitous peak of Kauwādol, and Lohābar Hill (1,799 feet) in the head-quarters subdivision; the Powai, Dugul and Pachār Hills in the Aurangābād subdivision; and Sringirikh in the Nawāda subdivision.

The appearance of the different hills furnishes some striking contrasts. The hills on the south present the aspect of a series of a gentle undulations and spurs gradually rising up into the plateau of Chotā Nāgpur behind. They are completely covered with a soft clothing of vegetation, chiefly of *sāl* (*Shorea robusta*), *kend* (*Diospyros melanoxylon*), and other trees. On the hills scattered over the remainder of the district, the vegetation has gradually been cut down or lost owing to the erosion of the clay, and the rocks and the boulders are in many cases left completely bare. The effect is almost equally picturesque, as the hills stand out in rugged bareness. They are strangely different in colour and form. Some, like the Barābar Hills, are composed of giant black boulders piled one above the other, leaving great caverns beneath; others, like Maher, are of red rock, much weathered, with rounded sides and easy slopes; and others again, like the Jethian range, have steep rocky sides mounting to a knife-like ridge at the summit.

Scenery. The view from the Brahmajuni Hill at Gayā presents a striking picture of a lowland country dotted with hills. On a clear day in the rains the eye travels past the rugged ravines and rocks overlooking Gayā to a country green with crops and groves of palm-trees, with hills rising on all sides from the level plain. To the north the temple-crowned hill of Rāmsilā stands out in the near foreground, overlooking the waters of the Phalgu, and beyond it is the high crag of Pretsilā; in the distance the outline of the Barābar Hills can be seen, and close by them the solitary peak of Kauwādol. To the south-east is a long range of red rock stretching away to the north-east and sinking to the plain near Bodh Gayā, the shrine at which can be seen rising above the surrounding palm-trees; while Maher looms large in the further distance. To the west the landscape shows the imposing contours of the Pahrā Hill, and beyond it one detached hill succeeding another; and to the south a long wall of hills bounds the horizon so far as the eye can see.

Water-falls. Among these hills are several picturesque waterfalls, the most beautiful of which are the falls of the Mohāna and the waterfall at Kakolat in the long ridge running from east to west 10 miles south of Nawāda. The falls of the Mohāna are just beyond the border of the district, but can easily be reached from Kāhudāg; the first at Tamāsin are situated at the head of a deep valley, where the river plunges abruptly down a high steep face of black rock into a shady pool below, and then dashes down a gloomy gorge of strangely contorted rock; the lower falls at Hariakhāl present a scene of more placid beauty, as here the river, issuing through a picturesque glen, glides down a sloping slide of red rock into a still, large pool surrounded by high wooded banks. At Kakolat a hill torrent tumbles down a long series of cascades, buried in thick woods and extending far up the side of the hill till it makes a final leap over a precipice some 90 feet high near the foot of the crag, and then hurries down over a rock-strewn bed to the plains below.

RIVER SYSTEM. With a few exceptions, the rivers of Gayā are hill streams, taking their rise in the highlands of the Chotā Nāgpur plateau and flowing across the district from south to north in more or less parallel courses. To the west is the Son, forming the boundary of the district, and then come the Pūnpūn, Adrī, Madār, Dhāwā, Morhar, Jamunā, Phalgu, Paimār, Dhādhar, Tilaiyā, Dhanārjī and Sakrī. The only rivers which reach the Ganges are the Son and the Pūnpūn, the latter of which, after leaving Gayā, passes through the district of Patna and falls into the Ganges a few miles below Patna city. The others are mostly used up in the network of *pains* or artificial water-channels used for purposes of irrigation, expending themselves before joining the Ganges, or mingling in a huge *jhīl* in the Bārh subdivision of the Patna district. The Pūnpūn, Dhāwā, Jamunā, and Paimār rise below the hills and have deep clayey beds, but most of the others have beds of pure sand and low sloping banks, though in the hilly portion of their course their beds are rocky and their banks are steep and abrupt. Torrents during the rains, they carry down with them quantities of gravel and fine sand which they deposit lower down; and their beds being thus raised, they are well adapted for irrigation. This system of irrigation is perpetually modifying their courses, and the result is that many of the channels given in Rennell's map of Bengal in the 18th century cannot now be traced. The sudden rise and fall of these rivers is remarkable. After heavy rain in the hills, they become swollen torrents, but they fall as rapidly as they rise and become fordable again within a few hours. Their beds are so sandy and the current is so rapid that within a few months, sometimes within a few weeks, after the cessation of the rains, they are almost dry, and for the rest of the year they are reduced to tiny rivulets winding in tortuous courses over wide sandy beds. The most turbulent of these rivers is the Sakrī, but they are all liable to violent floods, and in spite of their great breadth occasionally overflow their banks. A short account of the most important of these rivers is given below.

The Son

The principal river is the Son, which rises, near the sources of the Narbadā and Mahānadī, on the elevated plateau of Central India. After a course of 325 miles through a high rocky tract, it debouches upon the Gangetic valley opposite Akbarpur in Shāhābād. It then runs a straight course of 100 miles through the plains of South Bihār, and finally joins the Ganges 10 miles north of Maner between Arrah and Dinapore. The Son nowhere enters the district, but bounds its whole length to the west. It first touches on Gayā opposite Akbarpur about 400 feet above the sea, and then running south, passes Bārun, Dāūdnagar and Arwal, and after that leaves the district. At Bārun it is crossed by the massive masonry dam which supplies a head for the Son Canals, and by the great bridge over which runs the Mughalsarai-Gayā section of the East Indian Railway.

During this portion of its course it attains a great width, which generally exceeds 2 miles and in places amounts to 3 miles; and another peculiarity of these lower reaches is the height of the eastern bank, where the strong westerly winds which prevail during the hot weather heap up the sand from the river-bed to a height of 12 or 14 feet above the level of the country, covering the bank with sandy barren dunes, and forming a natural embankment for many miles. But the most noticeable features of its course through the plains are its meagre stream of water at ordinary times as compared with the enormous breadth of the river-bed, its vast size, and its paroxysmal violence at periods of flood. Seen in the dry season, about April or May, the bed presents a wide stretch of drifting sand with an insignificant stream of water, barely 100 yards wide, meandering from bank to bank, and fordable in most places. But in the rainy season, and specially after a storm has burst on the plateau of Central India, the river presents an extraordinary contrast. It drains a hill area of 21,300 square miles, *i.e.*, a tract more than four times as extensive as the district of Gayā; the entire rainfall of this enormous catchment basin requires to find an outlet by this channel; and after heavy rain the river rises with incredible rapidity. The channel frequently proves unable to carry off the total flood discharge, amounting to 830,000 cubic feet per second, and the flood waters rush down so violently as to spill over its broad bed, and occasionally cause disastrous inundations in the low-lying plains on either side. These heavy floods are however of short duration, hardly ever lasting more than four days, after which the river rapidly sinks to its usual level.

The Son receives no tributaries of any importance from the point where it enters the district up to Bārun, where its waters are distributed east to the Gayā and Patna districts, and west to Shāhābād through the great irrigation system of the Son Canals; and between Bārun and its junction with the Ganges, the drainage sets away from it, so that no stream can join it north of that place. Its bed consists almost entirely of sand; but in a few parts clay is found and cultivated, and nodular limestone is also obtained in several places. Below the junction of the Koel a species of small pebbles or agates is found, many of which are ornamental and take a good polish; most of them consist of silica, both opaque and diaphanous, of a reddish or dark green tinge. In the Ain-i-Akbarī the Son is said to have the power of petrifying substances thrown into it, and to contain many *sāligrām* stones.

During the dry season there are many fords, but ferry boats generally ply for eight months in the year. The fall of the river-bed below Akbarpur varies only from 1·75 to 2·80 feet a mile, but at several places above Bārun rocks and rapids effectually stop river traffic. In its lower reaches also navigation is intermittent and of little commercial importance. In the rainy season native boats of large tonnage occasionally proceed for a short distance up-stream under favourable circumstances of wind and flood; but navigation is rendered dangerous by the extraordinary violence of the floods, and during the rest of the year is impossible for any but small boats owing to the small depth of water. The principal traffic is in bamboos and timber. The former are floated down, bound into rafts consisting of 10,000 or more lashed together—a tedious process in the dry weather, as they are constantly grounding, and the many windings of the stream render their progress extremely slow.

The Son possesses historical interest as being probably identical with the Erannoboas, which is mentioned by Megasthenes as "the third river in all India and inferior to none but the Indus and Ganges, into the latter of which it discharges its waters." Erannoboas appears a manifest corruption of the Sanskrit *Hiranyabāhu* or golden-armed, a name formerly given to the river and apparently derived, like the name Son (the river of gold), from the golden colour of the sand it brings down in flood. It formerly flowed far to the east and joined the Ganges near Fatwā in Patna district; and the ancient town of Pālibothrā or Pātaliputra (corresponding to the modern Patna) was situated at its confluence with the Ganges.

The old course* of the river may still be traced across the district in a sandy depression forming a series of *jhīls* in the rainy season. From Dāūdnagar it swept round to the north-east as far as Sonbhadr on the river Pūnpūn. From this place it followed the present course of the Pūnpūn, being joined by the Morhar about 4 miles to the west of Jahānābād, and then flowed to the north, finally joining the Ganges at Fatwā. It has gradually receded westwards, and made fresh channels for itself. In some old documents of the Delhi Empire, Nadī, a village in the Arwal thāna on the edge of one of these channels, which is now 10 miles from the river, is described as Nadī on the bank of the Son; and traces of old courses were noticed by the officers engaged in the construction of the Patna-Gayā canal, one of which was used in laying out its line. Old river-beds have also been found between Bankipore and Dinapore, and Mr. Twining, who was Collector of Shāhābād in 1801—04, mentions that in his time the river broke through the eastern bank in high flood and, flowing along what was recognized as its old channel, inundated the cantonment of Dinapore.

---

* For a more detailed account of the old course of the Son, *see* Reports Arch. Surv. India, vol. viii, pp. 6—9.

The Pūnpūn.

To the east of the Son the next river is the Pūnpūn, which rises in the extreme south of the district, and flows towards the Ganges in a north-easterly course, more or less parallel to that of Son. It is the only river running through the district which retains water throughout the year, and even in the dry season there is always some stream. Its water is extensively used by the adjacent villages for irrigation, and it is dammed at several places for this purpose, the principal *bāndh* or dam being at Kusreh in the Jahānābād subdivision, where it gives a head of water sufficient to irrigate a number of villages on its western bank.

The Pūnpūn receives many small feeders on its right bank, of which the Dhāwā, Batāne and Madār are the chief. These streams dry up during the hot weather; and even when full, the greater part of their water never reaches the Pūnpūn, being dispersed over the fields by artificial channels. Other tributaries of the Pūnpūn do not join it in this district. The principal of these is the Morhar, which, coming from the south, flows northwards past the town of Sherghāti, where the Grand Trunk Road is carried over it on two fine bridges spanning the two arms into which it here divides. After passing Tekāri it bifurcates; one branch taking a northerly direction to the district of Patna, while the easternmost, called the Dardhā, flows by Jahānābād, and during the rainy season floods a large tract of country round that place. Some high land to the north forces the excess of water to disperse itself over this part of the district, and it only reaches the Pūnpūn during high flood. The next stream, the Jamunā, flows from the south, between Gayā and Tekāri; then turns east, passing the Patna-Gayā Road at Makhdumpur, and flows on beyond Tehta, when it twists back and joins the Dardhā at Jahānābād.

The Pūnpūn is a sacred river, and it is the duty of the pilgrim to Gayā to shave his head on its bank and bathe in its waters on his way to the holy city.

The Phalgu.

The Phalgu, flowing north and south, intersects the district. It is formed by the junction, some 2 miles below Bodh Gayā, of the Nilājan and the Mohāna—two large hill streams, each of which is over 300 yards wide. The united stream flows on to the north past the town of Gayā, where it attains a breadth of over 900 yards. The Phalgu here impinges on a high rocky bank, on the steep sides of which are many *ghāts* leading down to the river-bed, while high above are the Vishnupad temple, with many minor shrines, and the houses of the Gayāwāls. It then runs in a north-easterly direction for about 17 miles, and opposite the Barābar Hills it again takes the name of Mohāna, and divides into two branches, which eventually flow into a branch of the Pūnpūn.

The Phalgu, like the confluent streams of the Mohāna and Nilājan, is subject to high floods; but of all three rivers the Mohāna is perhaps the most turbulent. The stone causeway by which it is crossed at Dobhī, which itself replaced a bridge destroyed during a heavy flood, has several times been wrecked; and further north the river has frequently overflowed its banks. When in high flood the Phalgu reaches up to the flooring of the wooden bridge at Gayā, and traffic has occasionally to be suspended; but at other seasons of the year it is nearly dry, and dwindles to an insignificant stream wandering through a wide expanse of sand dotted here and there with stagnant pools. A great part of the water is however diverted for the purpose of irrigation, and is distributed among the fields by a series of irrigation channels, the most important of which is the Jamuāma *pain*, opposite the Barābar Hills, which has converted the whole of the Jamuāma Mahāl into rich paddy-fields.

The portion of its course flowing by Gayā is sacred to the Hindus; it is the first holy site visited by the pilgrim, and here his first offerings must be made for the souls of his ancestors. According to the Gayā Mahātmya, the Phalgu is the embodiment of Vishnu himself. One tradition states that it formerly flowed with milk, and another states that Sīta offered *pinda* on its banks to Dasaratha, the father of Rāma. The story runs that the spirit of Dasaratha, warned to make haste ere the gates of heaven were closed, appeared to Sīta in the absence of Rāma and begged her to offer *pindas* on his behalf. Having no rice, she made a *pinda* of sand; and in order to justify her doing this instead of Rāma, she invoked the Phalgu, a Brāhman, a *tulsī* plant and a banyan-tree as witnesses that the rite had been duly performed. The banyan-tree alone was true to the trust; and as a punishment for its faithlessness, the Phalgu river was cursed and doomed to flow in a desert of arid sand.

To the east of the Phalgu the district is drained by a number of parallel rivers, of which the largest are the Dhādhar, Tilaiyā, Dhanārjī, Khurī and Sakrī. These five rivers have all broad sandy beds, the width of the four first named, where they are crossed by the Gayā-Nawāda Road, being 1,050, 425, 384 and 940 feet respectively. They are extensively used for irrigation, and all unite, under the name of Panchana, near Giriak in the Bihār subdivision.

GEOLOGY.* The greater part of the district is occupied by the Gangetic alluvium, but older rocks rise above its level, chiefly in the south

* The account of the Geology of Gayā was supplied by Mr. E. Vredenburg, Deputy Superintendent, Geological Survey of India.

and east. These rocks are composed for the most part of a foliated gneiss, consisting of a great variety of crystalline rocks forming parallel bands and known in the geological nomenclature of India as the Bengal gneiss, a subdivision of the Archæan system which contains the oldest rocks of the earth's crust. Scattered at intervals amidst the Bengal gneiss, there are in the east of the district several outcrops of another very ancient series, resembling that described in Southern India under the name of Dhārwār schists, and constituting another subdivision of the Archæan system. Owing to the predominance of massive beds of quartzite, these beds stand out as abrupt ridges, the principal being the long range stretching from near Bodh Gayā to Rājgīr and the hills in the south-east of the district. Not only are these rocks everywhere altered by 'regional metamorphism,' caused by the great pressure that has thrown them into close-set synclinal and anticlinal folds as expressed by the elongated shape of the ridges and high dips of the strata with the inducement of slaty cleavage, but they have further been affected to a great extent by 'contact metamorphism' from the intrusion of great masses of granite and innumerable veins of coarse granitic pegmatite, by which the slates have been further transformed into crystalline schists. In its more massive form the granite is relatively fine-grained and very homogeneous, and it weathers into great rounded hummocks that have suggested the name of "dome-gneiss" by which it is sometimes known, though the term "dome-granite" would be more appropriate. But it is the narrow sheets of the same intrusive group, where they cut across the metamorphosed schists as excessively coarse granitic pegmatites, that are of most practical importance on account of the mica which they contain, the south-east corner of the district being situated in the middle of the rich mica-bearing belt of Bengal. The Rājgīr Hills consisting of slaty schists and quartzites are less metamorphosed, but contact effects are well seen in the Maher hill, and in the detached spurs forming the south-western continuation of the Rājgīr range near Gayā, where idols and utensils are extensively wrought from the soft serpentinous rock of the converted schists.

The Tālcher rocks, which constitute the basement beds of the coal-bearing Gondwāna series, are seen at the small village of Gangti, 20 miles south-west by west of Sherghāti, and 4 miles west by south of Imāmganj, in the bed of the Morhar river, where they occupy a small outcrop entirely surrounded by alluvium.. This outcrop is of great interest as indicating the possibility of coal-measures existing beneath the alluvial formation in this part of the Gangetic plain.

BOTANY.

The alluvial country which forms the greater portion of the district presents in its botanical features a great contrast to the hilly tracts to the south. In the former sugarcane, poppy, rice and a great variety of other food-crops are extensively grown; the area under cultivation is bare or dotted over with clumps of bamboos and mango orchards; while the villages are frequently surrounded by groves of palmyra (*Borassus flabelliformis*) and date-palm (*Phœnix sylvestris*). Numerous more isolated examples of *Tamarindus*, *Odina*, *Sapindus* and *Moringa* also occur, associated with which one frequently finds in village shrubberies *Glycosmis*, *Clerodendron*, *Solanum*, *Jatropha*, *Trema*, *Streblus* and similar semi-spontaneous and more or less useful species. In the rice-fields which cover the low-lying lands, the usual weeds of such localities are found, such as *Ammannia*, *Utricularia*, *Hygrophila* and *Sesbania*. Elsewhere a dry scrub jungle is sometimes met with, of which the principal species are euphorbiaceous shrubs, *Butea* and other leguminous trees, and various examples of *Ficus*, *Schleichera*, *Wendlandia* and *Gmelina*. The grasses clothing the drier parts are generally of a coarse character, such as *Andropogon contortus*, *aciculatus*, *annulatus*, *foveolatus* and *pertusus*, *Aristida Adscensionis*, *Tragus racemosus*, *Iseilema laxum*, various *Anthistriœ*, and *sabai* grass (*Ischœmum angustifolium*). Throughout this tract the mango (*Mangifera indica*), *pīpal* (*Ficus religiosa*), and banyan (*Ficus indica*) are common, the other principal trees being the *bel* (*Aegle Marmelos*), *nīm* (*Melia Azadirachta*), *siris* (*Mimosa Sirissa*), *sisu* (*Dalbergia Sissoo*), jack-fruit tree) *Artocarpus integrifolia*) and red-cotton tree (*Bombax malabaricum*).

In the hills a different class of vegetation is met with. The solitary peaks and ranges, which break the surface of the level plain in the heart of the district, have been almost entirely denuded, but they are still clothed to some extent with low thorny scrub-wood and masses of cactus, which make the ascent by any but frequented paths a tedious process. On some of the hills, such as the Barābar Hills, there are a number of flowering shrubs and creepers, and after the rains the rocks are covered with graceful festoons of spiræa. Further south the cultivation is less extensive, the groves of palms near the villages are larger, and the bush jungle is more plentiful; it becomes a long belt of brushwood under the hills, stretching away from east to west, and studded in places with a number of stately trees, sole survivors of a former forest, which give it a park-like appearance. It rapidly passes into a submontane forest, extending up the slopes that lead to the edge of the table-land of Chotā Nāgpur, and resembling in many of its features the forest clothing the foot-hills of the Himālayas. This forest consists of stunted trees of no great height or girth, and it yields no timber of any size. But it is the main source from which the fuel-supply of the district is derived, and it is also rich in jungle products, from which the denizens of the jungle obtain a livelihood. The *kend* (*Diospyros melanoxylon*) yields the ebony of commerce; lac is obtained from the *palās* (*Butea frondosa*); *tasar* silkworms feed on the *āsan*-tree (*Terminalia tomentosa*); and the long coarse *sabai* grass is made into a strong twine. Perhaps, however, the most useful of all the trees which clothe the hills and the undulating slopes at their base is the *mahuā* (*Bassia latifolia*) which yields food, wine, oil and timber, and affords the lower classes a ready means of subsistence in times of dearth. From the flowers the common country spirit is distilled, and whether fresh or dried they furnish the poorer classes with wholesome food; from the fruit is pressed an oil largely used for the adulteration of *ghī*; and the tough timber is used for the naves of cart-wheels.

FAUNA.* The carnivora of the district comprise tiger, leopard, bear, hyæna, wild dog, wolf and other smaller species. The ungulata are represented by *sāmbar* (*Cervus unicolor*), spotted deer (*Cervus axis*), barking deer, *nīlgai* (*Boselaphus tragocamelus*), antelope, gazelle, four-horned antelope and wild pig.

Tigers (*Felis tigris*) inhabit the jungles of the southern ranges bordering on Hazāribāgh and Palāmau. They are not very numerous, but wander a great deal; one or two, however, may always be met with in certain favoured localities, such as Nawādih near Kauwākol, Dubaur, Singar, Dhanwa, Dhangain, Pinra near Sherghāti and Delho-Kachanpur near Deo. Man-eaters are unfortunately very destructive at times, and for years past a family of these brutes has haunted the range of hills between Gobindpur and Kauwākol in the Nawāda subdivision, where they have killed over 100 human beings in the last 5 years. Several have been trapped in pits by local zamīndārs, one of which may be seen in the Zoological Gardens at Calcutta, and two or three have been shot, but villagers are still carried off while grazing their cattle or cutting wood. The range covered by these pests is so extensive and the jungle so heavy that it is impossible to beat them out, and the only means of destroying them is trapping or sitting over kills. As an instance of the wandering habits of these tigers, it may be mentioned that about 1877 and again in 1904 a tiger has been found lying up in crops close to Nawāda, 15 miles from the nearest heavy cover and 9 miles from the nearest hills. In the first instance the unfortunate Subdivisional Officer was killed, in

* I am indebted to Mr. F. J. R. Field, Sub-Deputy Opium Agent, Gayā, for the account of the Fauna of Gayā.

the last his successor got off with a few rather serious scratches. Leopards (*Felis pardus*) are very numerous and commit great havoc among cattle and goats. The numerous isolated trap-rock hills dotted over many parts of the district, such as those at Pattharkati, Khizrsarāi, Rafiganj, Wazīrganj, the Barābar Hills and the hills at Gayā itself, are their favourite resorts, one or more being almost invariably located in each, but the larger hill ranges also give shelter to many. Their depredations are chiefly confined to cattle, goats and dogs, but one or two instances have been recorded of leopards which have taken to man-eating. On the hills surrounding Gayā itself no less than 16 have been shot within the last 15 years, and their tracks are sometimes seen on the roads of the station. As an instance of their boldness near Gayā, it may be mentioned that in one case a leopard jumped on a man drawing water from a well in a compound on the outskirts of the town, and both fell down the well together, the man being pulled out and the leopard shot. On another occasion a leopard appeared one evening on the golf links, but was scared away by one of a party playing there.

Hyænas (*Hyæna striata*) are very common, almost every trap-rock hill holding one or more. They do not as a rule do much damage, living chiefly on carrion, but they occasionally carry off goats and dogs, and one case is cited of a female hyæna attacking a wood-cutter and mauling him so badly that he died of blood-poisoning. Bears (*Ursus melursus*) are also numerous in all the jungly tracts along the hills and jungles; and many instances are known of their attacking wood-cutters and mauling them terribly. One authenticated case occurred in which a goat which had been tied up for a leopard was killed and eaten by a bear and her cubs. On a second goat being tied up, the bear was shot as she attacked it. They are very numerous during the time the *mahuā*-tree is in flower, when four or five may be seen in the moonlight feeding under the trees. Wolves are not very numerous, but certain localities nearly always contain a pair or two. They do great damage to goats and sheep, the latter in particular, but in this district they never attack human beings or even children. Wild pig (*Sus cristatus*) swarm in some of the hills, such as Maher and the range running from Giriak to Mora Tāl near Bodh Gayā, and are the cause of heavy damage to the ryots' crops. They come down nightly in great numbers, and no efforts to scare them away have any effect. The thick thorn-hedges which the ryots put round their crops afford no protection against their ravages, as the pigs go through these without hesitation, and even firing off of guns only moves them from one patch to another. They are literally a scourge to the villages lying under these hill ranges, and during the time the rice crop is ripening each plot has to be guarded by night watchers. In these two ranges they multiply exceedingly, owing to the fact that there are none of the larger carnivora, except a few leopards, to keep them down. The larger hills to the south have comparatively few wild pigs, owing to the number of wild dogs and tigers. A few are caught by low-caste villagers in pits, and, as they cannot be driven out of their hill fastnesses, pigsticking is impossible. Wild dog (*Cyon dukhunensis*) are numerous along the southern range of hills, where they do great damage to deer, which, partly for this reason, are on the decrease. Of late years also they have taken to killing cattle and goats, and as no rewards are given for their destruction, the natives will not shoot them, and European sportsmen very seldom come across them.

Sāmbar (*Cervus unicolor*) are not very plentiful, and are only found on the higher ranges along the southern boundary. Their horns run to a very fair size, an ordinary head being over 30 inches. Spotted or *chītal* deer (*Cervus axis*) are only found in certain localities, and are not very numerous. They are steadily on the decrease, as they are largely shot by local *shikāris* over water in the hot season. Barking deer (*Cervulus muntjac*) are rare, but are occasionally met with in the jungles of the southern hills. Four-horned antelope (*Tetracerus quadricornis*) are also rare. They frequent the same localities as barking deer, and are generally met with when beating for or stalking *sāmbar*. *Nīlgai* (*Boselaphus tragocamelus*) are only common in a few localities, such as the big grass *chars* of the Son river, but two or three are found here and there along the foot-hills of the southern range. Antelope or black buck (*Antelope cervicapra*) were formerly very numerous, all the high cultivated *tānr* lands holding big herds, but they are now fast disappearing. Where herds of 60 to 100 were once met with, only 5 to 10 are now to be seen. Gazelle or ravine deer (*Gazella bennetti*) are fairly numerous along the broken ground at the foot of the southern hills.

Game birds.

The game birds of the district consist of jungle, spur and peafowl, grey and black partridge, common rain, button, bustard and bush quail, and sand grouse (*Pteroclurus exustus* and *Pterocles fasciatus*). Lesser florican are occasionally seen, and one great bustard has been shot. Two varieties of geese are found, the greylag and bar-headed, and among ducks the red-headed and white-eyed pochard, pintail and gadwall are most numerous. Widgeon are rare, but the spotted-bill breed in the *chars* of the Son river. Besides these, the following are found: the shoveller, ruddy sheldrake, common blue-winged teal, whistling teal, cotton teal and the comb duck, the last three breeding here. Snipe of four varieties and golden plover are met along the Son, and kulan (*Grus communis*) and demoiselle crane (*Anthropoides virgo*) frequent the same locality. One Siberian crane (*Grus leucogeranus*) was shot some years ago. Most of the usual waders are met with.

The Son contains *buāli*, *tengrā*, *bachuā*, *rahū* and other small fish, and *mahseer* and *hilsā* are said to pass up when the river is in flood. The large tanks are stocked with *rahū*, *naini*, *katla*, etc. The fish-eating alligator or *gariāl* is common in the Son, as well as the mugger or snub-nosed crocodile, which also haunts large deep reservoirs in one or two localities. Fish.

The climate of Gayā is generally dry and bracing. It enjoys a long cold weather, which commences early in November and ends with the close of March, when the hot weather sets in with strong west winds, which blow until the end of May. Soon after this, the rainy season commences and lasts till the end of September; but as the beginning of this season occurs when a storm from the Bay of Bengal passes over Bihār, the commencement of the monsoon may be as early as the last week of May and as late as the first or second week of July. In the cold weather it would be difficult to find a more delightful climate. The days are bright and warm, and the sun is not too hot; as soon as it has set, the temperature falls, and a fire is at once a comfort and a necessity. The minimum temperature recorded at this season of the year is 38°·9 (January 8th, 1874). In the hot weather Gayā is the hottest place in Bengal. There is a fierce dry heat, which makes it almost compulsory for the European residents to sleep in the open, and the temperature has been known to rise as high as 116°·2 (June 18th, 1878). There is generally a strong west wind at this period, blowing from the sun-baked plains of Hindustān, which parches up all vegetation and raises immense clouds of dust; but this wind, in spite of its fierce heat, is a boon to the inhabitants, as the interior of the houses can be kept cool by means of screens of scented grass (*khas-khas tattis*), placed at the doors and windows and kept constantly wet. When this wind fails or gives place to an east wind, the air is moist and enervating, and the heat is extreme. In the rains humidity is comparatively low, and Gayā is as agreeable a station as any at that period of the year. CLIMATE.

Owing to its distance from the sea Gayā has greater extremes of climate than the south and east of the Province. Mean temperature varies from 64° in January to 93° in May, the average maximum temperature rising to 105° in the latter month. Owing to the hot and dry westerly winds which prevail in March and April, humidity is much lower at this season than at any other Temperature and humidity.

times of the year and averages only 51 per cent. of saturation. With the approach of the monsoon season, the air slowly becomes more charged with moisture, and humidity remains steady at from 84 to 87 per cent. throughout July and August. In September, when periods of fine weather alternate with the cloud and rain of the monsoon, humidity is lower; and with breaks of increasing length it gradually falls and reaches a minimum of 70 per cent. in November. There is then a slight increase, partly owing to the unsettled weather caused by the cold-season disturbances.

Winds.

From October until May the prevailing direction of the wind is from the west, but a marked change takes place with the commencement of the monsoon, which is generally caused by the first cyclonic storm which enters from the Bay of Bengal. The flow of the moist winds from the Bay is northwards over the eastern districts of Bengal proper, but afterwards they trend to the west owing to the barrier interposed by the Himalayan range; so that after the passage of the cyclonic storms, easterly and south-easterly winds set in and continue with but little interruption until the middle of September, when westerly winds again become common.

Rainfall.

During the months from November to May, fine dry weather prevails, with an almost entire absence of cloud and rainfall; and only a fraction of an inch of rain falls monthly. In normal years the monsoon breaks in June; and the heaviest rainfall occurs in July and August, varying from 12·1 inches in the former to 11·8 inches in the latter month. From the middle of September the monsoon current begins to fall off in strength; and if the westerly winds are stronger than usual, the storms coming inland from the Bay of Bengal recede eastwards, and rainfall is consequently deficient.

Statistics of the rainfall at the various recording stations are given below for the cold weather (November to February), the hot weather (March to May) and the rainy season (June to October). The figures shown are the averages recorded from the earliest year in which rainfall was systematically registered up to the end of 1905 :—

STATION.	Years recorded.	November to February.	March to May.	June to October.	Annual average.
Gayā	39-41	1·79	1·80	39·35	42·94
Arwal	15-16	2·00	1·96	38·75	42·71
Aurangābād ...	30-31	1·72	1·80	41·78	45·30
Dāūdnagar ...	14-16	1·68	1·11	37·62	40·41
Jahānābād ...	28	1·70	1·84	40·33	43·87
Nawāda	30-31	1·65	2·26	39·50	43·41
Pakrībarāwān ...	15-16	1·54	1·70	38·46	41·70
Rajaulī	12-16	1·84	2·21	41·03	45·08
Sherghāti ...	14-16	1·63	1·34	38·28	41·25

CHAPTER II.

HISTORY.

"To the present day," writes Dr. Grierson,* "the Gayā district is composed of two tracts—a northern and southern, with very distinct characteristics. The northern half of the district, together with the Patna district, is known as Magah, a corruption of Magadha, and is well irrigated and fertile. The southern half, which still locally bears the name of Rāmgarh, commences about 10 miles south of Gayā town, and is still imperfectly irrigated and covered with forests. Magah represents the ancient Magadha which received Aryan civilization from the north and west and was the area from which Buddhism spread over India. Rāmgarh has received such civilization as it has got in latter years, from the south and south-west. Magah to the present day is a Buddhist country. It is covered with ruins of temples, and, in frequent fields, Buddhist images are turned up by the plough. Buddhism never seems to have penetrated Rāmgarh. Indeed, during the time of Magadha sovereignty, that country must have been a dense forest inhabited only by wild tribes and by a few solitary hermits—outposts of Aryan civilization. The country is dotted here and there with rude forts which local tradition attributes, and no doubt rightly attributes, to the Kols or wild aboriginal tribes of Central India. In later years clearances were effected in it by enterprising immigrants from Rājputāna, who were the ancestors of such Rājput families as those of Deo and Chandragarh. By them the south of the district has been brought into civilization, but this 'zilla Rāmgarh' saw no Buddhist civilization and has no Buddhist remains. Magah is Buddhist, ancient, highly cultivated and thickly populated; Rāmgarh is Hindu, modern, half-cultivated and sparsely populated." In these words Dr. Grierson sums up the different characteristics of the southern and northern portions of Gayā, and his account clearly shows the difficulty of giving a connected history of the district as a whole. For the history of Magadha there are ample materials, whereas there are no records referring to the southern tract until comparatively recent times.

* Notes on the District of Gayā, pp. 3-4.

There is no notice of Rāmgarh even in the chronicles of the Muhammadan historians, and it was regarded by them merely as part of Jhārkhand, *i. e.*, the jungle tract—a vague term given to the territory extending from Bīrbhūm and Pānchet to Ratanpur in Central India and from Rohtāsgarh in Shāhābād to the frontier of Orissa. While therefore the northern part of Gayā has a long record stretching back to very early times, the south of the district is practically a land without a history.

PREHISTORIC PEOPLES.

Gayā was occupied in prehistoric times by aboriginal races, whose power is still attested by the remains attributed to them, the traditions of their rule and the names* they gave to places, while their descendants are still found in considerable numbers in the hilly tracts to the south of the district. These tribes gave place to Aryan immigrants at a later period than in the adjoining tracts to the north-west, and Magadha, a country roughly corresponding to the modern districts of Gayā and Patna, continued to be inhabited by non-Aryan tribes at a time when Tirhut and Oudh were under Aryan sway. It was regarded as a land filled with wild tribes hardly worthy of the name of men, and as late as the 6th century B. C. it is mentioned by Budhāyana as a country inhabited by people of mixed origin outside the pale of Aryan civilization. The ancient capital of this empire was Rājāgriha, the modern Rājgīr, where king Jarāsandha is said to have held sway at a date too remote to be fixed with any certainty. A halo of legend is attached to this monarch, and though the site of his capital is now buried in jungle, many traces of his power are pointed out in the great stone walls and causeways which skirt and climb the rocky hills round Rājgīr.

EARLY HISTORY.

Saisunāga dynasty.

It was from this place that Sisunāga, the founder of the Saisunāga dynasty, the earliest which can claim historic reality, exercised his dominion (*cir.* 600 B. C.) over Patna and Gayā; but nothing is known of his reign, and Gayā practically emerges into the light of history in the time (*cir.* 519 B. C.) of Bimbisāra, the fifth of his line. This king was the first to extend the frontiers of Magadha, which hitherto was a petty State corresponding roughly with the present Gayā and Patna districts; but the real interest of his reign is that it synchronized with the preaching both of Buddha and Vardhamāna Mahāvīra, the founder of Jainism. According to the Lalita Vistara,† Gautama Buddha came from Rājāgriha to Gayā at the invitation of its inhabitants, who were good Brāhmans and Kshattriyas, and spent some time

* *See* Dravidian and Kolarian place-names in Mirzāpur, Shāhābād and Gayā, by the Revd. F. Hahn, J.A.S.B., Vol. LXXII, Part III, No. 2—1903.

† *See* Buddha Gayā, by Rājendralāla Mitra, LL.D., C.I.E., Chapter II.

in contemplation on the rocky crest of Gayāsīrsa (Brahmajuni Hill), before he passed on to Bodh Gayā. Here he underwent the memorable spiritual experience at the end of which he attained enlightenment: much of his life was spent in this district after he began his mission, and it contains many of the scenes of his earliest preaching. His great contemporary, Mahāvīra, who was nearly related to the royal family of Magadha, also spent many years of his ministry within the limits of that kingdom; and there he succeeded in gathering a large following of monks, who were afterwards called Jains when they spread over the rest of India. Both Mahāvīra and Buddha died shortly after the close of the reign of Bimbisāra and early in that of his son, Ajātasatru, who made his way to the throne (*cir.* 490 B. C.) by the murder of his father. This crime involved him in war with the king of Kosala, whose sister was the wife of Bimbisāra; and the war ending in the triumph of the king of Magadha, he passed on to the conquest of Vaisāli (Basārh), the capital of the powerful Lichchhavi clan in Tirhut. From this time the whole country from the Ganges to the Himālayas appears to have acknowledged the suzerainty of Magadha.

Maurya dynasty.

The Saisunāga dynasty was extinguished about 400 B. C., and Magadha passed under the rule of the Nanda kings, who in their turn were replaced by the powerful monarchs of the Maurya line, under whose rule Pātaliputra (Patna) became the capital not only of Magadha, but of India. With the reign of the great Asoka (B. C. 272—232) Gayā again comes into prominence. Overcome with remorse at the horrors of the conquest of Kalinga, Asoka became a Buddhist and signalized his adherence to that religion by constructing a temple and monastery at Bodh Gayā, and by the deepest veneration for the sacred tree under which Gautama had obtained enlightenment. Under his patronage Buddhism spread far and wide, and one of the most notable events of his reign, so far as Gayā is concerned, was the great ceremony of transplanting a branch of the Bodhī tree to Ceylon. Brahmanism appears, however, to have flourished side by side with Buddhism, and Asoka's support of the rival creed is sufficiently attested by the brief inscriptions in the caves in the Barābar Hills recording his presentation of these rock-hewn cave dwellings to the Ajīvikas, a sect of non-Buddhistic ascetics. Whether they were Vaishnava ascetics or a penitential order closely connected with the Jains, they certainly had little or nothing in common with the Buddhists, and it is clear that Asoka was sincere in his declaration that he honoured all sects. In this respect he was followed by his grandson, Dasaratha, who similarly dedicated the three

Nagarjuni caves in these hills to the use of the same order of ascetics on his accession in 231 B. C.

Gupta Empire.

Shortly after his death came the downfall of the Mauryan dynasty in 184 B. C., when Pushyamitra, the commander-in-chief of the last Maurya, killed his master and usurped his throne. The Empire began to decline, as the outlying provinces asserted their independence, and in 157 B. C. Khāravela, king of Kalinga, succeeded in leading his army to the capital Pātaliputra, where he compelled the Emperor to sue for peace. With this exception, we know little of the history of Magadha down to the time of Huvishka of the Kushan dynasty (150 A. D.), a royal patron of Buddhism, who is believed by General Cunningham* to have furnished funds for the building of the great temple of Bodh Gayā. A gold coin of this king was found among the relics deposited in front of the Diamond throne; and whether the temple was built during his reign or not, it appears certain that Gayā was part of his dominions, which extended as far north as Kashmīr and the Punjab. It is not till the rise of the Gupta Empire that we find the next mention of Gayā in connection with the foundation of a splendid monastery at Bodh Gayā by the king of Ceylon, during the reign of Samudra Gupta, about the year 330 A. D.

The Chinese pilgrims.

The Chinese pilgrim, Fa Hian,† who visited India 70 years later in the time of Chandra Gupta Vikramāditya, has left a glowing account of the prosperity of Magadha under this dynasty. The towns were the largest in the Gangetic plain; the people were rich and prosperous, emulating each other in the practice of virtue; charitable institutions were numerous, rest-houses were provided for travellers on the highways, and the Buddhist monasteries were liberally endowed. The city of Gayā was empty and desolate, but at Bodh Gayā there were three monasteries, the priests of which were supplied by the people with all that they could desire. A more detailed account has come down to us in the account of his journey left by Hiuen Tsiang†, another Chinese pilgrim, who visited India between 630 and 645 A. D. and recorded observations more or less minute about every place he visited. The people of Magadha, he says, highly esteemed the pursuit of learning and respected the religion of Buddha profoundly. Magadha contained 50 monasteries with 10,000 priests, most of whom followed the Greater Vehicle, but there were also 10 Deva temples belonging to numerous sectaries of different persuasions. From this it is clear that the land had

* Mahābodhi, p. 21.

† Beal's Buddhist Records of the Western World.

recovered from the savage persecution of Sasānka, king of Central Bengal, a bitter opponent of Buddhism, who 30 or 40 years previously had dug up and burnt the Bodhī tree, destroyed the convents and scattered the monks, carrying his ravages up to the foot of the Nepalese Hills. This change appears to have been due to the power of Harsha, who ruled Northern India between 606 and 648 A. D., and was in his later days at least a devoted adherent of Buddhism and a liberal patron of its institutions. However that may be, the account of the Chinese pilgrim shows that Buddhism flourished in the country of Magadha under his rule, and that Gayā was crowded with splendid Buddhist shrines and peaceful monasteries. At Gunamati, one of the first places in Gayā visited by Hiuen Tsiang, which has been identified with a spot to the south of Dharāwat, there was a magnificent monastery containing 50 Buddhist priests; and south-west of this was the richly endowed convent of Silābhadra, standing by the side of a single sharp crag like a stūpa—a description which clearly points to the peak of Kauwādol. Thence the pilgrim went to Gayā, which he describes as well defended, difficult of access and thinly inhabited, but containing 1,000 Brāhmans, highly respected by the people everywhere, who were exempted by the king from service as vassals. On his way to Bodh Gayā he made a detour to Prāgbodhī, where he saw the stūpas erected by Asoka to commemorate all the spots trodden by Buddha, and then at Bodh Gayā itself he offered worship at the Bodhī tree. The temple was surrounded by a vast number of stūpas and minor shrines; the great monastery was occupied by more than a thousand monks of the Sthavira school of the Mahāyāna, who afforded ample hospitality to the monks of Ceylon; and the tree itself was visited on each anniversary of the Nirvāna day by the princes of different countries and by a pious multitude numbering thousands and tens of thousands, who bathed its roots with scented water and perfumed milk. Hiuen Tsiang then crossed the river to Bakraur, where there was a stūpa set up in honour of the scented elephant Gandhahasti, of which the remains still exist; and after leaving this place he marched north-east in the direction of Rājgīr, passing on the way Kukkuta-pāda-giri (Hasrā Hill), Yashtivana (Jethian) and the warm springs of Tapoban.

The Pāla Kings.

On the death of Harsha in 648 A. D., Northern India relapsed into anarchy; Pātaliputra, the former seat of the Empire, fell into ruins, and each small potentate carved out a kingdom for himself. Early in the 9th century (*cir.* 815 A. D.) a chieftain named Gopāla became ruler of Bengal, and, extending his power over Magadha, founded the Pāla dynasty. The Pālas were devout

Buddhists, and a number of inscriptions at Bodh Gayā, beginning with Gopāla and ending with Mahīpāla (1026-1060 A.D.) record the dedication of various images of Buddha. Gopāla founded a great monastery at Bihār, which had taken the place of Pātaliputra as a capital; and under his successors Magadha became a great centre of missionary enterprise, sending out emissaries to spread the faith over Central and Eastern India and even outside its borders. Not the least notable result of this activity was the revival of Buddhism in Tibet where Atisha, who had studied under the Abbot of the Bodh Gayā monastery, succeeded in reforming Lāmaism. Arriving in Tibet in 1038 A.D., he found Lāmaism much tainted by devil-worship, and founded a reformed order based upon a Buddhist model, which afterwards became the Yellow-cap sect, and now as the State Church holds the entire secular government of the country. Here he died in 1052 near Lhāsa, and the rock sculptures near his tomb show that he and his followers strove to reproduce in this northern climate the surroundings of their monasteries in Gayā.* At the same time, the fame of the sacred Buddhist sites in Gayā spread far and wide, and attracted pilgrims not only from all parts of India, but even from the distant countries of China and Burma. But though devout Buddhists themselves, the Pālas were tolerant towards Hinduism. Under their rule Brahmanism flourished, Gayā itself became well known as a place of pilgrimage, and the town was adorned with a number of temples erected to the Sun-god, Gadādhar and other deities.

Muhammadan Period.

In 1193 A.D. Gayā suffered, with the rest of Bihār, from the invasion of Muhammad Bakhtiyār Khiljī. The combined intolerance and rapacity of the Muhammadans were directed against the ecclesiastical institutions which were so numerous in this part of the country. The monasteries were sacked and the monks slain, many of the temples were ruthlessly destroyed or desecrated, and countless idols were broken and trodden under foot. Those monks who escaped the sword fled to Tibet, Nepāl and Southern India; and Buddhism as a popular religion in Bihār, its last abode in Northern India, was finally destroyed. Thenceforward Gayā passed under the Muhammadan rule, and its history is merged in that of the Province or *Sūbah* of Bihār, of which it formed an important

* Lieutenant-Colonel Waddell, I.M.S., C.I.E., writes in Lhasa and its Mysteries:— "The rock sculptures bore abundant evidence that Atisha and Indian monks of his class had been in this locality. For the carvings covering the rounded shoulders and cliffs along the roadside were more in the old Indian style, whilst the contour and general appearance of these dark be-lichened rounded granite hills reminded one forcibly of similar hills in the Buddhist Holy Land around Buddha Gayā, whence Atisha came."

part. The chronicles of Mewār mention, it is true, expeditions made in the 13th and 14th centuries for the recovery of the holy city of Gayā from the infidels, but these references must be attributed to the pious wishes of the chronicles and not to accomplished facts, as the hold of the Muhammadans over the pilgrim city remained undisturbed.

In the time of Bakhtiyār Khiljī and his immediate successors, South Bihār was included in the Bengal Viceroyalty, from which it was separated by the Emperor Altamsh, who placed it under a separate Governor named Alā-ud-dīn Jānī (1229 A. D.). It was shortly afterwards resumed by the ruler of Bengal, and continued to be part of the Bengal kingdom till 1320, when the Emperor Ghiās-ud-dīn Tughlak again separated it. In 1397 A. D. it was attached to the kingdom of Jaunpur, and a century later it became subject to the Muhammadan kings of Gaur. There is no specific mention, however, of Gayā itself, and we only know that the Jaunpur kings appear to have given *jāgīrs* to Pathān chiefs, and that Rājput and Bābhan zamīndārs also gained considerable influence and power. Towards the end of the first half of the 16th century, Gayā was under the regency of one of these Pathān chiefs, Sher Shāh, a military adventurer who held Sasarām in fief and thence spread his sway over the whole of South Bihār and eventually seized the throne at Delhi. On the downfall of his short-lived dynasty, Bihār was again formed into a distinct *Sūbah*, and long had a Governor appointed direct from Delhi; but under the later Mughal Emperors it was again incorporated in the great Bengal Viceroyalty and was governed by semi-independent Nawāb Nāzims through Deputy Governors.

Mughal *Sūbahdārs*.

As the reins of central control slackened, the local chieftains, taking advantage of the disintegration of the Empire, began to play an important part in the politics of the *Sūbah*, and usurped considerable power. As early as 1730 Alī Vardi Khān, who was the Deputy Governor of Bihār under Shujā-ud-daula, found it necessary to subdue these local potentates, whose independence had become a political danger. From the Riyāzu-s-Salātin* we learn that "invading the tracts of Sundar Singh, zamīndār of Tekāri, and Nāmdār Khān Muin, who, sheltered by dense forests and rocks, had not cared for former Nāzims, had neglected to discharge the duties of loyalty, and had never paid the Imperial revenue without coercion, Alī Vardi Khān set about chastising them, subdued their tracts completely, levied the revenues from them to the fullest extent, and reduced them to thorough subjection. And similarly

* Riyāzu-s-Salātin, translated by Maulavi Abdus Salam (1904).

punishing other insolent rebels, Alī Vardi Khān placed the ring of submission on their ears."

Thenceforward Gayā was frequently overrun by contending armies during the troubled times which witnessed the decay of the Mughal Empire and the rise of the British power. The district was divided among a number of powerful zamīndārs, who each kept up a small standing army; the Rājā of Tekāri was supreme in the centre of the district, Kāmgār Khān and his brother Nāmdār Khān in Narhat and Samai to the east, Bishun Singh, the zamīndār of Siris and Kutumbā, in the west, and the Rājā of Rāmgarh to the south. The latter was the most powerful chieftain of the hills, and the Viceroys of the Province had scarcely any control over him. Accordingly, it was decided to break his power; and an expedition was sent against him in 1740, the invading army being led by the father of the author of the Sair-ul-Mutākharin, assisted by the zamīndārs of Siris, Kutumbā and Sherghāti, as well as by the powerful Rājā of Tekāri. The fort of Rāmgarh was taken, and the allied forces advanced far into the hills, when the expedition had to be abandoned in consequence of the news that the Marāthās were marching through the hills in order to swoop down upon Bengal. The invasion of Bengal soon became a reality; and in spite of its distance from the principal scene of the fighting, Gayā suffered from the ravages of the Marāthā armies. In 1743 the great Marāthā chief, Bālajī Rao, marched through it on his way to Bengal at the head of 50,000 horse. From every place on the line of march he levied contributions; and all who refused to pay had their property plundered, their lands devastated and their tenants put to the sword. One zamīndār only ventured to withstand the invading force—Ahmed Khān, the grandson of Dāūd Khān, the founder of Dāūdnagar, who held the *parganas* of Anchhā and Goh in fief. He shut himself up with his family, his troops and all the merchants and moneyed men of the place in the fort of Ghausgarh, which he had built and fortified close to Dāūdnagar. The Marāthās sacked and burnt the town, and when they proceeded to use the materials to fill up the moat surrounding the fort, Ahmed Khān fled, and was only too glad to be allowed to purge his contumacy by a fine of Rs. 50,000. The Marāthās then continued their march through Tekāri, Gayā and Mānpur without opposition. They returned however 2 years afterwards, when Raghujī Bhonsla made a sudden sally to the north, in order to rescue some Afghān followers of Mustafā Khān, the rebellious general of Alī Vardi Khān, who had taken refuge in the hills near Sasarām after their defeat near Jagdīspur. On the way the Marāthās sacked and plundered the town of Tekāri and all the adjoining territory, after which they crossed the Son, and did not visit Gayā again till after they had effected a junction with the Afghāns.

The district remained quiet for a few years afterwards, with the exception of a small expedition led by Rām Narāyan, the Deputy Governor of Bihār, against Bishun Singh, zamīndār of Siris and Kutumbā, who had refused to pay any revenues after Sirāj-ud-daula's death and had annexed a considerable strip of territory. He made some resistance in his forts, but the Governor's army and train of artillery soon brought him to terms. Shortly after this small campaign, Gayā again became the centre of some serious fighting. The Shāhzāda or Imperial Prince, later known as the Emperor Shāh Alam, determined to establish his claims to the Province and invaded Bihār in 1760 with a mixed army of Afghāns and Marāthās. Here Kāmgār Khān joined him with a large army, and soon assumed a predominant part in the councils of war. Repulsed near Bārh by the English troops and the Nawāb's levies, Shāh Alam, who in the meantime had been proclaimed Emperor on the assassination of his father, fell back on this district, where he and his army ranged without opposition from Dāūdnagar to the environs of Bihār. In the Sair-ul-Mutākharin we find a graphic account of the ravages of his army. "Having nothing," it says, "to subsist upon but what he found in the fields and among the farmers of the flat country, both himself and his cavalry and cattle would have been exceedingly distressed had he sojourned for any length of time in one place; in such a case he would have suffered for want of grain and for everything requisite for an army. His authority was not acknowledged, and he was obliged to live by rapine and plunder, just as if he had been in the country of some stranger." Apart, however, from their necessities, both the Emperor and his trusted general, Kāmgār Khān, took a special delight in ravaging this part of country—the former because he was incensed at the refusal of the Rājā of Tekāri to join his cause, and the latter because he had a bitter animosity towards the Rājā and was only too glad to prolong a stay which ruined the lands of his personal enemy and spared his own. The Rājā had no sufficient force to withstand his enemies, but remained shut up in his fortress of Tekāri, and when at last he ventured forth, he was at once captured by 1,000 Mughal horse, which Kāmgār Khān had sent to waylay him.

At last, however, the approach of an English force under Major Carnac, with the allied troops under Miran, the son of the Nawāb Mīr Jāfar Alī, and the Governor Rām Narāyan, compelled the Emperor to give battle at Mānpur near the walls of Gayā. The battle was short but decisive: the English troops fell on the masses opposed to them with their usual impetuosity, and they gave way in confusion in spite of some opposition from a small force under the French adventurer, Monsieur Law, who had taken service with the native powers after the capture of Chandernagore and had joined the Emperor with a small train of artillery. The Emperor and Kāmgār Khān fled from the field of battle, and the troops under Law, discouraged by their flight and tired of the wandering life they had in his service, broke and fled. Law alone remained, waiting for the end, seated on a gun, and in this position he surrendered to Major Carnac on condition that he was allowed to keep his sword. This battle (January 15th, 1761) put an end to the war. The Emperor came to terms, and was escorted by the English to Patna, where he was installed in the English factory, and there formally conferred on Mīr Kāsim Alī the Viceroyalty of Bihār, Bengal and Orissa. On the defeat of the latter in the decisive battle of Buxar (1764), the British became masters of the Lower Provinces of Bengal, and Gayā passed, with the rest of Bihār, under British rule.

THE MUTINY.

Thenceforward Gayā has had an uneventful history, except for the Mutiny of 1857, when the peace it enjoyed under British rule was rudely broken. Ever since the commencement of the convulsions in Upper India, there had been indications of an unquiet spirit pervading all classes of the community. In the city itself the fiction that the bones or blood of swine and oxen had been mixed with the flour of the bazar was industriously disseminated, and attempts were made to corrupt the Sikh soldiery who were posted there, and to win them over to the rebel cause. There was however no overt act of hostility, and the disturbances only began with the abandonment of the station. Writing on the 28th July 1857, the Collector, Mr. Alonzo Money, reported that the mutiny of Dinapore had thrown Gayā into a ferment, but there was nothing to be feared from the towns-people, as they were surrounded by a new and strong police, and had a wholesome dread of the 45 English and 100 Sikhs. Still there was grave danger if any of the mutineers entered the district, as there were plenty of zamīndārs who would join them, if they once got the upper hand, though none were likely to hazard life and property before that. He was prepared, however, to meet any body of the mutineers under 300 or 350 about 2 miles from the town, and had "no doubt of giving them a good thrashing," while if they came in greater force, he would place the treasure in a brick-house, which was being provisioned, and would defend it with the same numbers.

On the 31st of July, he received a message from the Commissioner informing him of the defeat of Dunbar's party near Arrah, and saying that "Everything must now be sacrificed to holding the country and the occupation of a central position." The order desired him and the other civil authorities to come with all their force to Patna, making their arrangements as promptly and quickly as possible, and contained an injunction to remove the treasure, if their personal safety was not endangered by doing so. The residents were called together and informed of the orders, and at six that evening they and the troops started, leaving the station and all that it contained under the charge of the *daroga* and the *sūbahdār* of the *najīb* guard. The jail was full of criminals and the treasury contained 7 lakhs of rupees, but even this large treasure was left behind, because, as Mr. Money reported next day, he had neither carts nor elephants to transport it. When they had gone 3 miles from the town, Mr. Money and Mr. Hollings, an officer of the Opium Department, who felt acutely the shame of this abandonment of the station to anarchy and plunder, determined to return and see what could be done to preserve order and to save the Government property. Money halted the party, announced their intention, asked none of them to join him, and went back with Hollings alone. They found the station in the same order as when they left it 3 hours before; the treasury was untouched and still guarded; at the jail the guard were on duty and all was quiet. Many of the inhabitants welcomed them back with every expression of joy, and the Gayāwāls promised, with the help of the zamīndārs, to raise a force of 3,000 or 4,000 men to defend the town. Their position was however one of great danger. The *najībs* were brothers in blood, and probably in feeling, to the mutineers, and 7 lakhs protected only by themselves was a great temptation. Not much help could be expected from the indolent Gayāwāls; at any moment a band of mutineers might swoop down upon the town; the Bakr-Id was being celebrated, and if the Musalmāns chose, they could rise with impunity. Money at once began collecting pack-bullocks on which to carry away the treasure, and called in a detachment of the 64th, which was near Sherghāti. They at once responded to his call and marched in on the 2nd August. There seemed no prospect, however, of their being able to hold the town. On the 1st news had come that the mutineers from Dinapore had attacked and looted Arrah, killing every Bengali they could find, and that the residents were surrounded. The Gayāwāls, who considered their sacred city safe, had failed to fulfil their promise; the zamīndārs were either indifferent or disaffected; and of the promised levies, less than 100 men were forthcoming, and those the refuse of the villages, old, weak and useless. On the 3rd a letter came from an officer at Dinapore with an urgent message: "For God's sake, look out. The 8th Native Infantry have marched upon Gya, they say with one gun." A council of war was held, and as it was impossible to hold Gayā with the small force of 80 men, it was decided to fall back on the Grand Trunk Road with the treasure. The Government paper was burnt, the treasure was placed on the pack-bullocks already collected and on the carts which had brought the English soldiers, and at 6 o'clock that evening they started. Having seen the convoy safely started, Money returned to his house* to save a few things of value, but suddenly he heard shouts and yells, and a servant came rushing in to say that the jail was loose and the prisoners were near. He just had time to get to the stable and mount his horse, which was ready saddled, and to catch up the convoy. As in other places, so in Gayā, the removal of the treasure seems to have been the signal to the disaffected to break out into open mutiny, and scarcely had the party left the station than the *najībs* let loose the prisoners, and joining with them, pursued and attacked the troops, whom they overtook in the rocky pass on the Dobhī road near the present jail. They were repulsed with some loss, and the party then proceeded unmolested and uninterrupted down the Grand Trunk Road to the railway at Rānīganj, and thence to Calcutta, where Money delivered over the treasure he had saved.

Gayā was re-occupied on the 16th August without opposition by a force of 220 Sikhs and 35 men of the 85th, all the bad characters and released convicts making off as soon as the relieving force appeared. No other enemy had approached the place, but a great deal of damage had been done by those scoundrels with whom riot and disorder are a trade and profession. The houses of the residents had been completely dismantled, the Judge's and Magistrate's *kachahris* had been burnt, together with the record-rooms, and the marauders had destroyed all that was useless to them. The Treasurer, however, faithful to his trust, made over Rs. 4,000 which had been given to him for the expenses of the jail, etc., and some of the clerks had preserved several *tahsīldāri* books, which they had taken home to make up the quarterly accounts. Steps were at once taken to restore the authority of Government. The out-stations of Sherghāti and Nawāda, which had also been abandoned, were reoccupied, and a small

* Mr. Money's house was that situated at the south-west corner of the Cutcherry Road to the west of the Dâk Bungalow, and the jail was at this time in the north of the town. Mr. Hollings' house is at present the Collector's residence.

expedition, sent out to relieve the Tehta Sub-Deputy Opium Agency, which was reported as being besieged, dispersed a body of 200 rebels. On the 8th September, the 5th Irregular Cavalry, which had mutinied at Bhāgalpur invaded the district, plundering as they went. At length, after having destroyed the public buildings at Nawāda, they approached Gayā, and Captain Rattray proceeded to encounter them at a few miles distance from the station; but after a severe skirmish, in which they inflicted considerable loss on the Police Battalion, they evaded him and got to Gayā before he could reach it. Here they made an unsuccessful attack on a house* which had been fortified for the protection of the residents, but succeeded in breaking open the jail and liberating the prisoners. They failed in an attempt to plunder the town, and after murdering the Munsif of Bihār, rode off for Tekāri and the Son. Towards the end of October, fresh alarm was caused by the advance of two companies of the 32nd Native Infantry, which had mutinied at Bhāgalpur; but the mutineers continued their march through Jahānābād to the Son without visiting Gayā, and on the 22nd October Major English marched to its rescue with a detachment of the 53rd Regiment.

In the meantime a marauder, named Jodhar Singh, with a band of Bhojpur men, was doing much mischief in the north and west of the district, making grants of land to his followers and giving out that the British rule was at an end. He plundered and harassed the whole country round Arwal, killing all who opposed him, and finally a party of *najībs* was sent against him in the hope of putting an end to his depredations. This expedition failed in its object. Jodhar Singh retreated to his house at Khāmini, which was strongly fortified and garrisoned by 70 or 80 men armed with guns and matchlocks. The attempt to force an entrance was repulsed with some loss, and another attempt to set fire to the building having also failed, the assailants were compelled to fall back on Arwal. Elsewhere the authorities were more successful in restoring order, a number of rebels were tried and executed, a body of European Mounted Police was raised, an extra Police force of 250 men was sent to Nawāda, and in January 1858 Gayā itself was reinforced by 100 sailors and officers of the Indian Navy. In June a raid was made by the Shāhābād rebels, who crossed the Son with the supposed intention of attacking the fort at Tekāri, where 15 or 20 lakhs were deposited, but they contented themselves with plundering villages near Arwal

* This was apparently the Judge's house as in the Narrative of Events dated September 12, 1857, it is stated that "an entrenchment was made round the Judge's house, to afford a place of refuge, only to be occupied in case of need."

and destroying two factories belonging to the Solano family. It was fully expected that Gayā and its jail would be attacked; and, as the jail was considered untenable, 156 of the worst prisoners were sent to Sherghāti. The guards broke into mutiny within 6 miles of that place, shot their officer, and released their prisoners. On the 22nd June the remainder of the *najīb* guard reported that 200 rebels had come quietly to the jail in the night and released the prisoners. Two days afterwards the Jahānābād thāna was surprised, the Government buildings burnt, the *daroga* cut to pieces, and his mangled body hung up by the heels on a tree opposite the thāna. Jodhar Singh openly boasted that he would destroy every public building between the Son and Monghyr, and it was recognized that it was necessary to crush him without further loss of time. Accordingly, Captain Rattray, with a portion of his battalion, 300 Infantry and 50 Cavalry, crossed the Son, and after dispersing one party of the enemy near Arwal, gave his attention to the main body under Jodhar Singh. On the 4th July he came up with the marauders and at once engaged them at Kāsmā. The Sikhs fought with their usual gallantry; Jodhar Singh's force was completely defeated, with a loss of about 100 men; and this victory had the effect of clearing the whole of the district.

A more detailed narrative of the events of 1857 will be found in Mr. Money's report, which is printed as an Appendix to this chapter.

ARCHÆOLOGY.

Gayā is singularly rich in archæological remains. Not only are there a great number of temples of a very early date, but there is scarcely a village in which some fragments of ancient statuary are not found collected under a sacred *pīpal*-tree. The statues generally belong to the time of the Pāla kings (800—1200 A. D.), and are both Buddhistic and Brahmanical. They afford a good illustration of the connection between the two sects, which seems to have culminated in an intermixture of both, the result being that Buddhism became more and more Hinduized. The Buddhistic images are of especial interest, as, with the exception of the Græco-Buddhistic sculptures of Gandhāra, they are the only class of Indian Buddhistic art that has come down to us with a fair amount of completeness. The following is a brief sketch of the most interesting remains: a fuller description of the more important of them will be found in Chapter XIX.

In the head-quarters subdivision, the town of Gayā is crowded with Hindu temples and ancient remains, and a few miles to the south is the stately fane of Bodh Gayā with some of the earliest sculptures in India. Opposite Bodh Gayā, on the narrow neck of land dividing the Nilājan and Mohāna rivers, are the remains of a large stūpa at Bakraur, which has been identified with the ancient Ajayapura. Many Buddhistic images are found in the neighbourhood and also at Punāwān, 14 miles, and Dakhin Gāwan 16 miles east of Gayā. Two miles south-east of Punāwān is Hasrā Hill, identified by Dr. Stein with the Kukkuta-pāda-giri of Hiuen Tsiang and Fa Hian, where Kāsyapa, the greatest of Buddha's disciples, is said to be buried, the mountain having burst asunder to receive him. There are many scattered remains in the valley between the Sobhnāth Hill and Hasrā Hill proper, consisting of pillars, relievos and fragments of images or sculptures of undoubted Buddhist origin; while in the neighbouring village of Bishunpur Tanrwā are some finely cut images of a life-sized Buddha and two attendants. At Kurkihār, 3 miles north-east of Wazīrganj, is a large mound evidently marking the site of what must have been extensive buildings, from which many Buddhistic images, *chaityas*, relievos and other carvings have been dug. Not far from Kurkihār are Amaithī and Urel, where some Buddhistic and Hindu remains are found, and about 11 miles to the north-east lies the village of Jethian, identified with the Yashtivana of Hiuen Tsiang, in the neighbourhood of which there are several sites associated with the wanderings of Buddha. Beyond this (in the Patna district), but separated by a high ridge, lies the valley of old Rājàgriha (Rājgīr) fraught with many associations of ancient times and dynasties. Interesting remains also exist at Belā, 13 miles north of Gayā, at Paibigha, 6 miles north-east of Belā, and at Pālī, 3 miles south, and Kespā, 6 miles north of Tekāri. At Konch, 5 miles south-west of Tekāri, is a curious brick-built temple, the architecture of which indicates a Buddhistic model, and traces of Buddhistic influence are also observable in sculptures round about. Seven miles south-east of Gayā is the Dhongrā Hill, which is identifiable with the Prāgbodhi mountain of Hiuen Tsiang, with the remains of several terraces on the slope, and of seven stūpas on the ridge of the hill. At Guneri, 8 miles north-west of Sherghāti, are many Buddhistic images and remains, marking the site, apparently, of the *Sri Gunacharita* monastery. In the extreme north of the subdivision lie the Barābar Hills with their famous rock-cut caves. Not far from these hills to the west is the curious isolated rocky peak of Kauwādol, at the base of which is a huge stone-carved image of Buddha in a sitting posture, which probably marks the site of the ancient Buddhist monastery of Silābhadra.

In the Nawāda subdivision, at Sītāmarhi, about 7 miles south-west of Hasuā, is a cave hewn in a large isolated boulder of granite, where tradition relates that Sita, the wife of Rāma, gave birth to Lava while in exile. Many legends cluster round Rajaulī with its picturesque hills and pretty valleys. Durvāsa, Lomāsa, Gautama, Sringi and other Rishis are supposed to have lived in this neighbourhood, and hills are still known by their names; while Dubaur claims to be the birthplace of Lorik, the Goālā hero, whose feats are still sung by the country folk in numerous well-known songs. At Aphsanr, about 5 miles north of Wārisalīganj, are several remains, including a very fine statue of the *Varāha*, or Boar incarnation of Vishnu.

In the Jahānābād subdivision, about 3 miles north of the Barābar Hills stands Dharāwat, near the site of the Buddhist monastery of Gunamati, where there is a fine twelve-armed statue of the Avalokitesvara Bodhisatwa by the side of a large tank. South of this on the slope of a low ridge of hills are many remains and mounds, where clay seals inscribed with the Buddhist formula have been dug out. At Dapthu, 3 miles north of Hulāsganj, are some finely-carved images and ruins of temples, and not far to the south near the village of Lāth (so called from the pillar) is a large carved monolith of granite, 53¼ feet long with an average width of 3 feet, lying half buried in an open field. Opposite the Barābar Hills, at Jāru and Banwaria on the east side of the Phalgu river are the ruins of what must have been a large temple, and there are other remains of interest at Kāko, Ghenjan and Ner.

At Shamshernagar in the Aurangābād subdivision are the ruins of a fort and also a fine mosque, which has been repaired by the Archæological Department. A fine stone temple stands at Deo and a similar one at Umgā near Madanpur, both of which have traces of Buddhistic influence in their architecture. Large Buddhistic images and many remains are found near the Mānda Hills, and at Burha, 2 miles further east, are some finely carved and polished *chaityas* and images as well as some remains marking the site of a monastery. Deokulī, Cheon and the Pachār Hill also contain remains of Brahmanical, Buddhistic and Jain interest.

APPENDIX.

To

The Commissioner of Patna.

Gya, the 11th March 1858.

"Sir,

In forwarding my annual statement, I beg to submit a short abstract of the events and occurrences which have marked, in this district, the year 1857.

Here, as elsewhere, all was quiet for the first two months. On the 28th of April I came up as officiating Collector. The storm, which shortly after burst in the North-West, appeared unlikely ever to travel so far south as Behar. Nearer and nearer, however, it came, and its approach was preceded by that general feeling of disquiet and uneasiness which is the fore-runner and sign of all great convulsions, physical or moral. The news of the mutiny at Benares ran through the district like an electric shock. I firmly believe—and the opinion is borne out by those of intelligent natives here—that on the fate of Benares hung that of Behar. There were at the time fair grounds for apprehension. The respectable natives expressed alarm; the scoundrelism of Gya began to boast and talk. It became known later that the *budmashes* had dared to speak of the approaching hour when they too would revel in the murder of Englishmen and the dishonouring of English women. There appeared signs of a possible outbreak; the 15th of June was the day said to be fixed for it. I never could discover the exact grounds for this supposition, but it seemed generally credited. A telegraphic message was sent to Calcutta, and the order came up for a Company of H. M.'s 64th, then passing through Sherghotty, to march to Gya.

About this time, I was directed to assume charge of the Magistrate's Office in addition to my own. My first object was to intimidate and disperse the *budmashes*. I instituted strict enquiries into the mode of livelihood of every doubtful man, and having received orders from the Government and the Commissioner to entertain 50 men, Police, I placed them as a guard over the four main roads leading into the town, south, north and west; the east was sufficiently protected by the river. The duty of these watches was to apprehend a number of doubtful characters, whose names were entered in a list, and to detain and bring before me all sepoys and suspicious people entering the town in gangs or with arms. A strong pressure was thus exercised over the rogues of the place. Within one week they were either caught or had escaped out of the town. Our position was soon strengthened by a reinforcement of 120 Seikhs. Shortly after their arrival I heard that the people of the town refused to sit or smoke with them, calling them Christians. It was proved against a carpenter that he had told some Seikhs their food was mixed with pig's fat and bullock's bones ground. The rascal was hanged next day; and I made it known that any man refusing to smoke with a Seikh on the ground that he was a Christian, *i. e.*, had eaten adulterated food, should be flogged. After this no more complaints were made.

On or about the 10th July, the detachment of the 64th was ordered to proceed on the Grand Trunk Road. The day before its departure, I received a letter-express from the Commissioner, desiring me to detain the troops until the return of a spy whom he had sent to Tikaree. Information, it appears, had been given to Mr. Tayler that 200 guns were mounted at the Tikaree Fort, guns belonging to Modenarain Singh. My instructions, in case the report received confirmation from the second spy, were to surprise the Fort by a night march with the troops, English and Seikh. His second spy contradicted the first, and the detachment went to Sherghotty. The removal of the English troops materially weakened our position. No one believed in the troops at Dinapore. The 5th Irregulars were said to be shaky; more than all, just at that time the march of English troops up the Trunk Road was discontinued. A few days more, and the Trunk Road might not be safe. To me Gya was no longer a place for English ladies and children. The Judge being of the same opinion, we sent round a circular, advising all to make arrangements for the removal of their families. But the Indian Englishman is a very domestic specimen of his race. We got no thanks from either wives or husbands. None would move until the Judge's and my wife led the way, when a general exodus of ladies and babies took place.

I forgot to mention that, besides 80 men of the 64th, we had had 45 of the 84th. These last remained when the first went. Our force, therefore, now consisted of 120 Seikhs and 45 English.

Until nearly the end of July matters remained in abeyance. Natives and English were watching the struggles alone. Kooer Singh's intrigues in Arrah had, previous to this, attracted my attention. I had reported his having enjoined upon his ryots to be ready when called, and had given the Commissioner notice of his writing to two of the largest zemindars in this district. On the 25th of July, the three Dinapore regiments mutinied and marched off unhurt. Information of the long-expected event was sent to me express by the Commissioner, whose letter of half-a-dozen lines ends with "Look out—large numbers of them are said to have gone in your direction." We were too weak to encounter large numbers, and I therefore asked Mr. Tayler for reinforcements, if he had them to spare. Six weeks sooner the mutiny of Dinapore would have produced an outbreak at Gya; but the rabble and scoundrelism were now cowed and without leaders; all the notorious *budmashes* lay harmless in prison; the man who was considered their chief had been sent up to Patna; the news of the defection of the three regiments passed over Gya without awakening any local response. Still it was an anxious time. I knew many of my Nujeebs* to be untrustworthy. I had had reported to me secret meetings at which some of them attended. Although I knew that, in the face of such a force as we had got, they would not attempt active revolt, I thought it far from improbable they might some night march off westward, and before doing so help themselves to a portion of the treasure over which they mounted guard alternately with the Seikhs every 24 hours.

On the 31st of July I was sitting in my room, talking to the Subahdar of the Nujeebs, when a letter, marked "urgent and express," was put into my hand. I opened it. It was from the Commissioner. In few words it informed me of the defeat of Dunbar's party at Arrah, and continued: "Everything must now be sacrificed to holding the country and the occupation of a central position." It directed me and the civil authorities to proceed "at once with all our force secretly and expeditiously to Patna." It ended with an injunction to remove the treasure "if doing so endangered not life." "What does the Commissioner Sahib say?" asked the Subahdar. I made some excuse, and after a minute or two sent him off. I then despatched a circular round the station, and within an hour every one was present. It was agreed we should start at 5 that evening. Mr. Tayler now declares that he intended the treasure to be removed, and anticipated the delay which the move must cause. Such an impression could not result from the perusal of his order. The object he

* There were 2 Nujeeb Companies with a strength of 160 men at Gya.

prominently put forward was the defence of Patna as a central position, the means the rapid concentration of all available forces, which were to proceed " at once and secretly and expeditiously." Any delay would have been contrary to the spirit and letter of the order. If " everything was to be sacrificed to the occupation of a central position," it evidently would have been going counter to the wishes and plans of the Commissioner to hazard such occupation by the delay consequent on collecting carts and moving treasure. Thus at least I argued. I thought, and still think, I was carrying out the order of my superior as intended. At six we started. I spoke to the Darogah, the Subahdar and one or two of the respectable natives, and enjoined upon them to maintain order and tranquillity.

We had gone a mile beyond the town, when it struck me that, though bound to send the Commissioner every available soldier, I was not bound myself to help in holding a central position. Mr. Hollings and I returned, thinking it best to take the bull by the horns at once. I rode first to the jail, and called out the Sepoy guard of 80 men. I spoke to them and they answered, as Sepoys do answer, with every appearance and demonstration of loyalty. Then I went to the treasury. The guard turned out with muskets, not empty-handed as at the jail. I fancied too some of them looked sulky; however, I made them a speech in Hindoostanee, and they made protestations in return. We then went home. I despatched a sowar to Sherghotty with a telegraphic message, asking for instructions. Sherghotty was abandoned. Another sowar, with a letter from Captain Thomson of the 64th, caught up his detachment at Balwa, and he at once turned back for Gya. The two days and nights preceding his arrival were anxious ones. I feared the Nujeebs making away with the treasure and joining their mutinous brethren at Arrah. We were not idle, however, during that time. I called a meeting of all the chief Gyawals or priests of Gya, and they promised me assistance and support in men and arms. Mr. Hollings and I both went to office, as a mode of quieting the native minds. The Gyawals proved a rotten reed. One of them, Deonath Sijwar, sent a few useful men; the other sent old men and blind and halt, with nothing but rusty swords. It was clear the people would not help themselves. When I found this, and before the 64th detachment arrived, I pondered on what should be done. There were no means of communicating with Calcutta except by the slow medium of the post. I had to think and act as appeared best. It seemed evident, if the danger to Patna was so real as to require the few Seikhs and English at Gya to help in warding it off, the

80 men now arrived would also be sent for. Again it appeared just as much my duty to assist Mr. Tayler with this force as with the force I had sent him. But if this force went, now that I saw no reliance could be placed on the people, with it would go my remaining chance of saving the treasure. It was determined to go to Patna and take the treasure. Six hours before leaving, a note in pencil, written by a brother officer of Captain Thomson's, came from Dinapore:—" The 8th N. I. are in full march on Gya with one gun, they say." To go north was to meet this Regiment and lose the treasure; we resolved to go south and to Calcutta. That pencil note probably saved many lives. Had we gone north, and had the jail being let loose as we traversed the town, we should have been attacked through a long succession of streets and lanes, and been fortunate to escape with life. Going south, the road was all *maidan* from the treasury door. At six the party left. How I remained behind—how the Nujeebs broke open the jail gates—how prisoners and guard together rushed to my house—how fortunately I found my horse ready saddled and contrived to escape on his back—how the scoundrel mob followed us up to a pass between some low hills nearly 3 miles from Gya, and twice attacked us—how they ran after losing 5 or 6 of their body—and how, after a long and painful march in the midst of the rains, we succeeded, thanks to the untiring vigilance and laborious care of the English soldiers, in depositing 7 lacs at the Calcutta treasury—has been already fully detailed by me.

Repulsed and discomfited, the guard and prisoners returned, looted a little money left in the treasury for the food of the jail, and then dispersed—the former to Arrah, the latter to their homes. Silent but trembling the town remained that night; next morning in its full force awoke the spirit of the oriental savage; every scoundrel had dreamt of plunder during the night, and now awoke to verify his dream; boys of 10 or 12 strutted about with swords; the peaceful and wealthy, in proportion to the *budmashes* as 10 to 1, would, in any other country, have united against a common foe; but the elements of self-government do not exist in this country. The scum and scoundrelism of the city had it all their own way. One or two bands, under able leaders, levied only blackmail, and going from house to house, sold immunity and safety; others revelled in indiscriminate plunder; five or six of the Gyawals mustered their followers and sacked a whole quarter of the town. The unhappy Hindu *mahajuns* were the chief losers, preyed upon at once by the Mahomedan rabble of the lower town, and by these priests of the upper.

On the 16th of August Gya was re-occupied by the civilians ordered back from Patna, by 35 of H. M.'s 84th, and by 220 of Captain Rattray's Seikhs with their Commander at their head. The natives, at first afraid that the burning of the Government offices and the destruction of European property was to bring a bombardment upon the city, fled in all directions, those who had looted leaving in the streets, in fields and tanks, the produce of their plunder; but as soon as it became apparent that the return of the authorities was to maintain order rather than to exact a general retribution, confidence was restored. Ten days of anarchy had disgusted all quiet men with what they called the Hindoostanee Raj. They had seen how necessary to their honour and comfort was that strong hand of the white foreigner which they used to fancy pressed heavily. They had seen how not only in the town, but in the country, every element of disorder, violence and wickedness was rife, how the village ryots as well as the town *budmash* instinctively turned to plunder and violence, how rampant and how general was that spirit of the beast of prey which acknowledges no common bounds and no law save the indulgence of its passions. "Rather than live again under such thraldom," more than one respectable native has said to me, "I would turn Christian, if this was necessary to obtain the protection of Government."

There are two curious facts connected with the disturbances in this district: one is the influence of Kooer Singh, although not a zemindar in Behar Proper; the other, the universal identification of a Hindoostanee Government with license and plunder. "Hindoostanee Raj hooa, Kooer Singh ke Raj—loot, loot," were the cries with one zemindar attacked a weaker one, one village preyed upon a neighbouring hamlet, or a dozen scoundrels knocked down and fleeced a solitary traveller. There was here no influential land-holder to knead into one large festering mass all these various scattered pieces of corruption. The anarchy rose but in three places to the so-called dignity of rebellion. In the north-east portion of the district, Hyder Ali Khan, with a few followers, attempted to regain possession of the Rajgeer Pargana, formerly belonging to his ancestors. In September he was caught and hanged. The two Anti-rajahs raised a Lilliputian standard of their own. One is hiding, the other in prison awaits his trial. At Wazeergunge, some 12 or 14 villages united under one Kosheal Singh, a ticadar of many villages, and after going through the initiatory ceremony of some indiscriminate plunder, set up the flag of Kosheal. Many of these miserable fools have been transported, but Kosheal is still uncaught. In the western thannahs, three or four factories belonging to Mr. Solano, the only European land-holder or planter here, were destroyed. I must not omit to mention the noble conduct of two men whose courage and judgment saved the station of Sherghotty. Rujjub Ali, Darogah of that place, and Babu Anand Coomar Rai of the Executive Engineer's department, remained at their posts when the Police throughout the district hid themselves, and by their example and by collecting round them the well-disposed, succeeded in overawing the *budmashes* and in preventing all plunder. The property of the Government and of English residents was untouched.

I returned on the 25th of August. The eastern portion of the district was then in possession of the mutinous 5th Irregular Cavalry. These gentry seemed aware that Government had no force to direct against them. They travelled slowly, remained three or four days at one place, and appeared under no apprehension of pursuit. They had originally come in this direction from a belief that Gya was still devoid of all troops. Even when they discovered their mistake, they did not hurry their movements in the least. At Wazeergunge, 14 miles from Gya, they remained 3 days. Meanwhile they levied contributions all around both in food and money; the Government authority was in contempt, and I began to fear lest their presence might kindle in the district a mutinous flame more dangerous than the last. Anything seemed to me better than to sit still with 250 English and Seikhs, and let these scoundrels swagger and hold the country under our noses. We were not half their number, but the Government could give us no more men. On the 6th of September the cavalry moved south from Wazeergunge. This appeared to relieve Gya from danger of an attack, and to show the enemy were on the march to the Trunk Road. Captain Rattray proposed to attack. I had all along been for offensive measures and heartily approved, telling him I thought it his duty to go out. Go out we did, and on the 8th came up with the enemy. The military operations and their result I have nothing to do with. We did not thrash the enemy, nor did they thrash us, as the Press at the time insisted. We lost none killed, but 22 wounded, of whom 2 afterwards died. The enemy lost altogether (on the field and died afterwards from wounds) about 12 men; of wounded no account could be got. The sowars moving quicker than we could got first to Gya, released the jail, went off west. They still remained nearly a fortnight longer in the district. During this time they perpetrated atrocities of all descriptions. They had been joined by a well-known scoundrel, Inder Singh, and by his followers; all the *budmashes* of Gya had gone with them, and all the worse characters from the jail. Women taken from their houses and carried off, to be a few days later left on the road-side and their places taken by the results of a fresh raid, industrious men plundered of all they had, rape, robbery and murder marked the progress of these ruffians.

At last the 5th Irregulars crossed the Soane. They had not gone very long when the approach from the south of the Ramghur Battalion began to cause alarm. Many of the men of this corps are recruited from the neighbourhood of Sherghotty, Gya, and other parts of the district.. It seemed certain, from all I heard, that their intention was to come through Sherghotty to Gya. Our force here consisted of about 50 sick and wounded Seikhs, of whom not a dozen could walk, and 35 English of the 84th, of whom eight were sick and wounded. Clearly we could do nothing against the Ramghurrees if they came. To be ready to send off the treasure, therefore, I collected some elephants and had large strong bags made, capable of holding some thousands each. For the sick I ordered a quantity of doolies, and, as it was impossible to expect to get a sufficient number of bearers on a sudden emergency, I hired some hundred or so, and told the Seikhs they must take morning and evening airings for their health. They were delighted, and daily, till the 53rd smashed the Ramghurrees at Chuttra, a long line of doolies used twice a day to leave the billiard bungalow, then the Seikh hospital, with a freight of poor wounded and suffering men. At any moment they could have gone off and been half way to Patna before the Ramghurrees got sight of Gya.

It was evident that this district was to be the high road to mutineers from the east. In July I had pointed this out to Government and foretold that when they mutinied, the 5th Irregulars and the 32nd would take the favourite native road through Deoghur, Kurrukdeea, and Nowadah. The 5th chose it. Towards the end of October, three companies of the 32nd, having mutinied at Deoghur, followed in their steps. The marvellous, the providential folly which has characterized the whole mutiny, was the saving of these Provinces. Had the Dinapore Regiments, the Ramghur Battalion, the 5th Irregulars, and the 32nd gone together, nothing could for a time have withstood them. As soon as I knew of the mutiny at Deoghur, I directed the Deputy Magistrate at Nowadah to send in his hajut (or under-trial) prisoners to Gya. The number amounted to nearly 300. You are aware, Sir, that immediately after the 5th Irregulars had crossed the Soane, Captain Rattray and every available Seikh was sent out of this district to Dehree on the Soane. By greatly enlarging the number of police, I had attempted to create a force sufficient to cope with the spirit of plunder and disaffection, still every now and then breaking out in isolated villages; but the martial Rajpoots and Brahmins of the interior were more than a match for a few burkandazes, and I was glad to accept your proffered aid of some of the Nujeebs' corps from Patna. The 40 men you sent had gone to Nowadah. As long as no mutinous soldiers were near, I felt I might trust them; but on hearing of the defection of the three companies of the 32nd, I determined to call them back, and with them the hajut prisoners. They arrived safely. The number of prisoners under trial in my jail exceeded 600, and as guard I had these 40 Nujeebs and a quantity of burkandazes. This was to me a time of great anxiety. A large number of prisoners under trial for offences involving the severest punishments—a very small guard—men whose brothers had released my jail once before and attempted my life—three companies of mutineers on the road to Gya and not far from it—and at Gya itself a heap of sick and wounded soldiers, with less than thirty men fit for duty,—all this constituted a heavy charge and a serious responsibility. I thought of sending away my entire jail in irons to some spot near the Grand Trunk Road. I had the irons prepared. I began again giving the Seikhs their morning and evening airing, when by telegraph I heard that Major English and his victorious 53rd were ordered up to Gya. It still seemed doubtful whether they or the mutineers would be here first; the latter had got to Wazeergunge; 14 miles only separated us; Colonel English was 20 miles off at Sherghotty. I sent there a pressing message, and next day the glitter of English bayonets assured us all was safe. The mutineers now turned off from their westerly course and went north. Colonel English tried to cut them off at Jehanabad, but they gave him the slip and got away. Within a week they were followed by two other companies of the same regiment who had mutinied in the Rajmehal Hills. Against these latter we went on the 1st of November. A thirty miles march brought us early to Huswa—9 miles from Nowadah." * * * * * *

After describing how the British troops pursued the rebels through the Nawāda subdivision and then round to the west through the southern portion of the Patna district and through the Jahānābād subdivision as far as the Son, Mr. Money says they lost sight of the rebels after a march of 130 miles in 4 days and 5 nights, and adds:—

"This was the last inroad of mutineers this district saw in 1857.

One or two conclusions have forced themselves upon me in connection with such inroads. The first is, the absence of truth in the general impression that mutineers always possess excellent information. I believe, on the contrary, that their information is most scanty and untrustworthy. The 5th Irregulars were not aware, till they had approached near, that Gya had been re-occupied by the Government authorities. Each body of mutineers which crossed the district was influenced in its march by false reports. The first batch of the mutinous 32nd avoided Jehanabad because they were told a force lay there in wait. Their march was by zig-zag, the villagers, to avoid their visitation, turning them out of the direct line by lies and erroneous information.

As to accurate information for myself, I never found any difficulty in getting it. No body of mutineers passed through this district without my knowing the numbers, the exact quantity of elephants or camels they had with them, and their line of march. The moment I heard of a mutiny having taken place, I laid two lines of runners along the road the enemy would take to enter the district. These lines extended to 20 and 30 miles outside my district. In addition to these, I had lines of runners to various points in the district, where I thought the mutineers would march, and to the neighbouring thannahs. The Darogahs had similar lines to places within their thannahs. All this cost a good deal of money, for I paid well, but the results were satisfactory.

It has been much the fashion amongst a certain class of English in Calcutta and at home to attribute the mutiny of 1857 in part to misrule of the Government, to our civil institutions and the mode in which they are said to press heavily upon the people. I have taken pains to ascertain whether any foundation, however slight, existed for this assertion. As far as my own experience goes, it is entirely gratuitous. No sepoy in this district has ever excused his defection on any one of these pleas. Villagers and zemindars have questioned the Sepoys as to the reasons for their mutiny. Their answers have been many and various:—"Their religion was in danger,—it was intended to blow them away from guns,—many of them had been hanged without cause, and they feared a like fate,—their pay was in arrears." These and similar ones were the grounds assigned, but among his many lies the Sepoy never was fool enough to bring forward the plea of oppressive institutions and hardship to the people. The ryot, from his own knowledge, would have laughed in his face had he done so. It remains with those who wish to make capital out of the events of the last year, to explain the mutiny upon grounds untouched by even the leaders of the mutiny. I look upon the absence of any such arguments on the part of the mutineers themselves as the strongest proof that the people do not feel our institutions oppressive. Had there been a chance of response in the great heart of the nation, the cry would have been an excellent one to appeal to the country with, and men like the Nana would not have neglected the chance. But he knew such a cry would have fallen flat and awakened no echo. It may excite the ignorant at a London public meeting, but the Indian prince and the Indian ryot heed it not. I cannot understand why the Sepoy should not be allowed to know his motives and reasons. He has proclaimed them loudly enough and in various ways, so that those who run may read. When upon throwing off his allegiance, he releases jails, plunders treasuries, and indulges in rape and rapine, he displays the vices of all pampered soldiery and shows his object to be unbridled license. When, whether mutinying at Chittagong or in the Punjaub, he turns alike his steps to Delhi, he betrays the deep strength of the old traditionary feeling still alive within; his struggles in Oudh disclose a misguided patriotism; his murdered officers silently bear witness to the instinctive hatred of race; and when, as I have seen, a young lad with tears in his eyes confesses to having believed his religion in danger, it is plain how large a part of the history of 1857 religious fanaticism has to answer for. But the want of arrangement, the absence of simultaneous action prove that there is no one broad common ground of complaint." * * *

I have, etc.,

A. Money.

CHAPTER III.

BUDDHA AND BODH GAYA

BUDDHA. THE district of Gayā may with justice be described as the Holy Land of Buddhism owing to the number of places it contains which are associated with the life and teaching of the great founder of that religion. It was here that Sākya Muni spent long years of penance and meditation before he attained the ideal he had set before him; here he finally won Buddhahood, *i.e.*, became free from the circle of re-births, and here he gained some of his earliest disciples after this great triumph. It was to this district that he turned at an early stage in his searchings after truth. Failing to find enlightenment in the ecstatic meditation affected by the teachers of Brahmanical philosophy, he determined to secure peace by a course of self-mortification, and with this intention wandered forth from Rājāgriha (Rājgir) to a wood in this district called Uruvilvā. Here, with five other ascetics, he entered on a fast lasting six long years, at the end of which he realized that the mortification of the flesh had brought him no nearer to the truth he sought, and that penance and austerity were not the means of obtaining deliverance from the evils and sufferings of life. He resumed his former diet, and when his five companions left him in anger at this change of life, he determined to give himself up to meditation in silent solitude. The tradition handed down by the Chinese pilgrim, Fa Hian, relates that he came to a cave, where he sat down and prayed that he might be granted a sign to show whether he was to arrive at the condition of perfect wisdom. Immediately his shadow appeared on the stone wall, the earth shook and the mountain quaked, and he heard the voices of the *Devas* telling him that that was not the place where he could obtain enlightenment. He then passed on towards the village of Senāni and met on his way a grass-cutter, who offered him some bundles of grass, which he accepted. Having arrived at the Bodhī tree, he scattered the grass on the ground and sat down, vowing that though his skin, nerves and bones might waste away and his blood dry up, he would not leave the place until he obtained perfect enlightenment.

He then began a long vigil, giving himself up to higher and higher forms of meditation. A great struggle between good and evil ensued. He was assaulted by the hosts of evil, by fiends and demons of all kinds, and then, finding that they had no power to shake him, Māra, the spirit of sensuous desire, tempted him with the pleasures of the flesh; other temptations followed, all of which he conquered; and finally, as day broke, the light of knowledge burst upon his mind. In the first watch of the night of this final struggle he gained a knowledge of all his former states of existence, in the second of all present states of being, and in the third the knowledge of the chain of causes and effect; at the dawn of day his spiritual illumination was complete, he knew all things, and became Buddha, the enlightened. After obtaining this perfect enlightenment, Buddha went to a place a little to the north-east, and thence looked for a week at the sacred Bodhī tree without removing his gaze from it. Between this place and his seat under the Bodhī tree he spent a week walking to and fro, from east to west, wonderful flowers springing up in the places on which he set foot. After four weeks near the Bodhī tree, the master left it and meditated for another seven days under the goat-herd's banyan-tree, and then went to another spot where Muchilinda, the serpent king, coiled his body round him as he sat in meditation, and formed a canopy over his head to protect him from the rain. He then passed on to the Rājāyatna tree, where he remained another week, on the last day of which he made his first converts—Tapussa and Bhalluka, two merchants from Orissa who happened to pass by. Shortly afterwards Buddha went to Benares and began his life-long mission; but, after sending out his 60 disciples to preach to the people, he returned to Uruvilvā. Here he converted three brothers, hermits with matted hair who worshipped fire, known as Uruvilvā Kāsyapa, Nadī Kāsyapa, and Gayā Kāsyapa, together with 1,000 Brāhmans who were their disciples. Accompanied by these, he went to the Gayāsīrsa Hill, where he preached his "burning" sermon on the fires of the passions. In this fire sermon, which is said to have been suggested by a fire seen from the rocky crest of the hill, Buddha gave a key to the meaning of Nirvāna. He pointed out that all things are burning with the fires of the passions and lusts, and that a wise man, becoming weary of the world of sense, frees himself from passion. When free he realizes that his object is accomplished, that he has lived a life of restraint and chastity, and that re-birth is ended. In this way, Buddha, comparing all life to a flame, brought home to his hearers the duty of extinguishing the fire of lust, and with it the fire of existence, and impressed upon them the importance of monkhood and celibacy for the accomplishment of that object. After staying for some time near Gayāsīrsa, Buddha wended his way with his numerous followers to the court of king Bimbisāra at Rājāgriha. Henceforward he passes away from the scene of the great consummation, and the record of his life in this district is confined to the neighbourhood of Yashtivanā, where we are told that he displayed great spiritual wonders for the sake of the *Devas* and expounded the law for three months.

The detailed descriptions which the Chinese pilgrims have left of the *topographia sacra* of Gayā have enabled many of the sites visited by Buddha to be traced with some certainty. The name of Uruvilvā has been perpetuated in the name Urel, a village close to Bodh Gayā; on the Dhongra Hill some $2\frac{1}{2}$ miles from the great temple of Bodh Gayā, a cave marks the place on the Prāgbodhi mountain where Buddha was warned that he must not stay; and pilgrims still worship at Mucharin, the spot where Buddha was sheltered by the snake-king Muchilinda. Brahmajuni, the rugged hill towering above the town of Gayā, has been identified with the hill called Gayāsīrsa; Jethian is the modern name of Yashtivana; and, close by, Tapoban with its hot springs marks the spot where the master walked for exercise. An account of these places will be found in Chapter XIX, and the present chapter will be devoted to the history of Bodh Gayā, the Gayā of enlightenment, or as it is sometimes called Buddha Gayā, the Gayā of Buddha, or Mahābodhi, the great enlightenment—a name which is also given to the *Bodhīdrūma* or sacred *pīpal*-tree.

HISTORY OF BODH GAYA.

Early history.

It was under this tree that Sākya Muni attained Buddhahood; it is the most sacred of sites to Buddhists, and worship has consequently centred round it from the earliest period of Buddhism. The tree became celebrated as the tree of enlightenment, and is now the most sacred symbol of the Buddhists, who regard it as many Christians do the cross. In the 3rd century B. C. Asoka built a monastery and erected a temple near it, giving 100,000 pieces of gold for the building. One of the bas-reliefs of the Bharhut stūpa (2nd century B. C.) gives a representation of the tree and its surroundings as they then were. It shows a *pīpal*-tree, with a stone platform in front, adorned with umbrellas and garlands, and surrounded by a building with arched windows resting on pillars, while close to it stood a single pillar with a Persepolitan capital crowned with the figure of an elephant.

From a Burmese inscription found in the residence of the Mahanth of Bodh Gayā we know that this temple became ruinous with lapse of time and was replaced by another, identified by

General Cunningham* with the present temple, which, in his opinion, was built on the site of that erected by Asoka and was set up during the rule of the Indo Scythian kings in the 2nd century A. D., though other authorities attribute it to the 5th century A. D. In the reign of Samudra Gupta a great monastery was constructed close to this temple by the Cingalese about the year 330 A. D. This monastery was built by Meghavarna, the Buddhist king of Ceylon, in consequence of the complaints made by two monks whom he had sent to do homage to the Diamond Throne and to visit the monastery built by Asoka at Bodh Gayā. On their return, they informed the king that they could find no place where they could stay in comfort, and the king resolved to found a monastery where his subjects could reside when on pilgrimage. An embassy was sent to Samudra Gupta and the required permission having been given, Meghavarna erected a splendid monastery to the north of the Bodhī tree. This building, which was three storeys in height, included six halls, was adorned with three towers, and surrounded by a strong wall 30 or 40 feet high. The decorations were executed in rich colours with high artistic skill, the statue of Buddha, cast in gold and silver, was studded with gems, and the subsidiary stūpas, enshrining relics of Buddha himself, were worthy of the principal edifice. About 600 A. D. Sasānka, the king of Central Bengal, who was a worshipper of Siva and a fanatical enemy of Buddhism, dug up and burnt the Bodhī tree, but it was replanted by Purnavarman, king of Magadha, who surrounded it with a wall in order to prevent it being cut down again. When Hiuen Tsiang visited the place in the first half of the 7th century, it was a young and vigorous tree, the temple was intact, and its precincts were crowded with hundreds of stūpas and *chaityas* erected by kings, princes and other great personages.

Mediæval history.

After this we have the records of the erection of several minor temples and of the dedication of statues at various periods down to the flourishing period of the Pāla kings in the 9th and 10th centuries. Under the rule of these Buddhist kings, the stream of Chinese pilgrimage, which had been so great in the 7th century during the reign of the powerful Buddhist monarch, Harsha Vardhana, again set in, and the sacred tree was visited by numbers of Chinese pilgrims, who have left many memorials of their visits. In the 11th century two missions were sent over to Bodh Gayā by the Burmese king, first in 1035 and then again in 1079, and the temple, which had fallen out of repair, was completely restored between the years 1079—86 A. D. The Buddhist religion appears

* Mahābodhi, from which this account of Bodh Gayā is mainly derived.

to have fallen on evil times in the 12th century, and there is a noticeable absence of inscriptions and votive offerings. A number of works, however, were carried out by Asokavalla, king of Sapādalaksha, *i.e.*, Siwālik, either a northern kingdom including the hill country of Kumāon and Garhwāl or the whole of Northern Rājputāna: indeed, one inscription found in Gayā expressly states that an appeal was made to him in consequence of the decay of the law of Buddha.

At the end of the 12th century the whole country was desolated by the Muhammadan invasion; and though Bodh Gayā is not mentioned in the records of their ravages, it seems very unlikely that it escaped when the great monastery at Bihār was sacked and its monks were slain. The gilt copper umbrella, containing a record of the first Burmese mission, which was found carefully hidden underground when the temple was restored, was probably buried at this time, when everything of value that was not secreted must have been either carried off or destroyed; and to the savage iconoclasm of the invaders must be due the many headless and broken statues found here. But though the monastery was sacked and desolate, pilgrims continued to visit the shrine, and we find records showing their presence in the early years of the 14th century. These poor pilgrims however were no longer able to build temples or dedicate stūpas as their predecessors had done, and their records are limited to rough sketches of themselves and their offerings boldly scratched on the granite pavement slabs of the temple. General Cunningham considers that from this time both the holy *pīpal*-tree and the temple were appropriated by the Brāhmans, though he gives no arguments in favour of this view, except the finding of a round stone (originally the dome of a stūpa), which formerly stood in front of the temple, with the feet of Vishnu carved on its face and a date corresponding to 1308 A. D. inscribed on its side. In any case, however, the place must have fallen under Brahmanical influence with the downfall of Buddhism, though it was still visited and has been visited up to the present day by Buddhist pilgrims performing Buddhist rites.

Except for these intermittent visits, the temple stood deserted during the 6 centuries following the Muhammadan conquest, and gradually became more and more ruinous. At the end of the 16th century a Hindu ascetic, attracted by the sylvan solitude of the place, came and settled near the temple and founded a *math* or monastery of the Hindu sect of Girs, one of the seven Saivite orders established by Sankara Achārjya. About the year 1727 the then Mahanth or abbot of the monastery received by royal *farmān* from the Mughal Emperor, Muhammad Shāh, the grant of the village of Tārādih, where the ruins of the temple stood, and thus acquired possession of the shrine. In spite of this circumstance, the temple was not used for worship by the Hindus; it was neglected and slowly but steadily crumbled away. In 1811 Buchanan Hamilton described it as "in the last stages of decay compatible with anything like a preservation of original form"; on the ground-floor was "a monstrous mis-shapen daub of clay," with a motley row of images taken from the ruins and built in front of it so as to hide part of the deity; the sacred *pīpal*-tree was still an object of worship and frequented by the pilgrims of Gayā, but a stair had been built on the outside of the temple, "so that the orthodox may pass up without entering the porch and thus seeing the hateful image of Buddha."

Modern history.

In the early part of the 19th century archæologists began to make enquiries into the history of Bodh Gayā, and it was visited by a Burmese mission in 1833; but it was not till 1884 that the ruins were restored. In 1876 Mindoon Min, king of Burma, being anxious to restore the temple and to construct a building on the adjacent ground for the accommodation of a number of Buddhist priests who wished to settle there for the performance of religious service at the shrine, obtained the permission of the Government of India to depute a party of Burmese officials and workmen for the purpose. It soon appeared however that this work was being done without due regard to archæological fitness, and, after an investigation made by Dr. Rājendralāla Mitra, Government took the work of restoration into its own hands and completed it in 1884 at a cost of two lakhs. Government placed the building which they had thus restored under the Public Works Department and appointed an overseer as custodian of the temple. They have undertaken and paid for such repairs as have been found necessary ever since, and have also kept in repair the adjoining Burmese rest-house, which was originally built from Burmese subscriptions.

Of late years the Buddhists have been endeavouring to recover this ancient shrine, one of the objects of the Mahābodhi Society, which was founded by Buddhists of Ceylon in 1891, being to secure possession of the Bodh Gayā temple for the Buddhists. In 1893 an endeavour was made on behalf of the Society to obtain a lease or conveyance of the temple from the Mahanth of Bodh Gayā; and on the failure of these negotiations, the Secretary of the Society invoked the assistance of the Bengal Government, but was informed that Government could take no measures for the furtherance of the general objects of the Society, and that there was perfect freedom of worship for all Buddhists at Bodh Gayā. In the same year the Secretary had been entrusted, when in

Japan, with an historical image of Buddha for enshrinement in the temple, and in 1895 he proceeded to place the image in the temple without permission. This action was resented by the disciples of the Mahanth, and a disturbance ensued which resulted in the removal of the image* and the expulsion of those who were enshrining it. A protracted criminal prosecution followed, which ended in the conviction of some disciples of the Mahanth in the local Courts; but they were acquitted by the High Court on appeal, on the ground that it was not established that the complainant and his companions were lawfully engaged in religious worship when they were disturbed, and that the accused had therefore committed no offence under section 296, Indian Penal Code. The Mahanth's position in regard to the temple was discussed at length in the various judgments recorded in the course of these proceedings; and the High Court found that the Mahanth was in possession, was sole superintendent of the temple, and took all the offerings both of Hindus and Buddhists. They stated, however, that it might be conceded that the Mahābodhi temple was a Buddhist temple, that, although it had been in the possession of Hindu Mahanths, it had never been converted into a Hindu temple in the sense that Hindu idols have been enshrined or orthodox Hindu worship carried on there, and that Buddhist pilgrims had had free access and full liberty to worship in it. At the same time, they observed that the evidence showed that since July 1894 the Mahanth and his disciples had been carrying on a sort of spurious Hindu worship of the great image of Buddha on the altar of the ground-floor, and that the image had been dressed in a way that made it repugnant to Buddhist worshippers. These proceedings in the criminal courts produced much irritation and bitterness between the two sects. The attempt to place the image in the temple was regarded by the Hindus as being intended to assert and establish a right to the building, and they have consequently become less tolerant. The Buddhists have not ceased to press for larger privileges and to complain of the present state of affairs, and on the other hand the Mahanth has continued to assert his authority and his right to control the worship.

The present position of affairs is somewhat anomalous. The temple was originally a Buddhist shrine, but for a long time past has been in the possession of a Hindu Mahanth belonging to an order founded by one of the bitterest enemies of Buddhism. It had fallen into complete ruin and would soon have disappeared had not Government restored it at its own cost; in consequence, they

* The image is now in the Burmese rest-house to the west of the temple.

maintain a custodian for the care of the building and see to its repairs. The Mahanth controls the worship and receives the offerings made by Buddhists and Hindu pilgrims, Government maintaining an attitude of impartiality on all religious questions affecting the shrine. The Buddhists perform the rites of their religion at the shrine and under the Bodhi tree, just as Buddhists of different countries have done for centuries past, but Hindus also make offerings under the tree, as it is recognized as one of the 45 *vedis* or places which Hindus visit while performing the religious ceremonies for the salvation of their ancestors which centre round the holy city of Gayā. This Hindu reverence for the tree is very old, but side by side with it there is a Hindu cult of very recent growth, as Hindu worship, which has been pronounced to be of a spurious and unorthodox character, is offered at the shrine itself.

Remains at Bodh Gaya.

The temple.

In its main features the present temple represents the structure as it must have existed as early as 635 A. D., when the Chinese pilgrim, Hiuen Tsiang, saw it. It consists of a main tower, rising to the height of 180 feet, in the form of a slender pyramid which springs from a square platform, on the four corners of which are similar towers of smaller size. The outside walls have niches for the reception of statues, and access to the temple is obtained through an eastern gate supported by pillars, which opens on to an ante-room in front of the sanctum. At the western wall of the sanctum is an altar upon which is placed the principal image, a large mediæval statue of Buddha with various other images on each side. The main figure has been gilded over, and the Hindu custodians of the shrine have marked its forehead with the sectarian mark of the Vaishnavas, in order to represent it as the Buddha incarnation of Vishnu. In the upper floor another chamber contains a statue known as Māyā Devī, the mother of Buddha. The features of the temple described by Hiuen Tsiang correspond so clearly with that of the present structure that there can be little doubt that the shrine he visited is the same as that now standing. He described it as built of bluish bricks with a facing of plaster; in the four faces were several tiers of niches, each containing a gilded statue of Buddha; the walls were covered with beautiful sculptures, festoons of pearls and figures of *rishis;* and the architraves, pillars, doors and windows were ornamented with gold and silver chasing, in which pearls and precious stones were inserted. The magnificent adornments of the temple and the hundred of images enshrined in the niches have long since disappeared, but otherwise the structure is the same. Its dimensions correspond with those described by Hiuen Tsiang, it is built of blue bricks with a coating of plaster, and the four faces present several tiers of niches rising one above the other;

in some of these Buddhist figures were found as late as the time of restoration, and even the entrance on the east side was found to be a later addition, as stated by the Chinese pilgrim.

The discoveries made during the restoration show that this temple was built over Asoka's temple, and some remains of the latter were, in fact, found in the course of the excavations. A throne of polished sandstone was discovered with four short pilasters in front, just as in the Bharhut bas-relief; two Persepolitan pillar bases of Asoka's age were found flanking it; and the remains of old walls were laid bare under the basement of the present temple. When this restoration was undertaken, the temple court was covered with the accumulated debris of ages and with deposits of sand left by the floods of the river Nilājan. The courtyard was cleared, the temple completely restored, the portico over the eastern door and the four pavilions flanking the pyramid were rebuilt, and the great granite Toran gateway to the east, which dates back to the 4th or 5th century, was again set up. The model used in restoring the temple was a small stone model of the temple as it existed in mediæval times, from which the design* of the building as it then existed could be traced with some certainty. The work has been subjected to much adverse criticism, from which it might be presumed that visitors would find a temple robbed of its age and beauty, with a scene of havoc around it. The reverse is the case; the temple has been repaired as effectively and successfully as funds would permit, and the site has been excavated in a manner which will bear comparison with the best modern work elsewhere. Rising from the sunken courtyard, the temple still rears its lofty head, a monument worthy of the ancient religion it represents; the Vajrāsan throne is in its old place; and the shrine is still surrounded by the memorials erected by Buddhist pilgrims of different countries and different ages.

The Bodhī tree.

A few yards to the west of the western wall of the temple stands the *pīpal*-tree, which is known as the Bodhī tree (*Bodhīdūrma*), *i.e.*, the tree of enlightenment or the tree of wisdom. This tree is the oldest historical tree in the world, and has had an eventful history. It was first cut down by Asoka in his unregenerate days, but after he became a believer in the law of Buddha he lavished an inordinate devotion upon it. His queen, jealous of this attachment and grudging the jewels which Asoka offered to the tree, again had it cut down, but for a second time it was miraculously restored to life.

* In his "Lhasa and its Mysteries" Lieutenant-Colonel Waddell gives an interesting comparison between the temple as it was before restoration and the great pagoda by the side of the temple at Gyantse in Tibet, which is locally known as the Gandhola, the old Indian title of the Bodh Gayā temple, and which is said to be a model of that temple transplanted to Tibet.

The intense veneration in which the tree was held even at this early date is shown by the gorgeous ceremonies which took place when a branch was transported to Ceylon in the reign of Asoka. From the Buddhist chronicles we learn that the whole way from Patna to Bodh Gayā was cleared and decorated, and that a splendid urn of solid gold was made for the reception of the sacred shoot. The Emperor himself, attended by a long train of elephants, chariots, horse and foot, escorted the urn to the tree, which its votaries had enriched with all manner of gifts. Gems sparkled from among its leaves, rows of flags and streamers waved from its branches, and it was laden with fragrant blossoms, the offerings of devotees. After elaborate ceremonies, a branch was lopped off, placed in the urn, and then escorted with much pomp to the coast. A bas-relief on the eastern gateway at Sānchi pourtrays the scene. In the middle is seen the Bodhī tree with Asoka's temple rising half-way up it. A procession with musicians is carved on both sides, and to the right a royal person, perhaps Asoka, is dismounting from his horse with the help of a dwarf. Above is another sculpture which shows a small Bodhī tree in a pot and a long procession on its way to a towered city.

For a third time it was destroyed by Sasānka, who cut it down, dug up its roots, and burnt it with fire, in order that not a trace of it might be left. Soon afterwards it was restored by Purnavarman, who followed his great ancestor Asoka in his devotion to Buddhism; and a wonderful account is given of miraculous resuscitation. In a single night the tree sprang up to a height of 10 feet, and then, fearing that it might again be cut down, the king surrounded it with a wall of stone 24 feet high, by which General Cunningham understands that the new tree was placed on the terrace of the temple, which is over 30 feet above the original ground level. When Buchanan Hamilton visited the temple in 1811, he found the tree in full vigour, but judged that it could not be more than 100 years old. By 1875 this tree had become completely decayed, and in 1876 it was blown down during a storm. Many seeds however had been collected, and one of the offshoots of the parent tree was ready to take its place and was planted.

There can be little doubt that the same expedient has been followed ever since the tree obtained its sanctity, and that the present tree is a lineal descendant of that under which Buddha obtained perfect wisdom. It was destroyed several times, and, though the Buddhist chroniclers have concealed the fact by miraculous accounts of the way in which it was restored on each occasion, there can be little doubt that the life of the tree was perpetuated by dropping a seed in a fork or hollow of the dying trunk. The *pīpal* is a quick-growing tree, and there must have been a long succession of fresh trees raised from seed of the parent tree from the time of Asoka down to the present day. In 1861 traces were found of a succession of platforms below the high terrace on which the tree then stood, and in 1880 General Cunningham found two large pieces of an old *pīpal*-tree 3 feet below the level of the Diamond throne and 30 feet below the level of this terrace. As the whole mass of the buttress at the back of the temple had been standing on this spot for more than 12 centuries, General Cunningham considered it not improbable that these two fragments might be part of the tree which was cut down by Sasānka in the beginning of the 7th century.

The Diamond throne.

Under the Bodhī tree is a sandstone slab known as the Vajrāsan or Diamond throne, which still retains its original position of Buddha's seat (*Bodhimanda*) and the reputed centre of the universe. It derives its name from the fact that it is regarded as having stability, indestructibility and capacity of resisting all worldly shocks. The throne consists of a polished slab of grey sandstone with a surface carved with geometrical patterns, circular in the middle, with a double border of squares. All the four outer faces are richly carved with pigeons, conventional flowers * and the geese of Asoka's pillar capitals. General Cunningham is of opinion that it must have been exposed to view on all four sides in an open building, and once formed the upper slab of the sandstone throne inside Asoka's temple. It rests on a brick platform ornamented with boldly moulded figures of men and lions; and judging from the round faces, full lips and easy pose of the figures, General Cunningham assigns the pedestal to the time of the later Indo-Scythian or earlier Gupta kings. In the middle of one of the faces the restorers found a ball of clay enclosing a rich treasure, which helped to fix the date of the temple, as it contained gold impressions of a coin of Kuvishka, who was a liberal patron of Buddhist ecclesiastical institutions in the latter half of the 2nd century A. D. This treasure included gold flowers studded with sapphires, shells of gold, pearls, coral, crystal, sapphires, rubies and emeralds ; and even the plaster of the throne was composed of powdered coral, mixed with sapphires, crystal, pearl and ivory, and bound together with lime. The throne itself should probably be ascribed to the time of Asoka, as the geese and other conventional ornaments are

* Lt.-Colonel Waddell points out that the plinth of the throne of the Grand Lāma in the Potala at Lhāsa is "ornamented with the same simple diaper-worked flowers like marguerites." *See* Lhasa and its Mysteries, p. 391.

exactly the same as those found on the capitals of the Asoka pillars.

Dr. Rājendralāla Mitra* was of opinion that the true Diamond throne was the massive chlorite slab which has rested for many years in a shed to the east of the shrine, known as the temple of Vāgeswarī Devī. This stone, which is to be removed to the temple precincts, is a circular blue slab streaked with whitish veins, the surface of which is covered with concentric circles of various minute ornaments, the second circle being composed of conventional thunderbolts (*vajra*), and the third being a wavy scroll filled with figures of men and animals. These circles occupy a breadth of 15 inches, leaving in the centre a plain circle, inside which is a square. General Cunningham, however, believes that this is the stone described by Hiuen Tsiang as "a blue stone, with wonderful marks upon it and strangely figured," which stood before a large *vihārā* to the west of the Bodhī tree. This stone was the seven-gemmed throne made by Indra on which Buddha sat after his enlightenment, but the Chinese pilgrim added sadly:—"From the time of the Holy One till the present is so long that the gems have turned into stone."

The Asoka railing.

The ancient stone railing containing the pillars mentioned above certainly belongs for the greater part to the time of Asoka's reign, and forms one of the oldest sculptured monuments in India. According to Hiuen Tsiang, Asoka surrounded the Bodhī tree with a stone wall 10 feet high, and this measurement corresponds with the height (9 feet 10 inches) of the pillars still existing, while the pillars themselves bear inscriptions in Asoka characters. The enclosure of Asoka's temple was 250 feet in extent with 64 pillars, whereas the circuit of the present railing is not less than 520 feet, which would have required double the number of pillars; and it appears therefore that the original railing of Asoka was re-arranged and its circuit enlarged to suit the greater dimensions of the surrounding enclosure of the great temple which replaced Asoka's chapel. The remains of 62 of the pillars of this greater enclosure are *in situ*, a large number being of granite and the remainder of fine sandstone; about half a dozen more have been removed to Kensington and the Indian Museum at Calcutta; and 23 more, which have until recently been in the various courts of the *math* at Bodh Gayā, are to be restored to their proper place round the temple.

The pillars of the railing have been replaced as far as possible, and the original design can still be traced. The inner faces of the coping stones are ornamented with long strings of animals,

* Buddha Gayā, pp. 142—144.

some natural and others quite fabulous, such as winged horses and fish-tailed elephants, lions and rams; the outer faces are decorated with continuous bands of flowers. The carved rail-bars, which are fitted into almond-shaped holes in the sides of the pillars, are ornamented on both sides with circular bosses or medallions containing capitals of pillars, flowers, and kings' busts. The pillars themselves have at the top and bottom of each face semi-circular medallions containing half flowers or small scenes of various kinds, and in the middle of each face there is a full circular medallion ornamented in the same way. The sculptures are vigorously carved, the variety of subjects represented being astonishing; some have only figures such as crocodiles, winged horses, grotesque faces, kings' heads, and lotus flowers, while one curious figure is somewhat like a mermaid; others, which represent scenes of ordinary life, might have been carved at the present time, such as a boat being poled through a mass of lotus leaves and a ploughing scene in which a pair of bullocks draw the plough. Others again pourtray mythical or religious subjects. The Bodhī tree is shown adorned with umbrellas and garlands; on another medallion the *dharmachakra* or Wheel of the Law is set up on a throne with two attendants in the act of worship; a *Deva* is represented flying over the battlements of a city, with a garland in his outstretched hand, towards a Bodhī tree before which a man is kneeling in adoration; and on a pillar near the south-east corner there is a full-length mutilated figure of a Yakshinī clinging to a tree with her foot supported by a male figure. One of the best preserved shows the householder Anāthapindika and his servants covering the whole surface of the Jetavana garden at Srāvasti with square golden coins, while a servant comes up to them with a basket full of more coins. In another, showing the famous Kalpadrūma or wishing-tree, two arms are seen extended from the tree, one holding a plate with food and the other a pitcher towards a man who is stretching out his arm to receive them; in another Indra's harper stands before the Indrasilā cave in which Buddha's seat can be seen. The most interesting, however, of all the sculptures is on a pillar which has recently been removed from the adjoining Hindu monastery. It shows a figure of the sun-god standing on his chariot drawn by four horses, with two attendants shooting arrows to right and left, and is clearly an adoption of similar types of the Greek Apollo.

The Jewelled Cloister.

The only other remains now extant of so early a period are the bases of some columns on a brick wall about 3 feet high to the north of the temple. These mark the promenade where

Buddha walked for 7 days after the great consummation, and where flowers sprung up beneath his feet; they are the sole traces left of the Jewelled Cloister, a long pavilion covering the path which Buddha once trod, the columns of which were hung with garlands of flowers and strings of jewels. Twenty-two pillared bases are still *in situ*, each marked with a letter of the Indian alphabet of Asoka.

To the visitor unacquainted with Buddhist countries one of the most interesting sights at Bodh Gayā is the vast number of stūpas ranged round the temple in the sunken courtyard. It was the custom of Buddhist pilgrims to leave as memorials of their visits stūpas, which varied in size and magnificence with the wealth of the votaries. Hiuen Tsiang has left it on record that the precincts were crowded with them, and during the excavations made at the time of restoring the temple thousands of stūpas of all sizes were found, some built of stones and bricks, others great monoliths; others again, whose number could be counted in hundreds of thousands, were small clay stūpas, from 2 or 3 inches in height to the size of a walnut, which would appear to have been the number of offerings of poor pilgrims who could afford no more. As the soil silted up and the level of the courtyard rose, later stūpas were built over the tops of the earlier ones in successive tiers of different ages, and temples were found standing on broken stūpas, and stūpas resting upon ruined temples. So great was the number of these successive monuments, and so rapid the accumulation of earth and stones, that the general level of the courtyard was raised about 20 feet above the floor of the temple. A great number have been set up again in the courtyard, and here the memorials of pilgrims of different ages can still be seen, beginning with rude, rough monoliths of early periods, and ending with the tall ornamented spire of the mediæval ages, surmounting a dome with an elaborately carved basement. The earlier stūpas appear to have been crowned with umbrellas of stone or copper gilt, but were severely simple and unadorned; in the later ones the dome, which was originally the principal feature of the stūpa, became a mere top, below which figures of Buddha were placed in rows of niches, and the umbrella above the dome became a tall spire of successive tiers of umbrellas. Stūpas.

The great statue of Buddha which is enshrined in the sanctuary on the lower floor of the temple was set up during the restoration to replace a brick and mortar statue which had been placed there by the Burmese. By far the greatest number of the figures of Buddha represent him seated under the Bodhī tree, but the ancient examples are very few, and nearly the whole of Statues.

the sculptured figures belong to the mediæval period and are not earlier than the period of the Pāla kings (800—1200 A. D.). They belong to the latest phase of Buddhism and afford a striking illustration of what that religion had become before its final overthrow.

Other remains.

Scarcely more than one quarter of the old site has been excavated; but, as far as can be judged from the present state of the ruins, the entire area of the main enclosure of the temple has been laid open. It was filled with an enormous amount of smaller shrines, *chaityas*, votive stūpas and the like, the foundations of which are still extant. South of the temple is an old tank, called *Buddha-pokhar*, which may be the tank excavated by the brother of the Brāhman who is said to have built the temple, and north-west, at a place now called Amar Singh's fort, remains of the ancient monastery mentioned above have been discovered. Very little of these remains can, however, be seen at present, and here as in other places further excavation on a systematic scale may yield valuable results. It is possible also that many treasures may be found in the local *math*, as the neighbourhood of the temple was probably the quarry for the materials used in constructing it. It has been the receptacle for many fine statues and is known to contain remains of archæological and historical interest. From this monastery the great image of Buddha was brought to its place in the sanctum; some of the pillars of the Asoka railing until recently supported a verandah inside it; a long Sanskrit inscription was found here in the ground with a hole bored in it, on which the lower tenon of a gate played; and here too were found the Burmese inscription recording the restoration of the temple in 1709—86 A. D. and a Chinese inscription of the same century recording the erection of a Pagoda near the Diamond throne by the command of the Chinese Emperor.

CHAPTER IV.

THE GAYA PILGRIMAGE.

Sanctity of Gaya.

Gaya is one of the great places of pilgrimage in India and has especial sanctity in the eyes of Hindus. It is their belief that it is incumbent on every Hindu to visit Gayā and there make offerings for the souls of his ancestors. By so doing, the spirits of the deceased obtain deliverance from hell and admission to the paradise of Vishnu, while their descendants themselves acquire personal merit and absolution from some of the deadliest sins of the Hindu code. From the moment the pilgrim starts from his home, the deliverance of his ancestors begins; he is said to be making a ladder to heaven for them and himself; and the offerings at the holy sites crowded in and round Gayā assure their salvation and his own blessing. To save the spirits of the dead from torment is the first duty of a son, and the performance of the *srāddha* or funeral ceremonies at Gayā is regarded as a certain means to secure that end.

The Gayā legend.

The sanctity of Gayā is based on a legend contained in the Gayā Mahātmya, which forms part of the Vāyu Purāna. This legend relates that a giant demon, named Gayā Asura, performed a rigid penance for a thousand years. The gods, anxiously fearing that they could give no sufficient recompense for his piety, came to him and asked what reward he wanted; his request that he might be the holiest of all things was granted, with the result that all who saw or touched him went to Heaven. Yama, the God of Hell, finding that he was monarch of an empty realm, appealed to the gods. They persuaded Gayā Asura to allow a sacrifice to be performed on his body; the sacrifice (*jajna*) was accordingly performed, but the demon was not yet laid. Yama then brought a sacred rock from his home, which he placed on the demon's head, and all the gods sat on his body, but still the demon moved. At last Vishnu was called in; he struck Gayā with his club and removed with this blow, as the account euphemistically has it, all his fatigue and pain. Gayā Asura begged as a last boon that the gods should abide for all time on his body, and that this should be the holiest of spots, within the limits of which all men might obtain salvation by offering *srāddha.* His prayer was granted, and his body became the holy ground of Gayā.

At the time of this great sacrifice Brahma, seeing that the Brāhmans refused to accept the offerings, incarnated the Gayāwāl Brāhmans in fourteen gotras to assist in the sacrifice. On its completion he made them gifts of mountains of silver and gold, and tanks and rivers of milk and honey, on the one condition that they should never accept gifts for *srāddha.* Yama, however, after performing *srāddha*, gave them gifts of gold and jewels secreted in betel-leaves. Brahmā therefore cursed them, and their mountains turned to stone, their rivers and tanks to water. They threw themselves on Brahmā's mercy ; in pity, he promised that, though the precious mountains and rivers were for ever lost, they should have their one means of livelihood in the gifts of devotees who performed *srāddha* at Gayā, and that, though void of knowledge and learning, they should be respected and worshipped by all.

In this legend Dr Rājendralāla Mitra* finds an allegory of the triumph of Brahmanism over Buddhism, and points to the similarity between the character of Gayā Asura and the practice of Buddhism as it appeared to Hindus. He argues that the benevolent demon, like the Buddhists, made salvation too easy a matter, and was therefore an enemy to Brahmanism, while the followers of Buddha were as pious and self-mortifying as the Asura, and like him did away with Brahmanism and all sacrifice. The distance covered by Gayā's body is, he considers, perhaps an allusion to the area over which Buddhism obtained, the crushing of the good devil represents an appeal to force, and the rock placed on his head corresponds in extent to the present Gayā. Analogy is found in similar legends, such as that of the ogre Mochana, who tried to force his way into the assembly of the gods at Benares, and had almost entered the city, when its guardian, Bhairo Nāth smashed his head in with his club. The demon prayed that, as he was so near success, Mahādeo should allow him a place in the holy city ; the prayer was granted and the demon deified. Here, too, it has been held that the story of the struggle points to a religious strife between Brahmanism and Buddhism, which ended in a compromise, the latter religion not being entirely rooted out, but incorporated in Brahmanism.

Another fact which lends support to this theory is that the same legend is current in the distant Province of Orissa, once, like Gayā, a noted centre of Buddhism. Writing in 1822, Stirling† says in his description of Jājpur, a town in the district of Cuttack:

* Buddha Gayā, pp. 10—18.

† An Account of Orissa Proper or Cuttack, by A. Stirling.

"Jajipur is farther esteemed from its being supposed to rest on the navel of the tremendous giant or demon, called the Gaya Asur, who was overthrown by Vishnu. Such was his bulk that when stretched on the ground, his head rested at Gayā, his navel (nabhi) at this place, and his feet at a spot near Rajamendri. There is a very sacred well or pit within the enclosure of one of the Jājipur temples, called the Gaya Nábhi or Bamphi, which is fabled to reach to the navel of the monster, and into it the Hindu pilgrims throw the *Pinda*, or cake of rice, and sweetmeats, which is offered at particular conjunctions as an expiation for the sins of their ancestors." Here too it is said that Brahmā performed a great sacrifice, importing a vast number of Brāhmans from Kanauj to officiate, and this great *jajna* is perpetuated in the name of the town. The king with whose name the revival of Brahmanism in Orissa is usually associated had his capital at Jājpur, and leaving aside the mythical element, there is good reason for believing that he imported a number of pure Brāhmans from Kanauj, the stronghold of Brahmanism in Northern India, with the object of reviving the Brahmanical faith and of supplanting the Buddhism which had a firm hold on the country. The similarity between the legends attaching to the two towns is at least very striking, and it may well be that in both places they point to the former prevalence of Buddhism and to its assimilation with the triumphant cult of Brahmanism.

The antiquity of Gayā pilgrimage.

There is at any rate no doubt that the sanctity of Gayā as a pilgrim city dates back to an early age, and that it was visited by Hindu pilgrims even under the rule of the Pāla kings, when Buddhism still had its royal patrons and was in a flourishing condition. The evidence of inscriptions is particularly valuable in this respect, as they show clearly that the sacred *tīrthas* or places of pilgrimages at Gayā existed at a date long anterior to the time when the present temples were erected, and that Gayā was known as a pilgrim city at least as early as the 10th century* A. D. An inscription of that century near the Akshayabat or undying fig-tree mentions the tree, and shows that it was then one of the *vedis* or holy sites visited by pilgrims. In another unpublished inscription Vajrapānī, the Governor of Nayapāla

* Mahāmahopādhyāya Hara Prasād Sāstri informs me that it is probable that Gayā did not acquire a pan-Indian celebrity before this time, and points out that Gayā is not mentioned among the great places of pilgrimage in the sloka-*Ayodhyā, Mathurā, Māyā, Kāsi, Kānchi, Avantika, Purī Dvāravatī, chaiva saptaitāh mokshadayikāh, i. e.*, these seven are the givers of salvation, Ajodhyā, Mathurā, Māyā, Kāsi, Kānchi, Avanti and the city of Dvārakā. This couplet was composed probably in the 8th century A. D., and from the absence of any mention of Gayā, it appears that any importance it may have had then was only local.

(1060 A. D.), boasts of raising Gayā from a small place into an Amrāvati (city of Indra); and it may be conjectured that at this time the Gayāwāls developed their organization and regulated the worship. A third inscription* of later date throws more light on the Gayā pilgrimage. This inscription records a pilgrimage to Gayā which some Rājput minister, apparently from the north-west, undertook in 1242; and to commemorate its accomplishment the pilgrim says: "I have done Gayā. Witness thereof is Prapitāmaha." A statement of this kind, technically known as Sākshi-Srāvana, is incumbent on every pilgrim either at the end of his offerings at each *vedi* he has to visit, or at the completion of the whole pilgrimage, when he invokes the gods as witnesses that by completing the prescribed rites he has freed himself from the debts he owes his ancestors. In the ritual observed at the present day the Akshayabat and the temple of Prapitāmahesvara are the last spots visited by the pilgrims; and, as this record refers to the deity of the temple where the pilgrimage now ends, it seems clear that in one important point at least, the ritual observed at Gayā some 650 years ago was exactly the same as it is at the present day.

THE PILGRIMAGE. The first ceremony to be observed by the pilgrim is to shave at the river Pūnpūn, and on arrival at Gayā itself he is conducted before the Gayāwāl who is his family priest, and worships his feet. The Gayā *srāddha* then begins, and the pilgrim visits, if he is piously inclined, and has time and money to spare, all the 45 *vedis*, which lie within the holy ground extending for some 15 miles between the Pretsilā Hill on the north and Bodh Gayā on the south, and which centre in Gayā itself. It is absolutely essential, however, to offer *pindas* or balls of rice to the spirits of the dead in three places, viz., at the Phalgu river, the Vishnupad temple, and the Akshayabat or undying fig-tree. The Phalgu is said to be the embodiment of Vishnu itself, and is also peculiarly associated with *srāddha* ceremonies, as Sīta here offered a *pinda* of sand, in default of rice, to the spirit of Dasaratha, the father of Rāma. Here the pilgrim begins his round by a *sankalpa*, *i.e.*, a vow to perform all the rites duly, and this is followed by *tarpana*, or homage offered to the spirits of the departed, with water, *kusa* grass and sesamum seed. Then comes the full *srāddha* with balls of rice or barley-flour mixed with milk, water, flowers, sandal-wood, betel-leaves, etc., and small lighted lamps. The rites of bathing, *tarpana* and *pindadān* are repeated, one or more of them, at all the *vedis* subsequently visited. The Vishnupad temple

* Report Arch. Surv. Bengal Circle for 1901-02.

in the heart of old Gayā is one of the most sacred of all the Vaishnava temples in India; most of the later Sāstras enjoin that no one should fail to visit this holy spot at least once in his life-time; and in one of the Smritis the wish for numerous off-spring is commended on the ground that one of the many sons may visit Gayā and rescue his father from the horrors of hell by performing *srāddha* on the sacred imprint of Vishnu's feet. The outline of these foot-prints are still to be seen, encased in silver, on a large granite stone with an uneven top, which is much worn with the frequent washings it daily undergoes. The third of the three *vedis* which no pilgrim may omit is the Akshayabat tree. Coming to this at the end of his pilgrimage he offers *pindas* to the spirits of his ancestors and gifts to the Gayāwāl, before whom he prostrates himself in worship. The Gayāwāl touches him on the back and blesses him by pronouncing the word "*Suphal*," assuring him thereby that his worship has been "fruitful", *i.e.*, that he has secured salvation for his ancestors and blessings for himself. The gifts (*dakshinā*) which are the Gayāwāl's due having been paid and this blessing received, he is presented by the Gayāwāl with sweetmeats and a garland of sacred flowers as *prashādi*, he has the *tilak* mark placed on his forehead, and is free to go away in peace.

As regards the actual ceremonies observed, the following account written by Monier Williams,* which gives an interesting description of the rites, may be quoted:—"A party consisting of six men and one Gaywāl entered one of the colonnades of the temple and seated themselves on their heels in a line, with the officiating priest at their head. Twelve Pindas were formed of rice and milk, not much larger than the large marbles used by boys. They were placed with sprigs of the sacred Tulasī plant in small earthen-ware platters. Then on the top of the Pindas were scattered Kusa grass and flowers. I was told that the Pindas in the present case were typical of the bodies of the twelve ancestors for whom the Srāddha was celebrated. The men had Kusa grass twisted round their fingers, to purify their hands for the due performance of the rite. Next, water was poured into the palms, part of which they sprinkled on the ground, and part on the Pindas. One or two of the men then took threads off their clothes and laid them on the Pindas. This act is alleged to be emblematical of presenting the bodies of their departed ancestors with garments. Meanwhile texts and prayers were repeated, under the direction of the Gaywāl, and the hands were sometimes extended

The ceremonies.

* Religious Life and Thought in India, pp. 310-311, by Monier Williams, M.A., C.I.E.

over the Pindas as if to invoke blessings. The whole rite was concluded by the men putting their heads to the ground before the officiating Brāhman and touching his feet.

"The number of Pindas varies with the number of ancestors for whom the Srāddhas are celebrated, and the size of the balls and the materials of which they are composed differ according to the caste and the country of those who performed the rite. I saw one party in the act of forming fourteen or fifteen Pindas with meal, which were of a much larger size than large marbles. This party was said to have come from the Dekhan. Sometimes the Pindas were placed on the betel-leaves with pieces of money, which were afterwards appropriated by the priests; and sometimes the water used was taken out of little pots by dipping stalks of Kusa grass into the fluid and sprinkling it over the balls. At the end of all the ceremonies a prayer was said for pardon, lest any minute part of the ceremonial had been unintentionally omitted. Then finally all the earthen platters employed were carried to a particular stone in the precincts of the temple and dashed to pieces there. No platter is allowed to be used a second time. The Pindas are left to be eaten by birds and other animals, or reverently deposited in the river."

The pilgrims.

In the Gayā Mahātmya it is laid down that the Gayā *srāddha* is equally efficacious at all times of the year, but there are three seasons when pilgrims flock to the sacred city, viz., (1) the month of Asin (September-October), (2) of Pus (December-January), and (3) of Chait (March-April); these three seasons are significantly styled *fasils* or harvests. Pilgrims from Bengal and the East come chiefly in Chait, and pilgrims from the north-west and west of India in the month of Asin. According to the sacred books, Asin is the most auspicious month, and this is the great time of pilgrimage, when men of the Punjab and Bombay, Gwalior and the South come to the pilgrim city: in fact, it is estimated that at this time no less than 100,000 pilgrims visit Gayā. But considerations of convenience probably regulate the seasons more than anything else. The importance of getting in the rich rice harvest, for instance, probably deters the Bengal pilgrims from coming in the Asin season; and the pilgrims from Northern and North-Western India do not like being away from home while the *rabi* is being harvested. The pilgrims are also influenced by the occurrence of a *kāla suddha* (auspicious time) or *kāla asuddha* (inauspicious time), and the occurrence of an eclipse is the occasion for a great influx of devotees.

The pilgrims are of three classes,—those who come voluntarily, those who are brought by paid agents of the Gayāwāls, and those brought by professional pilgrim hunters acting independently of the Gayāwāls. Voluntary pilgrims come all the year round, and the principal Gayāwāls depute servants to the railway station to meet the trains and fetch those pilgrims who should come to them. By tacit consent, or as the result of immemorial custom, the whole of India has been parcelled out among the several families of Gayāwāls; and as a rule the pilgrims start from their home knowing the names of their respective Gayāwāls, or the names of their ancestors. Sometimes, however, the pilgrim does not know in the jurisdiction of which Gayāwāl he falls, and in such cases it not unfrequently happens that the servants of the Gayāwāls quarrel as to who should have the pilgrim; in previous years fights over the pilgrims occasionally took place at the railway station. In many cases the question can be settled at once by reference to the Gayāwāls' *khātās*, or books in which the names of their chief pilgrims and of the villages to which they belong are carefully recorded. When, however, a family of Gayāwāls has become extinct, as is sometimes the case, no such solution of the difficulty is possible; the pilgrim is, so to speak, intestate property, and opposing claims are put forward and hotly contested for the right of guiding him through the ceremonies and receiving his fees.

Many pilgrims are brought by professional pilgrim hunters who collect a number of persons wishing to perform obsequies at Gayā, and conduct them there. Disputes frequently occur in respect to these pilgrims, and the pilgrim hunters, taking advantage of these, manage to drive a bargain with a Gayāwāl, and generally receive, it is said, one-third to as much as one-half of the *suphal* gifts. The largest number of pilgrims, however, are brought by servants of the Gayāwāls sent out into the country expressly for the purpose. These servants are paid from 5 to 7 rupees a month, but in the case of Rājās and other important personages more highly-paid emissaries are sent. They start in the month of Srāban or Phāgun, taking *pedas* (sweet-meats) and other sacrificial offerings with them, realize arrears of remuneration due to their masters, collect pilgrims, and then return to Gayā, perhaps after several months. When they come to Gayā, the pilgrims lodge in licensed lodging-houses, which are generally owned by Gayāwāls. In this case the pilgrims are lodged free and are carefully tended by the Gayāwāls' servants, but if the houses are owned by others, they have to pay rent. Occasionally also the pilgrims put up outside the town.

There is no record of the number of pilgrims who visit Gayā every year. One hundred years ago it was estimated that they were not less than 100,000 annually, but when some of the great Marāthās, who were attended by armies rather than guards, came to the place, the number was doubled. At the present day, the number of pilgrims must be much greater owing to the ease with which Gayā can be visited, and it is said that their number is not less than 300,000 a year.

The pilgrim priests.

When the pilgrim has presented himself before the Gayāwāl, Brāhman *āchārjyas* are deputed to conduct him personally round the different *vedis*, and perform the necessary ceremonies. Some of these are the paid servants of the Gayāwāls and others are remunerated by a share of the gifts made by the pilgrims. Except in the case of important personages, the Gayāwāls themselves perform no ceremonies beyond those at the Akshayabat, and their function is merely to have their feet worshipped, to receive the pilgrims' gifts, and to certify that the offerings made have been effectual. It is this right to have their feet worshipped and to pronounce the pilgrims' "Vade in pacem" which marks the Gayāwāls' unique position, as without them the Gayā *srāddha* would be impossible. There is however another class of priests, known as the *Dhāmins*, who share the peculiar position of the Gayāwāl as priests presiding over these ceremonies. The Dhāmins alone have the right to officiate at the ceremonies performed at five *vedis*, Pretsilā, Rāmsilā, Rāmakund, Brahmakund and Kāgbali, the Gayāwāls having a monopoly of the remainder. These five *vedis*, the *pānchvedi* which comprises the second day of the pilgrims' tour, are all situated on or about the two hills, Rāmsilā and Pretsilā, which are peculiarly devoted to Yama and evil spirits. The general practice is for the pilgrim merely to promise gifts to the Dhāmins at these two hills, and, when he finally pays his dues and makes over his offerings to the Gayāwāl under the Akshayabat tree, the amount thus promised is deducted from them and made over to the Dhāmins, the Gayāwāl himself keeping one quarter of the amount. If the pilgrim wishes to make his offerings on the hill itself, the Gayāwāl's agent advances it and pays the Dhāmin three quarters of the amount on the spot.

Expenses of pilgrimage.

What a grievous tax these offerings formerly were may be realized from the following account given by Buchanan Hamilton. Writing in 1811 he says* :—"Although the number of pilgrims has been gradually increasing for these five or six centuries, there continued great checks on it until Mr. Law† introduced many new regulations to give them protection. At many different places on approaching Gaya the pilgrims found custom-houses, erected by

* Eastern India, by Montgomery Martin, vol. I, pp. 53—55.

† Mr. Law was Collector of Gayā at the close of the 18th century.

every land-holder or petty officer of government who had power enough to compel them to pay contributions, for which there was no rule but the means of payment and the power of exaction. Mr. Law therefore abolished the whole of these custom-houses, and having ascertained that four sorts of pilgrimage were usually performed, he fixed a certain sum to be paid for a license for each. One class of pilgrims visits only one place, and, on receiving a license to visit this, the votary pays 2 rs. $1\frac{3}{4}$ annas; another class visits two places, and pays 3 rs. $5\frac{3}{4}$ annas; a third class visits 38 places, and pays 6 rs. $4\frac{3}{4}$ annas; the fourth class visits 45 places, and pays 14 rs. $2\frac{1}{4}$ annas. Deductions are, however, made on all the licenses to Nepalese, who are not numerous, and on the highest licenses to persons who bring water from the Ganges to pour on the sacred places, who are considered as holy, and who are generally poor. These four classes of licenses are marked by seals of different colours, by which alone the persons generally employed as a check on imposition know the one from the other; and there is strong reason to suspect that many frauds are still committed, although there has been of late a considerable improvement of revenue. But the duty* to Government is a small part of the pilgrim's expense. The chief expense consists of the presents (*dakshina*), which must be made to the priests. The Bengalese, in fact, give chiefly grain, brass vessels, silver coin, and cloth; but sometimes they present cows. The presents nominally are in general quite different, but are trifles held in brass vessels covered with cloth, which in reality compose the most usual value of the present, and are sold to the next votary that comes. The Mahrattas give money, jewels, plate, fine cloth, elephants and horses. The very lowest person, performing his devotions at one place, cannnot spend less, including duties, than $3\frac{1}{2}$ rs.; those who worship at two places cannot spend less than 5 rs., but many spend 100 rs. The lowest rate of expense at the 38 places is 30 rs., and few there exceed 40 rs. The Bengalese, who worship at 45 places, usually expend from 40 to 200 rs.; some, however, spend as much as 500 rs., and some few great men have gone so far as 5,000 rs. Almost all the Mahrattas worship at the 45 places, and several every year give 5,000 rs., while great chiefs expend 40 or even 50,000 rs. These expenses are exclusive of the charges of travelling, and of what is exacted by numberless solicitations to which the pilgrims are exposed. Every one, so far as he is able, feeds the Brahmans who attend.

* This duty was a considerable source of revenue to Government. In 1812-13 the gross receipts were Rs. 2,76,890, and deducting the expenses the net revenue amounted to Rs. 2,33,440.

"No person can possibly go through the 45 places in less than 15 days, and persons of rank take from one to three months, during which, from morning till night, they are not a moment free from the most clamorous solicitations of religious mendicants, from 200 to 300 of whom, besides the priests, hover round the place with incredible diligence and importunity. When the votary has made his offerings and performed all his ceremonies the priest that attends him binds his thumbs together with a garland, and says that he will fine him on account of his ancestors. When the fine is paid, the Brahman unties the garland, and declares that the ceremonies have been duly performed; nor are the ceremonies considered as of any effect until this declaration has been made. Formerly it was the custom of the priest to keep the votaries' thumbs tied until he consented to give a sum that was considered adequate to his circumstances; but Government has declared that all contributions must be voluntary, and the collector of the duty or magistrate will, on complaint, compel the priest to perform his duty, and to accept of whatever the votary pleases. People, however, from distant countries, who do not know our customs, are still often much abused, of which while on Pretasila, I saw no less than two instances, two decent Brahmans from Malwa applying to me for assistance: one was stript even to the skin, and had his thumbs tied; the other was sitting in despair at the foot of the hill, the sum demanded being so exorbitant that he would not venture to ascend. The checks, however, on this violence have rendered it much less frequent, and have given great satisfaction, not only to the votaries, but to many of the more moderate priests, who perceive that the security given to the votaries has greatly increased* their number."

Whatever modes of extortion or pressure may have been used in former times, the Gayāwāls now confine themselves to the more specious methods of flattery, solicitude about personal comfort, and appeals to worldly and religious benefit. Other influences are seldom or never used, and the pilgrims generally pay their fees voluntarily, according to their position and means, and in accordance with what has grown to be as much a custom as any other part of their ceremonial observances. A poor pilgrim can, it is said, complete the orthodox round of the 45 *vedis* or sacred spots, and satisfy all authorized demands at a total cost of Rs. 15 to Rs. 20. The amount increases with the wealth or social rank of the pilgrim; and very large sums are occasionally paid by the wealthy, and quite voluntarily. One of the Peshwās of Poona is

* In the seven years 1798—1805 the number of pilgrims who received licenses increased from 17,670 to 31,114.

said to have paid a lakh of rupees in fees alone, and Randhir Singh of Kashmīr is said to have given presents in cash, ornaments, and other movable property to the value of 3 or 4 lakhs. The fees and gifts do not always consist of cash, as landed property, elephants, jewels, and movable property of many kinds are also given. More than two-thirds of whatever is expended by the pilgrim in the performance of his ancestor's obsequies is said to go into the pocket of the Gayāwāl, and his position is therefore one of affluence.

ORIGIN OF THE GAYA *Srāddha*.

It has already been mentioned that the Gayā legend possibly embodies an allegory of the triumph of Brahmanism over Buddhism, and it is noticeable that the Gayā ritual contains two features, of which one is possibly and the other is certainly of Buddhist origin, viz., foot-worship and the adoration of the Bodhī tree. One of the most important of the ceremonies observed at Gayā is the worship of the footprints of various gods, and especially of those of Vishnu. The latter is absolutely essential, but, besides this, the pilgrim is bound on the 6th day of his pilgrimage to offer up worship at no less than 18 other *padas* or sacred footprints in the precincts of the Vishnupad temple. Dr. Rājendralāla Mitra* has no doubt that the marks of Vishnu's feet enshrined in this temple were originally a Buddhist emblem. "In all Buddhist countries," he says, "carvings of Buddha's feet are held in great veneration. In many temples they occupy the most prominent place; and when the Hindus got hold of Gayā, the popular feeling in favour of the most sacred footprint there was so high that, unable to set it aside, the Brāhmans recognized it, under the name of Vishnu's feet, as the most sacred object of worship at that place; and thousands of Hindu pilgrims from the most distant parts of India to this day visit and worship it every year for the salvation of their ancestors." The same belief that the Brāhmans adopted the worship of Buddha's feet has been expressed, though tentatively, by General Cunningham† with reference to the large circular stone with two human feet carved upon it which lies in a small open temple of 4 pillars, in front of the Bodh Gayā temple. This temple is now called Buddha-pad, and General Cunningham was of opinion that "the feet may have been those of Buddha, which, on the decline of Buddhism, were quietly appropriated to Vishnu by the accommodating Brāhmans."

Foot-worship.

The Bodhī tree.

With regard to the Bodhī tree we are on more certain ground. It is one of the *vedis* which the Gayā pilgrim visits on the 4th

* Buddha Gayā, pp. 124-125.

† Report Arch. Surv. India, vol. I, pp. 9-10, 1871.

day of his rounds; and though the *pīpal*-tree to the north is now used more largely for the offering of *pindas*, there is no doubt that the Buddhist tree was appropriated as an object of adoration by the Hindus many centuries ago. When it was so appropriated, we have no means of knowing; but it seems certain that it was an object of attestation to the Hindus as late as the 7th century, for about 600 A. D. Sasānka, a devoted adherent of Brahmanism, dug it up and burnt it with fire, "desiring," Hiuen Tsiang says, "to destroy it utterly and not leave a trace of it behind." It appears probable that, following their usual policy, the Brāhmans adopted the tree as a suitable object for veneration on the decline of Buddhism, and in this way made a profitable use of the worship it received from the Buddhists. However that may be, the sacred book of the Gayāwāls, the Gayā Mahātmya, which forms part of the Vāyu Purāna, though it is most probably an addition of comparatively late date, contains a special invocation to the *pīpal*-tree at Dharmāranya (Bodh Gayā), which is described as the king of trees, planted by Dharmarāj (Buddha) himself. In the 16th century a pandit employed by the Chauhān zamīndār of Patna records the curious custom of Hindus embracing the Bodhī tree; and, as we have already seen, Buchanan Hamilton mentions worship being offered to it by Hindus in 1811, though he goes on to say that some zealous person had lately built a stair on the outside of the terrace from which the tree grew, "so that the orthodox may pass up without entering the porch, and thus seeing the hateful image of Buddha." The Sāstric authority for offering *pindas* under it is contained in the Tristhalisetu—a work written about 400 years ago by Narāyan Bhatta, who migrated from the Marāthā country to Benares during the tyrannical rule of the Nizām Shāhi princes of Ahmednagar. The pilgrims from places in which the Tristhalisetu is held in esteem still offer *pindas* under the Bodhī tree and have done so for more than three centuries, but, on the other hand, such offerings are not made by the Bengalis, Oriyās and Maithilīs, who do not know of the work.

Animistic features. Though these two portions of the Gayā *srāddha* appear to be Buddhistic in origin, it is impossible not to perceive how much more marked are the elements of this worship which appear to have been taken from a more primitive form of religion. Examination of the Gayā Mahātmya, the sacred book containing the legends of the origin of this cult and prescribing its ritual, leaves one impressed with the prominent place assigned to the powers of hell. The most striking feature of the Gayā Mahātmya, though in many respects Vaishnava in tone and in its invocation of Vishnu, is the emphasis laid on the necessity of propitiating Yama and of delivering the ghosts of ancestors from the lives of fiends and evil spirits. A long invocation, called the Pinda Kharasi, which is prescribed at the time of offering *pindas*, clearly embodies a belief in the necessity of propitiating the disembodied souls of those who have died violent and unnatural deaths. This *mantra* specifies those to whom offering should be made, viz., among others, those whose funeral rites have not been performed, those who have died through abortion, been burnt, been devoured by dogs, been poisoned or hanged; those who have committed suicide or been shot by arrows, died by drowning, of starvation or thirst; ancestors who have been lame or maimed, or who are roaming about as evil ghosts, or who "by the snare of their deeds" have made it difficult ever again to live human lives.

In the same spirit, offering at Pretsilā, *i.e.*, the Hill of Ghosts, is enjoined that Yama may not beat or bruise the ghosts of the dead, and his two hell-hounds must be worshipped at Rāmsilā that they may not bark and bay at the unhappy spirits. At Pretsilā again the pilgrim, sitting with his face to the south – the point of the horizon representing the realm of the God of Hell—is to throw *sattu* and *til* in the air and offer the following prayer: "May those of my ancestors who live the lives of evil spirits be pleased to take this *pinda* and be satisfied. May they accept the water given by my hands and go to heaven." Many of the other *vedis* or holy spots, which the pilgrim must visit, are similarly sacred to the God of Hell. On Dharmasilā Yama is said to be immovably settled; at Gayā there is a tank, named Baitaranī, the Hindu Styx, by bathing in which salvation is obtained; and at other holy spots offerings are ordered to be made to the hounds of Hell, to the four crows of Hell, and to the God of Hell himself with the prayer: "I offer this to thee, O Yama, for the deliverance of my ancestors".

It is noticeable moreover that the greatest rush of pilgrims occurs in the month of Asin, when the powers of the malevolent dead are most feared, and that the propitiation of evil spirits is practised particularly on the hill of Pretsilā. The guardians of this hill shrine, the Dhāmins, are an order of priests entirely distinct from the Gayāwāls, and the peculiar arrangement by which the Dhāmin gets three-quarters of the offerings made on the hill and the Gayāwāl the rest, possibly represents an old compromise between the more orthodox Brāhmans and the priests who officiated at the rites of aboriginal demonolatry practised on the jungle-clad hills: the existence of some rude stone circles near the foot of the hill, which are traditionally ascribed to the Kols, at least lends colour to the belief that it was once a centre of their worship. However this may be, the description of spirits invoked in the Pinda Kharasi and their invocation show that it is those spirits in particular who have met with a violent or unnatural end who are to be saved from the state of evil spirits; and indeed it is expressly stated that offerings are to be made to them whether roaming as evil spirits or suffering in the obscurest hell. Such a conception closely resembles the more vulgar demonolatry which consists in offerings to, and worship of the malignant spirits of the dead. This demonolatry is the prevalent form of religion throughout the district, and there appears to be much of the same belief, under the cloak of orthodoxy, in the Gayā *srāddha*. The conception of the state of evil roaming spirits, who are to be propitiated by offerings and worship is not distinctively Brahmanical, and it plays so prominent a part in the sacred book of Gayā that it appears a plausible hypothesis that at least in some respects the Gayā *srāddha* represents the adoption by Brahmanism of the popular demonolatry which preceded it and has existed side by side with it to the present day.

CHAPTER V.

POPULAR RELIGION.

THE district of Gayā occupies an interesting position in the religious life of India. On the one hand, it is well known as having been the birthplace of Buddhism and the scene of some of the earliest preaching of Buddha; and though Buddhism as an active form of faith has passed away from the hearts of the people, the sacred tree under which Sākya Muni attained Buddhahood still attracts devout pilgrims from distant countries. In striking contrast to the purity of the early Buddhist faith is a primitive form of religion, now prevalent in the district, which embraces aboriginal rites and beliefs roughly grafted on to a loose and elastic Hinduism. In the town of Gayā, again, there is a special form of orthodox Hinduism, which finds its manifestation in the Gayā *Srāddha;* but the really popular religion consists of the propitiation of evil spirits by offerings before stocks and stones.

TRACES OF BUDDHISM.

Buddhism appears to have never had any real hold in the southern part of the district, but was confined to the northern portion of the district, which is rich in Buddhist remains. The southern part of the district was probably jungle, hill and forest in the Buddhistic times, and was untouched by Buddhist civilization. In the north Buddhism remained in a more or less flourishing condition until its final extinction by the Muhammadans, and the vast number of images dating back to the Pāla kings (800—1200 A.D.) still bear witness to its popularity; while the very name Bihār (*vihārā* or monastery), formerly applied to this part of the district in place of the old Magadha, shows what a firm hold Buddhism once had over it. But there is now no sign that the existing religion of the people is in any way affected by Buddha's teaching, by the subsequent Buddhist cult or by its later ritualistic developments.

In the preceding chapter it has been mentioned that a trace of the influence of Buddhism may perhaps be detected in the sanctity ascribed to the Bodhī tree, and in the worship of the marks of Vishnu's feet. These however are concerned with the special form of worship observed in Gayā, and one looks vainly for traces of the Buddhist cult in other directions. Images of Buddha and other Buddhistic images and *chaityas* are found in temples of all kinds, under trees, and in the open air in all parts of the district, and are treated as different deities, lingas, etc. Such images have been enshrined in hundreds of temples, in temples of Siva, of Mahādeo, of Vishnu, of the Sun, of Sītalā, the goddess of disease, and others. Hundreds of *chaityas* have similarly been set up in *sivālās* filling the places of lingas. But this is simply because these images and *chaityas* have been found lying about and have been utilized by the Hindus as images of their own deities or as the linga of Mahādeo. They are worshipped by the ignorant Hindus, not as Buddha or as Buddhistic emblems, but as their own gods and symbols.

In the same way, stone images of Buddha dug up in the fields are not unfrequently set up to represent the various evil spirits propitiated by the lower castes, but the worshippers do not know that they are Buddhistic images. There must be something tangible to represent a godling or even a malignant spirit, and the image is something tangible that will serve their purpose, as they can rub vermilion on it or pour a libation over it or sacrifice a fowl, goat or pig before it. In all cases, the rites are Hindu and not Buddhistic, and no traces of Buddhism* are visible. At Bodh Gayā, it is true, the large stone image of Buddha on the ground-floor of the temple is worshipped by some low-caste Hindus in the neighbourhood, but this is a recent innovation, and no orthodox Hindu thinks of doing so or regards the worship as anything but incongruous and spurious. In Gayā, as in other parts of Bengal, Buddhism is dead as a separate and current religion. It was a branch that sprouted from the tree of Hinduism, grew vigorously for a considerable period, and then withered off.

POPULAR HINDU RELIGION.

The religion which is now prevalent among the mass of the people throughout the district consists of the propitiation of evil spirits, the genesis of which appears to be due to the belief of the peasant in malignant powers of evil. "The rude mind," it has been said, "with difficulty associates the idea of power and benignity. A shadowy conception of power that by much persuasion can be induced to refrain from inflicting harm is the shape most easily taken by the Invisible in the minds of men,

---

* In Dr. Grierson's Notes on the District of Gaya (p. 3) it is said that the inhabitants of the northern portion of the district "still worship a so-called incarnation of Vishnu whom they call *Baudh* Deo." Special enquiries were made during the census operations of 1901 as to the existence of this worship, but no traces of it could be found.

who have always been pressed close by primitive wants and to whom a life of hard toil has never been illuminated by any enthusiastic religious faith." The religion of the uneducated majority of the population is of this type. It is a curious mixture of Hinduism and Animism, in which the belief in evil spirits and godlings is the main ingredient. The common people have their shapeless stone or block to represent a spirit or godling to which they make simple offerings in the open air, while side by side with it is a temple to one of the regular gods of the Hindu pantheon with its carved image and elaborate rites. The latter, however, is not the real every-day working religion of the people, and the orthodox Hindu creed appeals but little to the peasants.

Worship of evil spirits.

The current belief is that there are a number of malevolent spirits who exercise their influence on the bodies and minds of men by means of demoniacal possession. Worship, therefore, consists of periodical propitiation of them in order to escape their attacks, or to induce them to relinquish the unhappy victims on whom they have descended. Man lives surrounded by powers of evil, inimical to his health and well-being, and success in life can only be obtained by propitiating the malignant spirits which beset his path at every turn. The personification of the evil spirit carries out this idea, as it is described as being fearful of shape and black of hue, tall as a palm-tree, with long projecting teeth and streaming dishevelled hair. In fact, the whole appearance of these fiends resembles very much that of the genii in the Arabian Nights. They live in desolate places and especially favour the jungle and wild hill country. They generally drop down on the unwary traveller from trees, and one, Panduba by name, comes out of rivers and tanks, and drags in and drowns the belated wayfarer.

Though they are said to have an incorporeal essence, they must have something to represent them and to receive the offerings of their votaries. Sometimes a little heap of earth, called a *pindi*, is formed; sometimes a brick is placed on a raised mound, sometimes a log of wood; sometimes a rough stone, and sometimes a hewn stone or even an old image. These are daubed with vermilion; libations and offerings are made to the spirits they represent; and occasionally a pair of clogs and a small wooden seat are placed before them. The lower castes attribute evil of all kinds to these spirits; illness is almost invariably ascribed to possession, and the remedy lies not in medicine, but in exorcism. The proceedings in case of possession are of a well-observed type. An *ojhā* or wizard, who is believed to command a spirit of greater power, is sent for, incantations follow, and offerings of sweetmeats or a goat are made. If the *bhūt* is obstinate and will not leave his victim, physical compulsion is resorted to; the man is soundly beaten, and red pepper and turmeric smoke are put to his nose. The idea running throughout the ceremony seems to be partly that the *ojhā's* familiar spirit will drive the other away, and partly that the spirit which causes the trouble may be cajoled into leaving his victim by means of offerings. It is noticeable that in the wilder tracts to the south of Gayā men of aboriginal descent are recognized as being peculiarly the intermediaries between these spirits and the human race, and often officiate when offerings are made.

Witches are regarded as occupying quite a different position to the *ojhā* or exorcist. The *ojhā* is a man of low caste with a recognized position and profession; he has not the power of the evil eye; and he is not feared therefore like the *dāin* or witch. He practises openly and his services can be hired, but witches work secretly and cannot be bribed. They are charged with cutting open children and taking out their liver, and also with the practice, commonly imputed to witches in the Middle Ages, of making images of flour to represent their enemies and piercing them with knives and needles. It is generally believed that at the time of the Dasaharā the witches assemble in some waste place, where they chant unholy incantations and dance naked. Here they meet with the spirits of the children whom they have decoyed and slain, and hold with them a witches' dance. The criminal records of the district contain numbers of cases of the murder of old women credited with the power of the evil eye.

A peculiar feature of the power of *ojhās* over *bhūts* is found in the actual purchase and sale of them, which is said to be practised by some low castes in the jungle-covered tracts to the south of the district. The *bhūt*, when under proper control, is a valuable possession and becomes a marketable commodity. When the sale has been arranged, the *ojhā* hands over a corked bamboo cylinder which is supposed to contain the *bhūt*; this is then taken to the place, usually a tree, at which it is intended that the *bhūt* should in future reside; a small ceremony accompanies the installation, liquor is poured on the ground or on the *pindis* erected there, the cork is taken out, and the spirit is supposed to take up his residence at the spot. The function of the spirit thus purchased is to act as the guardian of the village fields and crops. Should any person be hardy enough to steal from a field under his guardianship, he is certain to be stricken by the *bhūt*, and in a few days he sickens and dies. Usually, however, the knowledge that a field is under the protection of a *bhūt* is sufficient to keep off all marauders. Thieves have also been known to restore stolen property under the threat that otherwise a *bhūt* would be called down on them.

Though *bhūt* and *dānk* are the generic designations of all kinds of malignant spirits, their name is legion. In general, they are the spirits of those who have died a violent or unnatural death, *e. g.*, by suicide, drowning, murder, lightning, sunstroke, snake bite, a fall from a tree, etc. A particularly malevolent fiend is Kichin or Churail, the spirit of a woman who dies in child-birth, who may be known by the fact that her feet are turned backwards and that she has no mouth. She is specially feared by women, but sometimes she seduces young men and kills them by a slow process of emaciation. Baimat is the spirit of a child who dies soon after birth. When a Bhuiyā comes to an untimely end, he becomes a *gauhail* or village *bhūt;* a *pindi* is set up smeared with vermilion, and he is deified as Cheri. To the west of the district, where man-eaters have caused great loss of life, low-caste men killed by tigers are apotheosized under the name of Baghāut. The disembodied spirits of men of low caste who die unnatural deaths become Dāno, and similarly Brahm Pichās (*i. e.*, Brahm Pisāch, Pisāch being equivalent to spirit) is the ghost of Brāhmans who meet a violent end. The most famous however of all *dānks* or evil spirits in this district is one known as the Raghuni Dānk, which is located at the village of Tungi in the Nawāda subdivision. Legend relates that a Bābhan named Raghuni was working in his fields at Tungi one day with his *kamiyā* or hereditary serf. He sent the latter to his house, where he had left his sister, to fetch a basket of seed. The sister gave him the seed, and when she was lifting it on to his head, some of the red powder (*sindūr*) on her forehead was rubbed on to him. When he returned, Raghuni, seeing the marks of *sindūr*, suspected the two of an intrigue, and, after killing them both, committed suicide. All three became the Raghuni Dānk, a spirit which is represented by some *pindis* in a small hut at Tungi. It is by far the most potent spirit in the district and is worshipped in all parts of it; and, as an instance of its power, it is said that a European who outraged the spirit by having some shoes put on the *pindis* was at once punished by an illness which came on the same day.

Worship of godlings.

Allied to the worship of such spirits is the worship of godlings unknown to orthodox Hinduism. In some cases the god is a deified hero, such as Goraiya and Salais or Salesh, two bandit chiefs deified by the Dosādhs, and Lorik, the hero of the Goālās; in others extraordinary or gifted individuals, such as Kamālo Bībī mentioned below; and even *satīs* are commemorated with *pindis* and offerings of images of horses, moulded from clay. At the village of Nabīnagar in the Aurangābād subdivision there is a shrine sacred to a godling, called Sokhā Bābā, who is possibly a deified physician, as persons bitten by snakes are brought there in the hope that a cure will be effected. In other cases the godling appears to represent a tribal ancestor, such as Bān Singh among the Bhogtās, a caste of aboriginal descent in the south of Gayā; this god is regarded as the ancestor of the race; he has no idol or image, but only *pindis* put up in small huts, and is propitiated with sacrifices of goats in order that he may ward off wild beasts. Dharhā, a godling worshipped by low castes in the jungles, though said by many to be merely the spirit of a Dhāngar who has met with a violent or sudden death, is claimed by others as the ancestor of their tribe. They maintain that though a man who has died an unnatural death may become some other *bhūt*, he cannot become Dharhā, as the latter is a tribal god and distinct from other *bhūts*. The different accounts given serve to show how narrow a line divides the godling and the evil spirit, and the same spirit runs through the offerings made to Sītalā, the goddess of disease.

POPULAR MUHAMMADAN RELIGION.

The religion of a large number of the Muhammadans closely approximates to that of the Hindus. They freely indulge in superstitious observances and copy Hindu rites; some even join in the worship of the Sun and offer libations like Hindus; and one curious feature of the Shab-i-Barāt is the offering to deceased ancestors of puddings made of flour. The more ignorant have a pantheon of village gods; like Hindus, they resort to exorcism in case of sickness; and it is perhaps not too much to say that with them Islām is not so much a question of religion as of caste.

There are certain forms of worship common among Muhammadans which are neither based on the Korān, nor, apparently, adopted from the Hindus. The most common of these is the adoration of departed Pīrs. When a holy Pīr leaves this life, he is supposed to be still present in spirit, and his tomb becomes a place of pilgrimage to which persons resort for the cure of disease or the exorcism of evil spirits, or to obtain the fulfilment of some cherished wish, such as the birth of a child or success in pending litigation. The educated deny that Pīrs are worshipped, and say that they are merely asked to intercede with God, but it is very doubtful if this distinction is recognized by the lower classes. Here, as elsewhere, the adoration of the Pānch Pīr is common, a worship which is not confined to Musalmāns, but is also practised by Hindus; but there are also certain local Pīrs, such as Mansur Pīr, whose tomb in the compound of the Judge's Court at Gayā is visited by numbers who desire to be cured of diseases, and is specially frequented by litigants. At Miranpur Nadera is another *dargāh* erected over the remains of a saintly Pīr, where women who desire offspring come by night and tie shreds of cloth to a neighbouring tree. At Sihuli near Rafiganj the tomb of Saiyid Siālkoti is reputed to be particularly efficacious for casting out evil spirits; it is visited by Hindus as well as by Muhammadans, and his votaries seek to obtain the favours of the Pīr by offerings of cocks. Similarly at Bithu followers of both religions offer cocks and set up *pindis* before the tomb of Makhdum Shāh.

Closely allied to the adoration of Pīrs is the homage paid to certain mythical persons, of whom the principal are Sheikh Saddu and Kamālo Bībī. According to the legend current in this district, the former was a student at Morādābād, who found a lamp with four wicks and lit it. Four genii, thereupon, appeared and informed him that they were slaves of the lamp and were at his service: he used them for purposes of debauchery, but eventually he was caught in the embraces of a princess and killed by her father, who had been informed of the intrigue by his own familiar spirit. The spirit of Sheikh Saddu is worshipped all over the district. He takes possession both of men and women, who, when attacked, recite and sing; when this happens, Sheikh Saddu is propitiated with sacrifices of goats and cocks. Such persons are supposed to have supernatural powers, and in cases of sickness or trouble are often called in to find out the cure. Kamālo Bībī is the subject of many extraordinary legends. According to one account, she lived at Kāko in the time of a Buddhist Rājā Kanaka, who sent her a dish made of rats; when the dish was brought before her, the rats came to life, and she cursed the Rājā. At once Kāko fell in ruins, in which the Rājā was buried. Another legend relates that her husband tried to leave her and walked till nightfall when he stopped and slept. He woke up to find himself again at Kāko, and two other attempts at desertion also failed, owing to his wife's magical charms. Her tomb is resorted to by both Hindus and Musalmāns, and is regarded as a great place for exorcism or for the cure of any illness. Women constantly go there with small offerings, in order to obtain offspring, and tie up strips from their dress at the door of the tomb. A stone engraved with an inscription is smeared with oil by the pilgrims, who afterwards anoint themselves with it: this ointment is said to confer the gift of tongues, as they at once speak ecstatically. Another mythical personage whose celebrity appears to be due to his tragical end is Ghāzi Miā, for according to the legend current in Gayā, he perished in a fire on the eve of his wedding. His death is still commemorated by a fair held in May at Kenduā, 4 miles south of Gayā, which is attended by large numbers of Musalmāns. The worship of Sultān Shahid, which is observed by low-caste Hindus as well as by low Musalmāns, appears to be prompted by no such conception, and to be more distinctively Hindu. A *pindi* is erected to him near Devī's temple, and cocks are offered in his honour before the worship of Devī begins. It is explained that this worship is given to him because he is the body-guard, or, according to another account, the paramour of Devī.

All these cults seem to be of the same character as the popular religion which is common among the Hindus of this district. Sultān Shahid appears to be the male counterpart of Devī or to be some godling who has obtained his first step in the popular pantheon by being made the warder of the temple of the great goddess; the worship of Sheikh Saddu is apparently due to the common belief that those who die violent deaths become evil spirits; and the reverence for Kamālo and Ghāzi Miā is akin to the deification of persons who have been approved miracle workers, or who have died in some extraordinary or tragical way. They show clearly the extent to which the religion of the illiterate Musalmān has been permeated by the superstitious beliefs of his Hindu neighbours.

CHAPTER VI.

THE PEOPLE.

GROWTH OF POPULATION.

THE first census of the district was taken in 1872, when the area included within its boundaries was the same as at present, except for 6 square miles which were transferred three years afterwards to the adjoining district of Hazāribāgh. This enumeration disclosed a total population of 1,949,750, the average density being 413 persons to the square mile. The number of inhabitants recorded at the census of 1881 showed an increase of 9·1 per cent. on these figures, the population being returned at 2,124,682; but a large part of the increase is believed to be due to the greater accuracy of the enumeration, and this figure is therefore somewhat misleading. During the next ten years the population was practically stationary, and in 1891 it had risen only to 2,138,331, or 0·6 per cent. more than in 1881. The reason for this slow growth appears to be that the district suffered severely from the ravages of persistent fever throughout the decade, and that emigration increased greatly while immigration fell off. The result of the census was to show that Gayā lost nearly 150,000 by emigration; Calcutta, which in 1881 had among its residents only 15,767 person born in Gayā, having in 1891 altogether 32,412 natives of that district—a number double that contributed by any other district in Bihār. If the number of emigrants and immigrants is excluded, the net population shows a real increase of 2·8 per cent. for men and 3·0 per cent. for women.

Census of 1901.

This growth was not sustained, and the census of 1901 showed a marked decline, the number of inhabitants recorded being 2,059,933, or nearly 78,400 less than in 1891. This decrease was due to two causes—the outbreak of plague at the time of the census and the general unhealthiness which prevailed in the preceding ten years. In this decade conditions were on the whole unfavourable, and the state of the poorer classes was unsatisfactory. During the earlier years fever was very prevalent; and though its ravages were not so great in subsequent years, the death-rate was swelled by epidemics of cholera. In 1891-92 there was scarcity owing to the failure of the winter rice and spring crops, and again in 1896-97 some distress was caused by the short outturn, which was aggravated by the high prices of food-grains consequent on famine elsewhere. Besides this, the river Sakrī overflowed its banks in 1896 carrying away several villages in the Nawāda subdivision and covering the land with a deposit of silt. Thrice during the decade the number of deaths exceeded that of births reported, and the whole period was decidedly unhealthy.

At the same time, but for the appearance of the plague in the latter part of 1900, there seems no reason why the population should have decreased, as it did, by 3·7 per cent. The disease broke out in Gayā town in October, and by the time the final enumeration took place, it had spread with much virulence over the greater part of the district. The people of villages where plague appeared left their homes, taking refuge in temporary sheds constructed sometimes near and sometimes far away from the village sites; and large numbers moved away into other districts. The census results were consequently affected in three ways: firstly, by a mortality far in excess of that indicated in the death returns, secondly by the departure to their own homes of temporary settlers from other districts, and thirdly by deaths and desertions among the census staff, and partly also by the difficulty of enumerating panic-stricken villagers, who were daily and even hourly moving from the villages to escape the ravages of the disease. The loss due to the flight of natives of other districts may be taken as the difference between the immigrant population finally recorded and that recorded 10 years previously, or about 8,000 souls. The rest of the decrease must apparently be attributed almost entirely to plague mortality and the flight of the residents from the plague-stricken parts of the district. Enquiries made by the Magistrate showed that in the Tekāri thāna alone more than 11,000 persons had left their homes since the preliminary record, but that, in spite of exceptional difficulties, the work of enumeration had been carried out with great care and precision.

When we turn to the statistics for individual thānas, the responsibility of the plague for the loss of population which occurred becomes very apparent. Up to the date of the census, the epidemic had wrought most havoc in the Tekāri thāna, and this thāna sustained a loss of 19·8 per cent.; then come Atrī, Gayā town and Gayā thāna with decreases of 14·9, 11·3 and 6·5 per cent. respectively. On the other hand, the Nawāda subdivision, which was remarkably free from plague up to the date of the census, showed an increase in every thāna, and a small tract to the north-west, which benefits from canal irrigation and also escaped the ravages of the epidemic, added to its population. In the thānas to the south of the district there was also a decrease, for which however the plague was not to blame. In these parts the population is not progressive; in Sherghāti and Bārāchatti there has been a continuous decadence since 1881; and the falling off may be ascribed partly to long continued unhealthiness and partly to emigration to the adjoining districts of Hazāribāgh and Palāmau.

GENERAL CHARACTERISTICS.

Density of population.

In the district as a whole there are 437 persons to the square mile, as compared with the average of 400 per square mile for the whole of Bengal, and of 653 for the Patna Division; the pressure of the population on the soil is, in fact, less in Gayā than in any other district in the Division. Density of population is determined very largely by the physical characteristics of the two tracts into which the district is divided. It is least in the south, where the land is imperfectly irrigated and comparatively barren, and where a large area is still under jungle; in these tracts the population is very sparse, not rising to more than 278 to the square mile. In the north, where the soil is more fertile and a considerable area is protected from drought by an extensive system of artificial irrigation, the population is fairly dense, and the number of persons to the square mile is more than double that in the less favoured tracts to the south. Statistics of the population appear in the Statistical Appendix, from which it will be seen that the pressure of the people on the land is greatest in the highly cultivated tract included in the Jahānābād thāna, where the large number of 666 persons to the square mile is found, and that the minimum (257 persons to the square mile) is reached in the Bārāchatti thāna, in which there is a considerable area of hill and waste land.

Migration.

There is a large volume of emigration from Gayā, and the number of its emigrants far exceeds that of the immigrants. With the exception of emigrants who settle permanently in the adjoining districts of Palāmau and Hazāribāgh, this migration is generally of a temporary character. Every year large numbers leave the district in search of work on the roads, railways and fields, returning at the end of the hot weather to take part in the agricultural operations which commence with the bursting of the monsoon. Others find their way to Calcutta, Hooghly and elsewhere in Lower Bengal, where there is a demand for men to serve as *darwāns*, peons and the like, or as weavers in jute mills. An estimate derived from enquiries in typical villages made in the year 1888 shows that 0·7 per cent. of the rural population were thus absent from their homes; but there is every reason to believe that, now that railways have pierced the district in all directions, this annual exodus is very much greater. How large it is and how much it exceeds the volume of immigration may be seen from the fact that in 1891 over 200,000 persons born in Gayā were found in other parts of Bengal, while it had recovered only 54,000 by immigration. In 1901 nearly 59,000, or 2·8 per cent. of the entire population, were residing in Bengal proper at the time of the census, the emigrants to Calcutta alone constituting nearly two-thirds of the total number, while over 17,000 were living in the adjoining metropolitan districts. The immigrants from adjoining districts were found to be only half as numerous as the emigrants, and those from distant villages were outnumbered in the rates of 27 to 1; but these figures were affected by the prevalence of plague in Gayā. Emigration to the tea districts of Assam is not popular, and the average number of immigrants registered during the ten years ending in 1904 has been only 1,365. The number is insignificant, but in the Patna Division it is exceeded only in Shāhābād. Migration to the colonies is equally unimportant, the total number of emigrants during the decade 1891—1901 being only 1,423.

Towns and villages.

Gayā is essentially a rural district. The great majority of the population are engaged in agriculture, and the people have hitherto developed no tendency to flock into the towns. The tenant usually pays a part of his crops to the landlord in lieu of a money-rent, and village officials, such as the carpenter, blacksmith, barber, washerman and *patwāri*, are generally paid in kind at a fixed rate. Every householder has his grain store, by which he procures his luxuries in times of plenty, or averts famine after unfavourable seasons. There are no manufactures of importance; the old carpet, paper, and sugar industries have dwindled away; and agriculture is the one and prevailing occupation of all classes. No new centres of industry of any importance have sprung up; and the rapid development of commerce and manufactures which is so powerful a factor in the increase of an urban population is unknown. On the other hand, no less than three new lines of railway have been opened in the district within the last few years, and the trading classes have consequently set up business on the line of rail. The concentration of merchants in Gayā town has been marked, and some of the richer landholders, who formerly resided on their country estates, have taken up their residence in the town, and house rent is consequently rising. In spite, however, of the improvement which has taken place in the means of communication, only 5 per cent. of the population live in urban areas, *viz.*, in the eight towns of Gayā, Dāūdnagar, Tekāri, Aurangābād, Hasuā, Jahānābād, Nawāda and Sherghāti, the remainder of the population congregating in 7,871 villages. The three towns first named, which are municipalities, showed at the last census a decrease in the number of their inhabitants, which was very considerable in the case of Gayā and Tekāri, where plague was raging at the time. The aggregate urban population is 114,425, Gayā with 71,288 inhabitants accounting for nearly two-thirds of the whole number. None of the other towns have more than 10,000 inhabitants, and the population of Sherghāti is only 2,641.

Sex and age.

In common with other Bihār districts, Gayā has a marked excess of females over males, there being 1,037 females to every thousand males. The proportion of unmarried persons is also high, viz., 394 out of 1,000 males and 285 out of every thousand females, and is greater than in any of the districts lying south of the Ganges, except Shāhābād. The census of 1901 shows an abnormal sex proportion in the cases of Kahārs (males 49,978 and females 60,121), Jolāhās (males 32,169 and females 42,083), Kalāls (males 2,913 and females 4,199), and a few other castes. The reason for this is that the male members of these castes often remain absent from their homes in quasi-permanent employ elsewhere, leaving their female relatives behind. This explanation is supported by the statistics of persons born in Gayā but enumerated elsewhere, which also show a very striking disproportion of sex. In Calcutta out of 36,953 persons enumerated as born in Gayā, 27,981 were males and 8,972 females; in the 24-Parganas out of 6,037 persons, 4,146 were returned as males and 1,891 as females, and the same disproportion was found in other places in which emigrants from Gayā were residing at the time of the census. In spite of the large number of emigrants from the districts, the mean age of the population is comparatively high. This is only what is to be expected in a declining population where births are comparatively few in number, and having regard to the decrease in the population which has taken place, the wonder is that the average age has not risen to a higher figure.

Language.

The vernacular current over the whole district is the dialect of Bihāri Hindī known as Magahī or Māgadhī. Magahī* is properly speaking the language of the country of Magadha, which roughly corresponded to what is at the present day the district of Patna and the northern half of Gayā, but the language is not confined to this area. It is also spoken all over the rest of Gayā and over the district of Hazāribāgh; on the west it extends to a portion of Palāmau, and on the east to portions of the districts of Monghyr and Bhāgalpur. Over the whole of this area it is practically one and the same dialect, with hardly any local

* The sketch of Magahī is condensed from the account given in Dr. Grierson's Linguistic Survey of India, Vol. V.

variations, though it is acknowledged that the purest form of Magahī is spoken in Gayā, where it is the vernacular of 2,067,877 of the people. It is condemned by speakers of other Indian languages as being as rude and uncouth as the people who use it. Like Maithilī, it has a complex system of verbal conjugation, and the principal difference between the two dialects is that Maithilī has been under the influence of learned Brāhmans for centuries, while Magahī is the language of a people who have been dubbed boors since Vedic times. To a native of India, one of its most objectionable features is its habit of winding up every question, even when addressed to a person held in respect, with the word '*re.*' In other parts of India this word is only used in addressing an inferior, or when speaking contemptuously. Hence a man of Magah has the reputation of rudeness and his liability to get an undeserved beating on that score has been commemorated in a popular song. Magahī has no indigenous literature, but there are many popular songs current throughout the area in which the language is spoken, and strolling bards recite various long epic poems, such as the song of Lorik, the cow-herd hero, and the song of Gopīchandra, which are known more or less over the whole of Northern India. The character in general use in writing is the Kaithī, but the Devanāgari is also used by the educated classes.

Muhammadans and Kāyasths here, as elsewhere in Bihār, mostly speak the Awadhī dialect of Eastern Hindī (literally the language of Oudh), which Dr. Grierson considers is possibly an example of the survival of the influence of the former Muhammadan court of Lucknow. It is estimated that in Gayā 64,500 persons speak Awadhī; and this dialect is also used as a sort of language of politeness, especially when Europeans are addressed, by the rustics, who have picked it up from their Musalmān friends and imagine it to be the Hindustāni of polite society. The Devanāgari and the Kaithī characters are both used in writing Awadhī; and the Persian character is also occasionally used by the educated classes.

Character of the people. Dr. Grierson points out that the three great dialects of Bihāri Hindī fall naturally into two groups, viz., Maithilī and Magahī on the one hand and Bhojpurī on the other, and that the speakers are also separated by ethnic differences. Magahī and Maithilī and the speakers of these two dialects are, however, much more closely connected together than either of the pair is to Bhojpurī, and Magahī might very easily be classed as a sub-dialect of Maithilī rather than as a separate dialect. They are the dialects of nationalities which have carried conservatism to the excess of uncouthness, while Bhojpurī is the practical language of an energetic race. "Magadha," he says, "though it is intimately connected with the early history of Buddhism, was far too long a cockpit for contending Musalmān armies, and too long subject to the head-quarters of a Musalmān province to remember its former glories of the Hindu age. A great part of it is wild, barren and sparsely cultivated, and over much of the remainder cultivation is only carried on with difficulty by the aid of great irrigation works widely spread over the country, and dating from prehistoric times. Its peasantry, oppressed for centuries, and even now, under British rule, poorer than that of any other neighbouring part of India, is uneducated and uninterprising. There is an expressive word current in Eastern Hindustān which illustrates the national character. It is '*bhades*' and it has two meanings. One is 'uncouth, boorish,' and the other is 'an inhabitant of Magadha.' Which meaning is the original, and which the derivative I do not know; but a whole history is contained in these two syllables."

RELIGIONS.

Muhammadans.

By religion 89·3 per cent. of the population are Hindus (1,840,382), and practically all the remainder are Muhammadans. The latter, who form 10·64 per cent. of the people, are relatively more numerous than in any of the adjoining districts except Patna. The number of Muhammadans appears to be due to the settlement of soldiers of fortune in different parts of Gayā and to the influence they exercised over their Hindu subjects. The north-west of the district was long a centre of Musalmān power owing to the suzerainty of Dāūd Khān, one of Aurangzeb's generals and the founder of Dāūdnagar, who was given 3 *parganas* as a reward for his conquest of Palāmau. Tradition states that many Hindus in these parts embraced Islām during the reign of Aurangzeb, and this tradition is borne out by the fact that in several villages, which now contain Muhammadans, the inhabitants are said to have been originally Bābhans and Kāyasths. In the Nawāda thāna where the number of Muhammadans (29,798) is greatest, Nāmdār Khān and Kāmgār Khān, noted military adventurers of the 18th century, long exercised undisputed power. The former held 14 *parganas* and 84 *ghātwāli* tenures, which extended beyond the confines of the district into Patna and Hazāribāgh, and the village of Namdārganj in this thāna still commemorates his name; the latter was little better than a freebooter, and his forts are found in every part of the subdivision. In the south of the district there are a large number of Muhammadans of foreign extraction, including many Pathāns who trace back their descent to soldiers of fortune. They are subdivided into Rohilla Pathāns, who claim to be the descendants of Rohilla free-lances, and Magahiyā Pathāns, who say that their ancestors were Afghāns and that they derive the name Magahiyā from their long residence in the country of Magah. It is noticeable that the inhabitants of Kothī south of Sherghāti allege that they originally came from the Afghān valley of Kohāt, and Kothī is known to be the site of a Rohilla frontier fortress captured by Dāūd Khān in his advance against Palāmau in 1660. A further accession to the ranks of the Muhammadans is said to have occurred on the fall of Delhi in 1759 A. D., when many members of the Muhammadan nobility attached to the Mughal Court retired to their *jāgīrs* in the Gayā, Patna and Shāhābād districts, bringing a large number of followers in their train. But the pure foreign element is met with for the most part only among the higher classes, the lower classes being recruited mainly from local converts, and the vast preponderance of Jolāhās and Sheikhs gives good grounds for the belief that the majority are either the descendants of such converts or are of mixed origin.

Nearly all the Muhammadans of this district are Sunnis, but there are a few Shiahs in Gayā, Pālī and a few other villages. The followers of these two sects live in amity, and for many years past the only dispute between them has been about the carrying of the *mashk* and *tīr* in the Alam procession at Gayā. These emblems represent the tragical death of Abbās, the standard-bearer of the Imām Husain, at the battle of Karbala. Husain and his party had been without water for two days, and Abbās went, at the risk of his life, to fetch water from the Euphrates for the child of Husain, who was dying of thirst, and on his way back both he and his skin water-bag were pierced by an arrow. In commemoration of the death of Abbās, it is customary for the Shiahs of India and other Muhammadan countries to carry a standard (*alam*), to which is attached a leather water-bag (*mashk*) pierced by an arrow (*tīr*) from their houses or the Imāmbāra to the local Karbala during the Muharram procession. In Gayā the Sunni community, which entertains a deep-rooted aversion to the exhibition of these symbols, numbers about 10,000 souls, while the Shiahs are no more than 200; and in 1882 a disturbance took place which was only quelled by the interference of a large body of police. The carrying of these emblems was accordingly prohibited in the interests of law and order, in consequence of the feelings of passion and religious animosity which were excited among the Sunnis of Gayā, but since 1897 the spirit of toleration and friendliness between the two communities has rendered it possible to withdraw the prohibition, and the *mashk* and *tīr* have been carried in the Shiah procession.

At the last census the number of Christians was only 253. Three missionary societies work among the natives, viz., the London Baptist Missionary Society, the London Baptist Zanāna Missionary Society and the World's Faith Missionary Association. The Mission first named was started in 1882, and the work carried on consists of bazar preaching in Gayā, itinerant preaching in the district, the sale of the publications of the Society, and teaching in schools and bible-classes. The second Mission began work in Gayā town in 1891 and at Tekāri a few years prior to this; and the third was started in 1903. Christians.

An account of popular religion has been given in the previous chapter, and it will suffice here to mention the more remarkable of the religious movements which have occurred in recent years. These all took place in the year 1893, when there was an ebullition of religious excitement among the Hindus, which found expression in this as in other Bihār districts in the anti-kine-killing agitation, the ploughmen's begging movement and the tree-daubing mystery. RELIGIOUS MOVEMENTS.

The first movement appears to have been due to the activity of the Gorakshinī Sabhās or associations for the protection of cattle. These societies, the legitimate object of which is the care of diseased, aged, and otherwise useless cattle, started a crusade against the killing of kine, sent out emissaries to preach their doctrines, and collected subscriptions to further their objects. The relations between Hindus and Muhammadans soon became severely strained, and in various parts of Bihār the feeling aroused among the former manifested itself in the rescue of cattle from Muhammadans and in objections to their slaughtering cattle and selling the meat. At the beginning of 1893 the Gayā Gorakshinī Sabhā appeared to be confining its efforts to the establishment of asylums for the reception of neglected and starving cattle. But later in the year there was a sudden and dangerous recrudescence of the agitation for the prevention of kine-slaughter, in consequence mainly of a propaganda carried on by preachers, who gave themselves out as agents of the Sabhā, and began preaching at the various cattle fairs which were held in April. The trouble commenced with forcible interference on the part of Hindus with Musalmān purchasers of cattle at the Bisua fair held near Gayā, but fortunately there was no general disturbance, nor was any violence resorted to. Special police precautions were taken to prevent similar occurrences at other fairs held in the west of the district during that month, and nothing happened at them; but a drove of Commissariat cattle were attacked near Arwal on their way from the Deokund fair to Dinapore, and all were driven off. Anti-kine-killing agitation.

The minds of the ignorant people in the interior meanwhile got excited over the question, and there is good reason to believe that a great proportion of the Hindu zamīndārs of the district resolved to take effective measures to stop kine-killing on their estates. The result was a series of disturbances in several places in the interior, although not a single case came to notice in which Muhammadans made any wanton attempt to wound Hindu religious feeling. Fortunately for the peace of the district, no time was lost in getting additional police quartered for one year at the expense of the inhabitants in 31 villages round half-a-dozen centres where the principal disturbances took place. This had an excellent effect on both parties; and at the same time the leaders of the movement were brought to see that nothing but mischief would result from the lawless aspect it was assuming. Many people entertained great apprehension for the safety of Gayā town on the occasion of the Bakr-Id in the end of June 1893, and in one quarter of it the minds of the people were so excited that the shops were closed against Muhammadans for four days before the festival. Before it came round, however, all the leading members of the community on both sides, including the office-bearers of the Gorakshinī Sabhā, were enlisted in support of law and order, and the Bakr-Id passed off without the slightest disturbance anywhere in the district.

Ploughmen's begging movement. The ploughmen's begging movement, or, as it should more properly be called, the Mahādeo *pūjā*, was a curious exhibition of religious feeling which occurred soon afterwards. All ploughmen, the story goes, were obliged to give their cattle three days' rest and go round the neighbouring villages begging. With the proceeds three wheaten cakes were prepared—one for the ploughman himself, one for his cattle, while the third had to be buried under their stalls. This penance was performed by the people in consequence of a rumour that it had been imposed by the god Mahādeo to expiate the sin committed by the agricultural community in overworking their cattle. For some time the people continued to carry out, with scrupulous care, the orders which they supposed had been given them by their god. The remarkably elaborate nature of this penance gives reason, however, to suppose that it had been carefully thought out; and its inception and spread among the villagers has been attributed to the efforts of those interested in the Gorakshinī agitation to keep the movement afloat.

The tree-daubing mystery. Tree-daubing was another widespread movement, the meaning of which gave rise to much speculation. By the most reliable reports it commenced about the latter end of February 1894 in the north-east corner of Bihār in the neighbourhood of the Janakpur shrine which lies across the border in Nepāl. The movement consisted in marking trees with daubs of mud, in which were stuck hairs of different animals, buffaloes' hair and pigs' bristles predominating. It slowly spread through the Gangetic districts, eastwards into Bhāgalpur and Purnea and westwards through many of the districts of the United Provinces. It appeared in a few places in this district, where it was traced in several instances to wandering gangs of *sādhus*. As an explanation of the movement, it was suggested at the time that the sign was intended as an advertisement of the shrine of Janakpur; and this view was accepted officially. Others, however, held that the marks originated merely with cattle rubbing themselves against trees.*

PRINCIPAL CASTES.

The numbers and distribution of all the castes exceeding 25,000 persons are given in the Statistical Appendix. Among the Muhammadans Jolāhās (74,252) and Sheikhs (66,782) bulk most largely, and the only higher caste numbering over 25,000 is the Pathān (25,939). Among the Hindus the most numerous of the higher castes are Rājputs (110,949), Brāhmans (64,350) and Kāyasths (39,038). Many of the functional castes are well represented, such as Kahārs (110,099), Chamārs (81,179), Telis (58,385), Kurmīs (40,683), Barhis (38,828), Hajjāms (38,415) and Pāsīs (38,248). A large proportion of the people are of aboriginal descent, and four distinctively indigenous castes, the Bhuiyās (111,831), Musahars (54,559), Rajwārs (53,189) and Kharwārs (9,720) amount to one-ninth of the total population. The Goālās or Ahīrs are by far the largest caste, as they account, with a strength of 305,846, for no less than one-seventh of the people; and there are 6 other castes numbering over 100,000, viz., the Bābhans (163,108), Koiris (145,343), Bhuiyās (111,831), Rājputs (110,949), Kahārs (110,099) and Dosādhs (108,084). These seven castes alone account for more than a half of the aggregate number of persons residing in the district. A short account of each is given below.

Goālās.

The hereditary occupation of the Goālās is that of herdsmen, but with this they combine cultivation, and a large number have given up pastoral pursuits altogether and are only tillers of the soil. They have attained an unenviable reputation as cattle-lifters and furnish more than their proper quota of the jail population. Once every year they offer a peculiar form of worship to Basāwan in order that disease may be averted from the cattle. On the night of the 15th Kārtik, rice is boiled in all the milk

* For a fuller discussion of the subject, *see* The Tree-daubing of 1894, Calcutta Review, January 1898.

left in the house, and the mixture, called *khīr*, is then offered to Basāwan. All the cattle are left without food, and next morning their horns are painted red and red spots are daubed on their bodies. They are then turned into a field and ranged round a pig which they gore to death.

Bābhans.

The Bābhans or Bhuinhārs are usually land-holders and cultivators, and some of them, like the Mahārājā of Tekāri own large estates. They claim to be Brāhmans, and call themselves Ajāchak Brāhmans, *i. e.*, Brāhmans who do not take alms (*jāchak*) in contrast to the ordinary Brāhmans whom they call Jāchaks or almstakers. Like Brāhmans, they will not hold the plough but employ labourers for the purpose. Various traditions as to their origin are current. One is to the effect that they are descended from Brāhmans who took to agricultural pursuits, and one of the titles they claim is zamīndār Brāhman. Another tradition relates that in the war between Parasu Rāma and the Kshattriyas, the latter pretended to be Brāhmans and so saved their lives, as it is a sin to kill a Brāhman. They gave up their lands without fighting and henceforward were called Bhuinhārs. Another local legend declares that at a great sacrifice offered by Jarāsandha, king of Magadha, a sufficient number of Brāhmans could not be obtained, and the Dīwān therefore palmed off some men of the lower castes as genuine Brāhmans. The Brāhmans thus manufactured, failing to gain admission into their supposed caste, had to set up a caste of their own, the name of which (Bābhan or Bāhman) is popularly supposed to mean a sham Brāhman. This tradition, it need scarcely be said, is not recognized by the Bābhans themselves, and like the other legends, it has clearly been invented to explain the claim of the Bābhans to be Brāhmans.

In the estimation of the general Hindu public, they now constitute a separate caste, and their degradation probably dates back to the time when Buddhism was overthrown. It has been pointed out that Bābhan is merely the Pālī form of Brāhman, and that the word is often found in Asoka's edicts. It has therefore been conjectured that those now known as Bābhans remained Buddhists after the Brāhmans around them had reverted to Hinduism, and so the Pālī name continued to be applied them; while the synonym Bhuinhār or Bhumihāraka is explained as referring to their having seized the lands attached to the old Buddhist monasteries. This theory is borne out by the Brahmanical titles of Misr, Pānre and Tewāri which are used along with the Rājput titles of Singh, Rai and Thākur; and by the fact that in this Province they are practically confined to the area covered by the ancient empire of Magadha, which long remained the centre of Buddhism.

The Koiris call for only a brief notice. They are skilful and industrious cultivators, who are the best tenants to be found in the district. They are a purely agricultural caste, who also work as market-gardeners and rear such crops as vegetables, chillies, potatoes and poppy; they are proud of their position as adroit cultivators, and are indefatigable field-workers. Koiris.

The Bhuiyās of Gayā are an offshoot of the large Dravidian tribe of Bhuiyās which still numbers nearly two-thirds of a million. They appear to have come originally from the Tributary States of Chotā Nāgpur and Orissa, where the organization of the tribe at the present day is more complete than elsewhere. In this district they fell under the domination of people stronger than themselves, and found their level as landless labourers working in the fields. Cut off geographically from the original nucleus of the tribe, and socially degraded on account of their unclean habits of food, they are now one of the lowest of all the castes, but treasure among themselves the old tribal name of Bhuiyā. Bhuiyās.

The physical characteristics and the traditions of the Bhuiyās vary considerably in different places, but they all affect great reverence for the memory of Rikhmun or Rikhiāsan, whom they regard, some as a patron deity, and others as a mythical ancestor, whose name distinguishes one of the divisions of the tribe. It seems probable that in the earliest stage of belief Rikhmun was the bear-totem of a sept of the tribe, and that later on he was transformed into an ancestral hero, and finally promoted to the rank of a tribal god. However this may be, his cult is peculiar to the Bhuiyās, and serves to link together the scattered branches of the tribe. Here in Gayā, the Bhuiyās claim descent from Rikhiāsan, or Rukhminia as they call him, and two legends are current to explain the name of the caste. One relates that Rukhminia brought the land (*bhumi*) under the plough near the Dhaulagiri mountain, and that he and his descendants were consequently called Bhuiyās, though members of the caste also style themselves Rikhiāsans. The other is that an embankment having been breached by a flood, no one was able to repair it and save the crops from destruction, until Rukhminia came with his four brothers and rebuilt it in a single night. This act gave him the name of Bhuiyā or saviour of the land—a designation which was not regarded as in any way disparaging until a river god managed to get the Bhuiyās to eat the flesh of an unclean beast in revenge for the repair of the embankment. Thenceforward Rikhiāsan and his descendants were a despised and degraded race. Other legends relating the cause of their fall to their present low position are common in Gayā, *e.g.*, that they were created by

Mahādeo to do the work of menials, and that once upon a time a dead body having to be removed from Mahādeo's house, no one but the descendants of Rukhminia would obey his orders and carry it out. All the legends however point to the Bhuiyās having been a great cultivating caste which became degraded on account of their uncleanly habits and manners.

Rājputs. The Rājputs of Gayā, like the Bābhans, generally follow agricultural pursuits. They were probably among the earliest Aryan settlers in the district, which they wrested from the aboriginal tribes which had hitherto held it. They generally observe the same forms of worship as orthodox Hindus of good caste, but pay especial honour to Devī, a reverence explained by a legend about the special favour she showed to a Rājput, Jagat Deo Singh. When he was in attendance before the king at Delhi, Devī appeared as a woman dressed in sorry ragged raiment, and informed the king that only Jagat Deo could present her with suitable clothing. The king said he would give double what Jagat Deo did, and Devī thereupon put his and Jagat Deo's devotion to the test, by ordering Jagat Deo's head to be cut off. This having been done, she asked for the head of the king's son, which the king refused, and she then restored Jagat Deo to life.

Kahārs. The Kahārs follow the occupation of cultivators, *pālki*-bearers, household servants and labourers. According to tradition, field-labour is their hereditary calling. The legend is that king Jarāsandha built a tower, close to which was a garden at Giriak on the northern border of the district: this tower, which is still known as Jarāsandha's *baithak*, has been identified by General Cunningham as a Buddhist stūpa erected over a goose in the monastery of Hansa Sanghārāma. The garden was nearly destroyed by drought, and Jarāsandha offered the hand of his daughter and half his kingdom to any one who watered it in a single night from the Ganges. The chief of the Kahārs undertook the task, built a great embankment, and lifted the water by swing-baskets from the Bāwan Ganga, a rivulet running at its foot. The work was all but done, and Jarāsandha was in despair at having to marry his daughter to a Kahār, when the *pīpal*-tree came to his rescue and, assuming the form of a cock, crowed loudly. The Kahārs, thinking it was morning, fled at once, leaving their task unfinished, in fear of the king taking vengeance on them for presuming to seek an alliance with him. The king, however, gave them their wages, $3\frac{1}{2}$ seers of food, and that amount has ever since been the Kahār's daily wage.

Dosādhs. The Dosādhs also support themselves by labour and cultivation, but many of them are notorious thieves, and as a community they are reckoned among the criminal classes of the district. They are, as a rule, of a low type and appear to have traces of an aboriginal descent. The main features of their worship are the sacrifice of pigs and the libation of liquor, and their ceremonies generally terminate in a drunken feast on swine's flesh. Like the Dosādhs and Dhāngars of Northern India, they observe a curious ceremony in honour of Rāhu, the demon of eclipse. A long shallow trench is dug outside the village, and the officiating Dosādh, called the *bhagat*, sleeps in a hut close by on the night before the ceremony. Near the trench two long bamboo poles are erected with two swords fastened, edge downwards, across them. The trench is filled with mango wood, over which *ghī* is sprinkled, and the wood is then burnt. When the flames have burnt down, the *bhagat* passes over the live embers followed by the assembled people. This passing through the fire is regarded as a kind of exorcism; only those who are possessed by an evil spirit are affected by the fire, and any burn is a sign of their deliverance from demoniacal possession. Near the trench is a pot full of *khīr* (rice boiled in milk), which when boiling must be stirred by the bare hand of the *bhagat*. The latter mounts the swords, and sacrifices a boar and a pig, the flesh of which is then devoured by the worshippers together with the *khīr*. The remnant, if any, is burned before the next sunrise. This ceremony is generally performed in Māgh (January–February), but it is not necessarily periodical, as it is resorted to in order to obtain deliverance from any illness or trouble.

CHAPTER VII.

PUBLIC HEALTH.

VITAL STATISTICS.

A COMPARISON of vital statistics for any but recent periods is rendered impossible by the changes in the system of registering births and deaths which have taken place from time to time. In 1869 the duty of reporting deaths was imposed on the village *chaukīdārs*, and in 1876 the system was extended to births; but the returns received were so incomplete that they were soon discontinued, and, except in towns, deaths alone were registered until 1892, when the collection of statistics of births as well as of deaths was ordered, and the system now in vogue was introduced.

So far as they can be accepted, and they are sufficiently accurate for the purpose of calculating the approximate growth of the population and of showing the relative healthiness or unhealthiness of different years, the returns submitted since that year show that during the nine years ending in 1900 conditions were generally unfavourable. During the earlier years fever was very prevalent, and twice (once in 1892 and again in 1894) the number of reported deaths exceeded that of the births. Later on the ravages of disease were not so severe, but in 1897 the outbreak of cholera again caused the deaths to exceed the births. Taken as a whole, the births during this period exceeded the reported deaths by about 60,000. In six of these nine years the death-rate exceeded 30 per mille, and in 1894 the ratio was as high as 47·24 per mille, the highest percentage ever recorded in this district. On the other hand, the birth-rate, though it never fell below 30 per mille, never rose above 40 per mille, except in the two last years, when it reached the high percentages of 50 and 43 per thousand. Since 1900, owing to the opening of new lines of railway and the comparative prosperity which has resulted, the population has been far more progressive, in spite of the terrible visitations of plague to which it has been subject; and the increase in births has been very marked, the ratio ranging from 42·6 to 51 per mille; the latter figure, which was reached in 1904, represents a higher birth-rate than any previously recorded in Gayā. The excess of births over deaths in these 4 years has been nearly

86,000, and would indeed have been still greater, had not the number of the latter been swelled by the unusual mortality of 1901, when the death-rate rose to 45·68 per mille. This increase in the number of births is all the more noticeable, as the death-rate in the quinquennium 1900—04 was 37 per mille as compared with 32 per mille in the previous 5 years.

PRINCIPAL DISEASES. Fever.

According to the returns submitted year by year, by far the greatest mortality is due to fever, but the ignorant *chaukīdār* responsible for the returns is far from being a medical expert. Drawn as he often is from the lowest dregs of the people, he can diagnose only a few well-known diseases like cholera and small-pox, and many others are indiscriminately classed under the general head of fever. It may, however, safely be assumed that when the mortality ascribed to fever is unusually high, the greater part of the excess is due to malarial affections, and it is noticeable that in seven out of the last ten years the average mortality from fever in the district has exceeded that for the Province as a whole. Year by year the number of deaths from fever varies between 40,000 and 60,000, and it has been known to rise to over 70,000. This occurred in the unhealthy year of 1894, when fever accounted for a mortality of 33·52 per mille; and only once in the decade (in 1898) has the death-rate fallen below 20 per mille. Regarding the types of fever prevalent the Civil Surgeon, Major C. E. Sunder, I.M.S., writes:—"The commonest type of fever in this district is what for want of a better name has been called 'simple continued,' and which the writer believes to be due to the vicissitudes of temperature occurring in the district, to which the heat mechanism of the body is unable to accommodate itself, and it is therefore thrown out of gear. Malaria accounts for about 33 per cent. of all the fevers. This figure is based upon microscopical examination of the blood in about 200 cases, and must be accepted with reserve. When found the malarial organism is usually the 'benign tertian,' in two generations causing a quotidian, and not a true tertian ague. The 'malignant tertian' is uncommon, and the quartan parasite is rarely found. Almost all the other specific fevers occur in Gaya, but the only one that calls for notice is typhoid, which certainly does occur among natives, as has been verified clinically and by *post mortem*. Of the eruptive fevers measles is exceedingly common, and chicken-pox and small-pox come next. Typhus has not been seen."

Plague.

Bubonic plague first appeared in epidemic form in the district in October 1900. It broke out in the town of Gayā, but subsequently spread over almost the whole of the district, and continued its ravages up to May 1901. The mortality during this period was appalling; and though the returns show that only 1,133 deaths were due to plague in 1900 and 10,790 deaths in 1901, there is no doubt that much of the mortality reported as due to fever was really caused by plague. The deaths ascribed to the latter disease suddenly increased by 11,000 in 1901 and as suddenly dropped by 22,500 next year—a most suspicious variation; and it is reported that the actual number of deaths caused by plague in these eight months was over 26,000. Since then plague has been an annual visitation, though there has not been such heavy mortality as during the first epidemic. Some sporadic cases appeared in 1902, and in the next year the disease recurred with great severity, the total number of deaths aggregating 1,009, in spite of the immunity of the district during the months June to October. There was then a recrudescence of the disease, and the epidemic continuing to prevail until late in the year, the mortality rose in 1904 to nearly 7,000. It raged with even greater virulence in the beginning of 1905, in the first three months of which it accounted for over 10,000 deaths, the severity of the epidemic being aggravated by unusual cold and storms in January and February.

Throughout these years the disease has pursued a regular course, decreasing or disappearing entirely in the hot and rainy weather months, reappearing after the rains, and reaching its climax in the cold weather. In his report for 1904 the Civil Surgeon states:—"Plague may now be considered as having become endemic. The outbreak that began in November 1903 lasted well into the year under report, and cases continued to occur until the hot days of April. It now appears always to be at its worst in the cold months, and directly it appears in the town, an exodus of the people takes place, which spreads the disease still further. Even stricken patients are carried away in the exodus. Disinfection, dessication and evacuation are adopted, but the first can seldom be done thoroughly on account of the opposition, the second seems of as little use, and the last, while saving the individual in the present, does nothing to obviate reinfection in the future."

To this it should be added that inoculation has found more favour among the people of Gayā than anywhere else in Bengal, and especially during the first epidemic in the cold weather of 1900-01. At first they were doubtful of its value; but after its effects had been experienced, they came forward with great readiness to be inoculated by the Civil Surgeon and the trained medical officers deputed for the purpose, and during this epidemic some 23,000 persons were inoculated of their own free will. These operations afforded striking evidence of the value of the measure as a preventive of plague. In Gayā town some 3,716 persons were inoculated up to the 31st March 1901; of these, 31 were subsequently attacked by plague, but only 4 persons died, and three of these died within 10 days after inoculation, *i.e.*, they may have had the disease before inoculation, as the plague germ is supposed to incubate for 8 or 10 days, so that a person may not develop signs of the disease till after that period. Among the uninoculated inhabitants of the towns about 2·8 per cent. were attacked and 2·7 per per cent. died; and taking all cases of suspected fever as well as admitted plague, 8·3 per cent. were attacked and 8·2 per cent. died, whereas among the inoculated 1·2 per cent. were attacked and 0·2 per cent. died. In other words, taking only cases admitted to be plague, the proportion of deaths among the uninoculated was 14 times as great as among the inoculated; and taking all deaths from suspected fever as well, the greater part of which were undoubtedly caused by plague, we find that the proportion of deaths among the uninoculated was 41 times greater than among those protected by inoculation. In the district as a whole, there were 42 cases, so far as authentic information can be obtained, in which those who had been inoculated died, and only one person—and that a doubtful case of plague—died after the 10 days' period: in the case of the uninoculated most of those who were attacked died. The readiness with which the people took to inoculation was almost entirely due to the popularity of the local officers and the wholesome influence they exercised; and though the striking results attained during the first epidemic have not been repeated, inoculation still continues to be more popular than elsewhere in the Province; in 1904 the number inoculated (840) was as great as in all the other Bengal districts.

Other diseases.

After fever and plague, the greatest mortality is caused by cholera, which appears in epidemic form at times and carries off large numbers of the people. During the last decade it has raged with especial virulence every three years, causing a mortality of 7·64 per mille in 1894, of 3 per mille in 1897, of 5·79 per mille in 1900, and of 2·76 per mille in 1903. Small-pox also visits the district every year, but its ravages are not very severe, the death-rate due to it only exceeding 1 per mille in 1897 and 1902. Dysentery and diarrhœa are fairly common, but the only diseases specially prevalent in the district are cataract, stone, hydrocele and lymph scrotum, as well as other reputed filarial diseases. An enquiry has been made with the object of testing the interesting hypothesis that the prevalence of stone is due to a deficiency of salt in the diet of the people; and though there appears to be no doubt that common salt is deficient in their usual diet as judged by ordinary physiological standard diets, the data obtained were insufficient to establish any definite conclusions. In the opinion, however, of the Civil Surgeon it seems beyond dispute that hard water and an excessively dry climate are potent factors in the etiology of lithiasis. Similarly, the glare and dust accompanying the hot dry climate of Gayā predispose to cataract, and blindness is unusually common, the proportion of persons afflicted being 145 per 100,000 among males and 138 per 100,000 among females. The number of persons suffering from elephantiasis is also great, and in Gayā town particularly it is a common sight to see numbers both of men and women walking about the streets with enormously swollen legs and feet. Lepers are also unusually common, and at the census of 1901 it was found that leprosy was more frequent than in any other Bihār district, 102 per 100,000 males and 16 per 100,000 females being lepers. The great disproportion is probably due mainly to the fact that male lepers travel further from their homes and leave their homes in greater numbers in order to beg at Gayā, where a long string of men in all stages of this loathsome disease may be seen on the way to the Vishnupad temple imploring the charity of the passers-by.

SANITATION. Outside the municipalities proper methods of sanitation are almost unknown, in spite of the measures taken by the District Board to clear rank undergrowth, fill up unhealthy hollows and sweep selected villages. The tendency of the people is towards aggregation, and instead of living in hamlets, each nestling within its own belt of trees, as in Bengal, they cluster in closely-packed villages, usually consisting of a main street with narrow and ill-ventilated side lanes. The sanitary conditions are extremely primitive, while the apathy of the people and the unwholesome habits to which they are rooted render the task of village sanitation on any appreciable scale most difficult. Within municipal areas there is a regular system of conservancy, night-soil and other refuse are removed, and steps are taken to protect the sources of water-supply, but none of them have a regular system for the supply of pure water or an adequate scheme of drainage. Like the villages, they suffer from crowded and badly-aligned blocks of houses intersected by narrow lanes, and the mortality from plague, dysentery and cholera is generally greater than in the rural areas. In the town of Gayā special sanitary precautions are necessitated by the large influx of pilgrims every year, and the Lodging-house Act is in operation. The lodging-houses provided for pilgrims are licensed; they are regularly inspected, and measures are taken to see that their sanitary arrangements are adequate and that an improper number of pilgrims are not accommodated in them. As cholera often follows the pilgrim train, the Lodging-house Fund also maintains a cholera hospital, at which cholera and other contagious diseases are treated.

VACCINATION.

The opposition to vaccination was formerly very strong, and 35 years ago it was reported that nothing short of compulsion would ever induce the people to submit to the operation. The popular belief was that vaccination provoked the goddess Sītalā, who presides over small-pox, to visit the offence with small-pox in a deadly form, and the objection to vaccination was consequently very deeply rooted in the minds of the people. This prejudice has passed away, as the people now realize its efficacy, and, though vaccination is compulsory only in municipal areas, it has steadily gained ground except among a few bigoted classes. More than 20 per cent. of the population were protected against small-pox in the seven years ending in 1905, and during the ten years 1895-96 to 1904-05, the number of successful vaccinations increased from 43,000 to over 61,000; the average during the last four years of the decade was as high as 64,000. In spite of the fact that plague has created additional difficulties and impeded the work considerably, the ratio of persons successfully vaccinated in 1904-05 was 29·46 and in the preceding five years 28·30 per thousand of the population. Statistics of vaccination from 1892-93 to 1901-02 will be found in the Statistical Appendix.

MEDICAL INSTITUTIONS.

Thirty years ago there were only five dispensaries in the district, viz., the Pilgrim Hospital at Gayā and four branch dispensaries at Aurangābād, Jahānābād, Nawāda and Sherghāti. There are now three hospitals at Gayā itself—the Pilgrim, Cholera and Zanāna Hospitals, and 12 dispensaries in the outlying parts, situated at Arwal, Aurangābād, Dāūdnagar, Deo, Fatehpur, Jahānābād, Khizrsarāi, Nabīnagar, Nawāda, Rafiganj, Sherghāti and Tekāri. The number of persons served by each dispensary is 98,092, and in 1904 the average number of patients treated was 66 per mille of the population. The total number treated annually has risen from 52,000 in 1894 to 99,000 in 1904 and the daily average number from 668 to 1,071. The amount expended on dispensaries during the five years 1899—1903 was over $2\frac{1}{2}$ lakhs of rupees,—a sum exceeded only in two other districts in Bengal (Dacca and the 24-Parganas); Rs. 72,000 was received from subscriptions, and the ratio of these subscriptions to the total expenditure was thus 28·31 per cent.—a somewhat low proportion. Besides these institutions, there are 441 medical practitioners; of these only 54 have diplomas.

By far the largest number of patients are treated for fever and next to that for skin diseases; ear diseases and venereal diseases come next in frequency, followed by eye diseases. Cataract operations are very numerous, and during the five years 1896—1900 successful operations of this nature were performed in the case of 874 males and 543 females—a total exceeded only in the adjoining district of Shāhābād. All the hospitals and dispensaries, except those at Deo, Fatehpur, Khizrsarāi, Nabīnagar and Rafiganj, have accommodation for in-patients; they contain altogether 95 beds for men and 73 beds for women. Statistics of the daily attendance, indoor and outdoor, during the years 1892—1901 will be found in the Statistical Appendix; and a statement of the receipts and expenditure, and of the principal diseases treated at each dispensary in 1904-05, is given at the end of this chapter.

Gayā Pilgrim Hospital. The premier medical institution in the district is the Gayā Pilgrim Hospital, so called because it is specially intended for the medical relief of the pilgrims who visit the shrines at Gayā or pass through it on their way to other sacred places; in recognition of the services thus rendered a large contribution is made to its upkeep by the Pilgrim Fund known as the Lodging-house Fund. There are two separate buildings, the one for male patients and the other for female patients, the former of which contains eye, surgical and medical wards; and there are altogether 80 beds, of which 50 are in the male ward, 22 in the female ward and 8 in the pauper ward. The hospital also contains a separate building for moribund patients, an operation room, well equipped with modern aseptic appliances and surgical instruments, and a laboratory in which clinical bacteriology is carried on. The principal cases treated are fever, and eye, ear, skin and venereal diseases. Practically every operation known to modern medical science has been carried out, but operations for cataract and stone in the bladder predominate.

Gayā Zanāna Hospital. The Lady Elgin Zanāna Hospital, which was established in 1895 for *pardānashin* women, is in charge of a lady-doctor. It is a large and well-equipped building, containing 28 beds, and is also provided with cottage wards. It has acquired considerable popularity in the district and is doing much excellent work.

Name of Dispensary.	Operations.	Diseases treated.				
		Fever.	Skin diseases.	Ear diseases.	Venereal diseases.	Eye diseases.
Gayā Pilgrim Hospital	1,912	1,126	2,428	2,098	1,028	1,480
Gayā Cholera ,, ...	525	731	464	821	323	163
Gayā Zanāna ,, ...	648	386	401	409	583	464
Arwal Dispensary ...	381	1,042	924	339	581	337
Aurangābād ,, ...	222	2,116	608	464	463	320
Daūdnagar ,, ...	286	739	620	404	210	218
Deo ,, ...	149	701	737	271	219	123
Fatehpur ,, ...	97	1,059	922	233	474	157
Jahānābād ,, ...	403	1,610	1,558	766	707	519
Khizrsarāi ,, ...	88	1,076	348	213	277	207
Nabīnagar ,, ...	181	887	1,211	506	78	186
Nawāda ,, ...	291	1,407	1,142	1,059	670	611
Rafiganj ,, ...	262	828	850	210	294	314
Sherghāti ,, ...	300	1,137	591	112	57	155
Tekāri ,, ...	704	1,427	514	460	347	983
Total ...	6,449	16,272	13,318	8,365	6,311	6,237

Name of Dispensary.	Receipts.				Expenditure.	
	Government contribution.	District Fund.	Municipal Funds.	Subscriptions and other sources.	Establishment.	Medicines, diet, buildings, etc.
	Rs. A. P.	Rs. A. P.	Rs. A. P.	Rs. A. P.	Rs. A. P.	Rs. A. P.
Gayā Pilgrim Hospital.	...	6,115 0 0	5,877 0 0	(a) 4,517 0 0	5,008 0 0	10,084 0 0
Gayā Cholera ,,	...	...	...	(b) 1,744 0 0	743 0 0	902 0 0
Gayā Zanāna ,,	...	3,300 0 0	600 0 0	7,233 0 0	5,962 0 0	1,888 0 0
Arwal Dispensary	300 0 0	546 13 9	...	300 0 0	943 4 6	203 9 3
Aurangābād ,,	...	723 14 11	...	236 11 0	453 8 0	507 1 11
Dāūdnagar ,,	195 0 0	...	522 3 6	122 12 2	467 5 8	372 10 3
Deo ,,	...	...	...	(c) 1,500 3 6	519 0 0	981 3 6
Fatehpur ,,	...	855 7 10	...	32 12 0	646 4 1	215 6 5
Jahānābād ,,	...	486 2 7	...	464 1 6	515 6 0	434 13 3
Khizrsarāi ,,	...	1,237 7 0	...	...	749 0 0	488 7 0
Nabīnagar ,,	...	831 0 0	...	...	510 0 0	321 0 0
Nawāda ,,	...	1,390 9 2	...	593 11 4	563 9 4	629 0 6
Rafiganj ,,	...	1,014 0 0	...	63 0 0	699 0 0	314 0 0
Sherghāti ,,	..	968 0 0	...	42 0 0	492 0 0	518 0 0
Tekāri ,,	...	...	...	(d) 3,751 9 2	3,011 14 6	739 10 8
Total	495 0 0	17,468 7 3	6,999 3 6	20,600 12 8	21,283 4 1	18,598 14 9

(a) Of this sum, Rs. 3,500 was contributed by the Gayā Lodging-house Fund.
(b) This hospital is maintained by the same Fund.
(c) This dispensary is maintained by the Deo Rāj.
(d) ,, ,, ,, by the Tekāri Rāj.

CHAPTER VIII.

AGRICULTURE.

GENERAL CONDITIONS.

THE average annual rainfall of Gayā is about 45 inches, but owing to the position of the district, it receives a full supply from neither monsoon, and the rainfall is frequently deficient, fitful or untimely. Besides this, the general slope of the country and the nature of the soil render the land very unretentive of moisture, and the local rainfall would therefore play a comparatively minor part in the agricultural industry of the district, were it not for artificial works of irrigation. Owing to the conformation of the surface, water is carried off so rapidly into the rivers that artificial measures for storing water and leading it from the rivers by channels (locally known as *pains*) are indispensable. It is this necessity that has given rise to the network of *pains* and the thousands of artificial reservoirs, called *āhars*, which are scattered over the district; and it is on these sources of supply that the people almost entirely depend, except in the west near the Son, where a considerable area is irrigated from the Patna-Gayā canal and its distributaries.

As already stated, the drainage flows northwards to the Ganges from the Chotā Nāgpur plateau on the south, finding its outlet through a series of rivers and hill torrents, nearly all of which dry up after the rains are over. The district is thus divided into a number of parallel strips, each of which again slopes down to the river-beds on either side. The high land in the middle, which is known as *tānr*, is of poor fertility; it can only be irrigated from *āhars*, and grows chiefly *rabi* and *bhadoi* crops. This *tānr* land is most extensive in the south, but towards the north, where the surface is more level, the land is more easily irrigable. Most of the fields are supplied with water from the channels taking off from the rivers as well as from *āhars*, and the low lands near the rivers are generally sown with rice, which is the principal crop grown.

TRACTS OF FERTILITY.

It has been explained in Chapter I that the district of Gayā may be roughly divided into two tracts, that to the north well irrigated and fairly fertile, and that to the south sparsely populated, densely wooded and indifferently cultivated. The northern portion of the district, which constitutes about two-thirds of the whole area, is fairly level and is mostly under cultivation. In the south the rise towards the hills of Chotā Nāgpur is more rapid; the country is more intersected with hills and ravines; and the proportion of sand in the soil washed down from the hills is much larger. Cultivation in this tract is consequently much more scanty, and a large area is composed of hill and scrub-covered jungle extending for several miles below the hills.

Though the district is divided broadly into these two large tracts, there are four minor subdivisions* with different degrees of fertility. The first, or fertile, tract comprises the Jahānābād subdivision and the western canal-irrigated strip of the Aurangābād subdivision, the whole tract consisting of Jahānābād and Arwal thānas, and of a portion of Dāūdnagar thāna. The western portion of this tract has the benefit of canal irrigation, while the northern and eastern portions are intersected by *pains* or irrigation channels leading from the rivers Morhar and Mohāna. Moreover, the greater part of this portion of the district was once the basin of the Son river itself, and the soil being largely composed of old alluvial deposit is naturally more productive than elsewhere.

The second, or moderately fertile, tract consists of two areas, the first being composed of thānas Gayā, Tekāri and Atrī in the centre of the district, and the second of thāna Nabīnagar in the extreme south-west. These areas have also the benefit of ample irrigation from several rivers, and there are very few villages which have not either a *pain* or sub-channel (*bhoklā*) leading off from some efficient source of water-supply.

The third, or less fertile, tract also consists of two areas—the first being the Nawāda subdivision, and the second the rest of the Aurangābād subdivision, consisting of thāna Aurangābād and of a portion of thāna Dāūdnagar. Only about half the villages in these two areas are sufficiently irrigated, and moreover, the *pains* that do exist only give an adequate supply of water in years of good rainfall.

The fourth, or infertile, tract consists of thānas Sherghāti and Bārāchatti, or the southern half of the head-quarters subdivision. Besides containing extensive tracts of jungle, there are few *pains*, and only about ten per cent. of the villages are irrigated. Hence paddy is little cultivated, as compared with the rest of the district, and is liable to failure in a moderately bad year.

In the northern tract the soil is generally alluvial, consisting chiefly of *pauru*, a loam with a small proportion of sand, and SOILS.

* See Grierson's Notes on the District of Gayā, pp. 81-82.

kewāl, a species of hard stiff clay, opening out, when dry, in gaping fissures, which make cross-country riding impossible. In the south a great part of the existing sub-soil has been deposited by diluvion from the hills, the rivers issuing from which carry along with them quantities of hard white and yellow sand; this accounts for the large proportion of sand in the soil and for the large areas which are almost entirely composed of sand. This sandy soil is called *balwat*, *balmat* or *balsundrī*. In some places also there is a white soil called *rehra*, which is rendered more or less useless by being impregnated with carbonate of soda; when the impregnation is so great as to render it unculturable waste, it is known as *ūsar*. The presence of carbonate of soda (*reh*) in paddy land does not, however, seem to make it infertile, the soda being presumably dissolved by the water. *Pauru* soil is best adapted for the cultivation of paddy, though in the area irrigated from the canals even sandy soils produce fine paddy; it requires irrigation, and gram is almost the only crop that can be raised without it. *Kewāl* clay is best suited for *rabi* crops, as it retains moisture longer, and the *rabi* has to depend to a great extent on sub-soil moisture.

PRINCIPAL CROPS.

The crops grown in Gayā are divided into three great divisions—the *aghani*, *bhadoi* and *rabi* crops. The *aghani* is the winter crop of rice which is cut in the month of Aghan (November-December), the *bhadoi* is the early or autumn crop, reaped in the month of Bhādo (August-September), consisting of 60 days' rice, *maruā*, *kodo*, Indian-corn, millets and less important grains; while the *rabi* crop, which is so called because it is harvested in the spring (*rabi*), includes such cold-weather crops as gram, wheat, barley, oats, and pulses. Out of the total normal cropped area, 57·5 per cent. grows *aghani*, 31·8 per cent. grows *rabi*, and only in 9·4 per cent. is *bhadoi* raised. The latter is, therefore, relatively an unimportant crop, and the people are mainly dependent on the *aghani* rice, and secondly on their *rabi* crops.

RICE.

Aghani rice.

Rice, which occupies a normal area of 1,338,300 acres, is the staple crop of the district. The *aghani* or winter rice forms the greater part of this crop, and is raised on over 1,318,000 acres. It is sown broadcast after the commencement of the rains in June or July on lands selected for seed nurseries, which have previously been ploughed three or four times. After four or six weeks, when the young plants are about a foot high, they are generally transplanted; each plant is pulled out from the land, which is soft with standing water, and planted again in rows in flooded fields, in which the soil has been puddled. After this the rice is left to mature, with the aid of water, till towards the end of September. The water is then drained off and the fields are allowed to dry for 15 days, and at the end of that time they are again flooded. It is this practice, known as *nigār*, which makes the rainfall, or failing that, irrigation essential to successful harvest. These late rains (the *Hathiyā*) are the most important in the year, as not only are they required to bring the winter crops to maturity but also to provide moisture for the sowing of the *rabi* crops. Should no rain fall at this period, or if water cannot be procured from artificial sources, the plants will wither and become only fit for fodder; but if seasonable showers fall or the crops are watered from *āhars*, *pains* or canals, the rice comes to maturity in November or December.

Some winter rice known as *bāog* is not transplanted; it is sown broadcast on low lands at the commencement of the rains, and also in years in which there has not been sufficient moisture to allow of transplantation at the proper time. The *bhadoi* rice, which covers 20,000 acres, is also sown broadcast in June or July and not transplanted; it is regarded as a 60 days' crop, and is generally harvested in August or September. There is another kind of rice, known as the *boro* or spring rice, which is sown in January, transplanted after a month and cut in April. It is grown only on marsh lands and in the beds of shallow streams, and the area cultivated with it is insignificant.

Other kinds of rice.

A noticeable feature of rice cultivation is the way in which it is conducted religiously according to lunar * asterisms (*nakshatras*). The seed-beds throughout the country are, if possible, sown within a period of 15 days, called the *Adra nakshatra*, which lasts from about the 20th June to the 5th July. Transplantation from the seed-beds goes on during the *Punarbas*, *Pukh*, and *Asres nakshatras* (18th July—15th August). The water on the fields in which the young plant has grown up after transplantation is regularly drained off in the *Utra nakshatra* (12th—25th September)—a period when, as a rule, there is little rain; and after the exposure of the soil to the air and sun, the usual heavy rain of the *Hathiyā nakshatra* (26th September—7th October) is awaited. After this, it is the universal custom to keep the fields wet during the *Chitra nakshatra* (8th—20th October); and at the commencement of the *Siwātī nakshatra* (21st October—3rd November) they are again drained, and the paddy is left to itself till the *Bisākha nakshatra* (4th—15th November) when it is cut.

---

* As the *nakshatras* are calculated according to phases of the moon, they vary slightly from English dates, but the greatest variation is only five days.

Although there are sometimes slight variations in the times of sowing and transplanting from those given above, yet the cultivators are always extremely strict in draining off the water from the fields in the *Utra nakshatra*. It may be said that every cultivator begins, if he possibly can, to let off the water on the first day of that *nakshatra*, and this is done, without any hesitation, in the country commanded by the canals, because the cultivator looks to the Irrigation authorities to supply him with water, whether the *Hathiyā* rain fails entirely or not. It is generally agreed that after this draining (*nigār*), rice plants cannot exist for more than from 15 to 20 days, unless watered, without rapid deterioration; and as no ryot will, under any circumstances, take water till the *Hathiyā nakshatra* has commenced, the Canal Department is called upon to irrigate within a very few days every acre under lease. If water is delayed a week after it is wanted at this stage, the crop suffers; if it is delayed three weeks, it withers beyond redemption.

BHADOI CROPS.

The *bhadoi* crops require plenty of rain with intervals of bright sunshine to bring them to maturity, and constant weeding is necessary for a good harvest. The time of sowing depends in the breaking of the monsoon; if the rainfall is early, they are sown in the beginning of June; but they can be sown as late as the middle of July without the prospect of the crop being lost. Harvesting usually extends from the 15th July to the 15th October.

The principal *bhadoi* crop is *maruā* (*Eleusine Coracana*), a valuable millet, occupying a normal area of 77,000 acres, which is sown at the commencement of the rainy season and cut at the end of it. It is partly sown broadcast and partly transplanted to ground that afterwards gives a winter crop. The grain is largely consumed by the poorer classes in the form of *sattu*, or is converted into flour and made into a coarse bread; in bad seasons, when the rice crop fails, it supports the people till the spring crops have been harvested.

Next in importance to *maruā* comes maize (*Zea Mays*), or Indian-corn (*makai*), which is raised on 63,000 acres; it is sown from the 20th June to the 20th July, and cut from the 15th July to the 15th August. Besides being consumed in the form of bread, or as *sattu*, the young ears while still green are often parched in the cob, and so eaten. Among millets *jowār* (*Sorghum vulgare*) is grown on 19,000 acres, and *kodo* (*Paspalum scrobiculatum*) is a favourite crop sown on poor lands early in the rains and reaped after they are over. It is a millet cheaper than rice, which is popular with the poorer classes, as it can be readily grown on an inferior soil; it is eaten boiled like rice or sometimes in *chapātis*, but is not very nutritious. The chief oil-seed grown at this time of the year is *til* or gingelly (*Sesamum indicum*) which is sown in July and reaped in September; its total acreage is about 10,000 acres. The castor-oil plant (*Ricinus communis*) is sown from the 20th June to the 1st August and is cut from the 29th December to the 30th April.

RABI CROPS.

Ploughing of the fields for the *rabi* crops commences early in the rains and is continued at convenient intervals, sufficient time being given to allow the upturned soil to be exposed to the air. In the case of clay soils in unirrigated parts, more frequent ploughing is necessary for all *rabi* crops, because otherwise the soil would become so hard that if there was no rain at the sowing time, a crop could not be sown. The time of sowing *rabi* is generally regulated by two circumstances—the heavy rains of the *Hathiyā nakshatra* (26th September to 7th October) and the approaching cold season. If sown too late, the plants will not become strong enough to resist the cold; if sown too early, the heavy rain will probably drown the seed and sprouting crop, and so necessitate re-sowing. The cultivators are thus anxious to sow as soon as the heavy rains have ceased, and the general rule is that the proper time for sowing most *rabi* crops is the *Chitra nakshatra* (8th to 20th October), and that it must not be delayed beyond the *Siwātī nakshatra* (21st October—3rd November). A sufficient supply of water is essential at this time; later on several waterings are required, and if there is no rain, the crops have to depend on well irrigation. They are finally harvested between the last week of February and the middle of April.

The most important of the cereals is wheat, which occupies altogether 134,000 acres. It is generally sown broadcast on sandy soil, and requires as a rule four waterings. It is frequently sown on lands from which a crop of early rice has been taken, and is often sown together with barley, or with gram, mustard or linseed. The stubble is grazed by cattle, and the pounded straw (*bhūsa*) is used as fodder. About half the area under wheat, or 70,000 acres, is occupied by barley (*Hordeum vulgare*), which is sown partly with wheat, partly by itself, and partly with pulse. Like wheat, barley is sown broadcast and requires four waterings.

The other great class of *rabi* crops consists of pulses, of which, gram or *būnt* (*Cicer arietinum*), is by far the most extensively grown, as a normal area of 96,000 acres is given up to it. Besides forming an excellent fodder for fattening horses, this pulse is eaten by the natives in all stages of its growth. The young leaf is eaten, and the grain is split and converted into *dāl*, or pounded into *sattu*. Among other crops may be mentioned peas, the *china* millet (*Panicum miliaceum*), *kulthi* (*Dolichos biflorus*) and various pulses and lentils, such as *rahar* (*Cajanus indicus*), *masuri* (*Ervum Lens*) and *khesāri* (*Lathyrus sativus*). The crop last named is frequently sown broadcast among the rice stubble. It requires no care, and the grain is eaten, in the form of *dāl* or as flour cooked in *ghī*, by the poorer classes. If eaten in excess, it produces a form of paralysis known as lathyrism.

Oil-seeds. Oil-seeds occupy an important position among the *rabi* crops. The chief is linseed (*Linum usitatissimum*), which is grown on a normal area of 80,000 acres. It now forms one of the chief articles of export, and every year many thousands of maunds are sent out of the district. The other principal oil-seeds are mustard and rape, which are raised on 22,000 acres.

OTHER CROPS. Cotton. The fibre crops of Gayā are inconsiderable, the normal area under cultivation being only 1,000 acres. Thirty years ago the cultivation of cotton was carried on to a considerable extent in the Jahānābād subdivision, and also in the Nawāda subdivision and to the west of the district about Dāūdnagar; and in the beginning of last century it was much more extensive, as the cloth factories at Jahānābād, Dāūdnagar and elsewhere created a demand for the raw product. The local cotton industry has now been ruined by the competition of imported piece-goods, and the area under cotton has shrunk till it now amounts to only 300 acres.

Indigo. Indigo is another crop the cultivation of which has been practically abandoned, though it has never really flourished in Gayā. In 1812 Dr. Buchanan Hamilton wrote that indigo was of little importance and its cultivation was on the decline. Later, however, European enterprise took up the industry, and several factories were established in the west of the district. There was a large indigo concern at Sipāh, commonly known as the Arwal concern, and a factory at Tararh near Dāūdnagar, with outworks at Pura, a hamlet of Kaler village on the Son, and at Baghoi on the banks of the Pūnpūn, the whole being known as the Dāūdnagar concern. The industry with difficulty survived the Mutiny, when all the factories were dismantled and the labourers dispersed, and from that time its growth rapidly declined until 1878, when the introduction of the Son canal system converted the poorest lands in this part into the most fertile. Indigo was then entirely dropped, giving way to zamīndāri management, a safer and more profitable undertaking. The cultivation is now practically extinct, and indigo is grown only on 100 acres.

Opium. Of the other crops raised in Gayā, poppy is by far the most important, as not only is the normal area under the plant considerable (51,000 acres), but the price obtained for the crude opium renders it a very valuable crop. The production of opium is a Government monopoly, and no person is allowed to grow poppy except on account of Government. Annual engagements are entered into by the cultivators, who, in consideration of the payment of an advance, agree to cultivate a certain quantity of land with poppy and to deliver the whole of the opium produced to the Government at a rate fixed according to its consistence, but subject to deductions for inferiority of quality. The best soil for poppy is loam, so situated that it can be highly manured and easily irrigated, and for this reason homestead land is generally selected. The cultivation requires much attention throughout the growth of the plant. From the commencement of the rains in June until October the ground is prepared by repeated ploughings, weedings and manuring, and the seed is sown in November. Several waterings and weedings are ordinarily necessary before the plant reaches maturity in February. After the plant has flowered, the first process is to remove the petals, which are preserved, to be used afterwards as coverings for the opium cakes. The opium is then collected during the months of February and March, by lancing the capsules in the afternoon with an iron instrument and scraping off the exudation the next morning. In the beginning of April the cultivators bring in their opium to the weighment centres of the different sub-agencies, where it is examined and weighed, and the balance due according to the Opium Officer's valuation is paid to them. Final adjustments are made in August, after the value of the drug has been ascertained by assay at the Patna Factory, where the final process of preparing the drug in balls or cakes is conducted.

There is a tendency for the cultivation of poppy to decrease, as year by year it is becoming less profitable to the ryots. The plant is delicate; a thoroughly favourable year comes only at uncertain intervals; and the cultivators have had to contend with a number of bad seasons. There is accordingly a marked tendency to withdraw from an industry so precarious and to substitute the more robust cereals or such paying crops as sugarcane, potatoes, chillies and vegetables. This movement has been quickened by the fact that the value of cereals has increased of recent years, while the price paid for the crude drug remains stationary; and in the decade ending in 1903-04, the area under poppy has decreased in the Gayā Sub-Agency from 58,900 *bīghas* to 41,000 *bīghas*, and in the Tehta Sub-Agency from 42,900 *bīghas* to 41,000 *bīghas*. Each of these Sub-Agencies is in charge of a Sub-Deputy Opium Agent, who sees to the execution of agreements to grow opium, supervises the payment of advances to the cultivators, and checks the weighment of the crude produce and the payment of the sums due to the ryots. He has to satisfy himself that the land engaged for is cultivated with and fit for poppy, to test the measurements of it, to make advances for wells and see that they have been dug, and generally supervise the cultivation and control the subordinate staff.

Sugar-cane.

The falling off in the area under poppy has been largely made up by the extension of sugarcane cultivation. In 1884 the area under sugarcane was estimated at less than 13,000 acres, but of recent years the crop has grown immensely in importance, and its cultivation has rapidly extended, so that the average area covered by it has increased to 30,100 acres during the five years ending in 1904-05. This increase is partly due to the introduction of the Son canal system in the west of the district, where sugarcane, potatoes and poppy, which could not otherwise have been raised, have been substituted for the ordinary food-grain crops. So great is the necessity of water for the growth of sugarcane that its cultivation in this tract before the era of the canals involved almost prohibitive labour on well irrigation, but this difficulty was removed by the regular supply of water afforded by the canals. Another powerful stimulus was given to the industry by the introduction of the iron roller mills worked by bullock-power, invented in 1874 by the proprietors of the Bihiā estate in Shāhābād, and hence known as the Bihiā mills. Some years indeed elapsed before their great superiority over the rude machines in use was recognized, but the ryot in spite of his conservatism learnt to appreciate their advantages; their popularity is now firmly established; and the old-fashioned appliances which necessitated the cutting up of the cane and extracted a mere fraction of the juice are now no longer seen.

Sugarcane is now one of the most profitable crops grown in the district in spite of the labour and expense its cultivation requires. It is a crop which not only exhausts the soil, but occupies the ground for a long period, extending over a year. It is planted during February or March, in cuttings of about a foot in length placed in rows about 2 feet apart. When the plant begins to sprout, it is well watered and the surrounding earth is loosened. Each plant grows into a cluster of canes, which are generally ready for cutting in January or February. The crop requires great care, and must have 7 or 8 waterings, even if the other crops have to do without water in consequence.

VEGETABLES AND FRUITS.

Vegetables are cultivated in garden plots for household use, and also on a larger scale in the neighbourhood of towns. The most extensively grown are the potato, egg-plant or *baigun* (*Solanum Melongena*), ground-nut (*Trichosanthes dioica*), and pumpkins (*Lagenaria vulgaris*) and gourds (*Benincasa cerifera*), which may be seen climbing over the roofs of the houses in nearly every village. Onions, yams and cucumbers are also common, and in the winter radishes, carrots and melons are cultivated. Among condiments the favourite is the chilli, but turmeric, coriander and ginger are also grown in considerable quantities. The most popular fruit is the mango, which grows freely and forms a valuable addition to the food of the people during the hot weather, though the flavour of the local fruit is decidedly inferior to that of the Mālda and Bombay varieties. Of the other cultivated fruits, the commonest are the plantain, lemon, *lichi* (*Nephelium Litchi*), jack fruit (*Artocarpus integrifolia*), custard apple (*Anona squamosa*) and *bel* fruit (*Aegle marmelos*). The *khajūr*-tree (*Phœnix sylvestris*) is cultivated abundantly for the sake of its juice, which is made into liquor; and the *mahuā* flower is used for the manufacture of country spirit, and is also eaten by the poorer classes, especially by those living near the jungles. The cultivation of the climbing vine call *pān* (*Piper betel*), the leaves of which are used to wrap up the *supāri* or areca-nut chewed by natives of all ranks and classes, is carried on to a considerable extent at Ketāki and some neighbouring villages in the Aurangābad subdivision, and at Tungi and Deodha in the Nawāda subdivision.

AGRICULTURAL STATISTICS.

The total normal area under different crops is 2,292,700 acres, of which 194,300 acres are cropped more than once, so that the net cropped area is 2,098,400 acres. The returns for the five years ending in 1904-05 show, however, that the average cultivated area is 1,921,200 acres and the net cropped area 1,726,900; the proportion under *aghani*, *rabi* and *bhadoi* crops being 52·5, 38 and 9·5 per cent. respectively, and the area under cereals and pulses 1,631,800 acres and under oil-seeds 182,900 acres. This difference is apparently due to the fact that the area actually cultivated varies every year, and is often less than the normal area—a result due in a large measure to the *bhāoli* system, under which the cultivator frequently does not take the trouble to cultivate all the land he holds. The average area irrigated from the canals during the same period was 53,500 acres, but the greater portion of the district is irrigated from *āhars* and *pains*, and the total area irrigated from all sources varies from 60 per cent. in the Sherghāti and Bārāchatti police circles to 90 per cent. in the Daūdnagar and Arwal thānas.

EXTENSION OF CULTIVATION. According to an estimate* made 30 years ago, the area under cultivation at that time was 1,728,006 acres, of which only 864,000 acres grew rice, while the uncultivated area was 1,419,000 acres. The normal cultivated area has now increased to over 2,000,000 acres, and that under rice to over 1,300,000 acres, while 158,000 acres are classed as culturable waste, and the area not available for cultivation is 655,800 acres, or about one-fifth of the total area of the district. This increase of cultivation is largely due to the great progress in the western portion of the district, where the canals have turned neglected waste into fertile fields. Speaking of Dāūdnagar in 1812, Buchanan Hamilton says:—"This division has been a good deal neglected, and the poorer lands are in general waste, and in the dry season look very dismal, being covered with stunted thorns without a pile of grass. Some of the best land even is neglected, and is chiefly occupied by poor-looking woods of the Palas (*Butea frondosa*)." His description of the country round Arwal is equally depressing, as he says:—"A great portion is neglected, and where the soil is poor, is chiefly overgrown with thorns of the stunted *jujub*. Where the waste land is rich, it is overgrown with harsh long grass, which in the dry season loses all vegetation." The appearance of this tract is now widely different, as it includes some of the best rice-growing land in the district, and the barren waste is now covered with fields of waving grain. Elsewhere there are large areas not yet brought under the plough, especially in the south. Much of the waste has, however, been reclaimed in recent years—a process which has been accelerated by the development of communications and the construction of new lines of railway; but in spite of this, the area still uncultivated is very large, and many parts of the district are undoubtedly capable of greater agricultural development.

IMPROVEMENTS IN METHODS OF CULTIVATION. The Bihāri is a conservative cultivator, and has an apathetic indifference to agricultural improvements. Various experiments have been made from time to time in the Government and Wards' estates with different varieties of manures, seeds and modern implements, but these experiments have had little influence on cultivation generally, and practically the only innovation which has found favour with the people is the Bihiā sugarcane mill mentioned above.

Rotation. The scientific rotation of crops is not adopted as a principle of agriculture, but as a matter of practice it is observed, especially in the case of the more exhausting crops, such as sugarcane, which

*See Food-grain Supply and Famine Relief in Bihar and Bengal, by A. P. MacDonell, 1876.

is never grown on the same land year after year, but is always alternated with other crops and generally with rice. A great part of the land growing winter rice bears that crop year after year, but sometimes a second crop of *khesāri* is raised, or if the land continues moist until harvest time, it may be ploughed and sown with gram and peas or barley. The *bhadoi* crops of early rice, maize and millets are also followed by a mixture of various pulses and oil-seeds with wheat and barley, the mixture of pulses and cereals serving the purposes of rotation, as the pulses belong to the leguminous family and enrich the soil with nitrogen.

Manures. Manure is largely used for poppy, sugarcane, potatoes and other garden produce, but not for other crops. Cow-dung is the most important manure, but its value is much diminished by the negligent manner in which it is stored, and the feeding of cattle is generally so poor that it is not rich in manurial constituents. Besides this, a great deal is lost by its conversion into fuel-cakes, as firewood is scarce, except in a few favoured localities, and its high price makes its use prohibitive for the ryots. For the most part, therefore, cow-dung only finds its way to the fields in the form of ashes; and the only other manure in common use consists of household refuse.

Land Improvement and Agriculturists' Loans Act From the figures in the Statistical Appendix it will be seen that loans under the Land Improvement Loans Act are taken by the people with fair readiness, and that the amount advanced under the Agriculturists' Loans Act is comparatively small. The latter are devoted to the purchase of seed and cattle, and the former to the improvement or extension of the means of irrigation, such as the maintenance and repair of artificial embankments, water-channels and reservoirs.

CATTLE. The cattle raised in the district, though hardy and suited to the climate, are generally of a very mediocre stamp; little or no care is taken in selecting bulls for breeding, immature or poor specimens being used; and the Brāhmanī, or dedicated, bulls are usually no better than their fellows, though the freedom with which they are allowed to graze keeps them in better condition. The cattle are especially small in the south, and in consequence of their poor physique, three bullocks, viz., a pair under a shaft and a leader attached in front of the shaft, are constantly used to draw a loaded cart. The stock has little chance of improvement, as besides the want of careful and systematic breeding, there is difficulty in obtaining pasturage. In the thinly-cultivated tracts to the south, there is much pasture land and sufficiency of grass for the herds, but elsewhere the ground retains litlte moisture during the hot weather, and the grass being parched up by the burning sun, fodder is scarce. Nearly all the land available has been given up to cultivation; and the cattle have to be content with the scanty herbage found in the arid fields or are stall-fed on chopped straw.

Buffaloes are employed for the plough, especially when deep mud is being prepared for the transplantation of paddy, and are also used for slow draught work, but their chief value is for the milk which they yield in large quantities. Sheep are extensively reared by the Gareri caste, especially near the hills, where there is fallow land for pasture, and the wool is largely used in the manufacture of carpets, rugs and blankets. Goats are bred almost in every village, and pigs of the usual omnivorous kind are kept by the low castes, such as Doms, Dosādhs, Bhuiyās and Musahars. The only horses are the usual indigenous ponies; they are generally undersized and incapable of heavy work, but they are very hardy and those used for *ekkās* often have astonishing endurance and a great turn of speed.

Veterinary assistance.

The diseases most prevalent among cattle are rinderpest and foot-and-mouth disease; over 1,000 cases of rinderpest and 550 cases of foot-and-mouth disease were reported in 1903-04. Veterinary assistance is afforded by itinerant Veterinary Assistants, and also at a veterinary dispensary which the District Board maintain at Gayā; 70 horses and 81 cattle were treated as in-patients at this dispensary in 1904-05, and 352 horses and 644 cattle as out-patients.

CHAPTER IX.

NATURAL CALAMITIES.

In common with other Bihār districts, Gayā is liable to suffer from scarcity, when the rainfall is deficient or untimely, and from floods, when it is excessive. The effects of anything but a very serious failure of the monsoon are, however, counteracted by a wonderful system of irrigation, and, though there has been scarcity in some tracts, the present generation has not known the protracted agony of a widespread famine. The people are also practically immune from the disaster of great inundations. The rivers, being for the most part hill-torrents, rise rapidly in flood after heavy rainfall, but their beds are so wide and the drainage slope so rapid that, even when they burst down in flood, they rarely overflow their banks, and, as they fall almost as fast as they rise, inundations are of short duration and cause but little damage.

Floods. Local floods are occasionally caused, by the rivers breaching their banks owing to abnormally heavy rain in the hills, and also when a river leaves its old course and appropriates the channel of a *pain* or artificial irrigation canal. More serious floods are fortunately rare. Writing in 1877, Sir William Hunter said that there had been only one considerable flood within the memory of that generation—and this had occurred 37 years previously—but the water remained stationary for one day only, and the flood subsided in 9 or 10 hours. In more recent times the district has been equally free from inundation, and the only floods which call for notice are those which took place in 1896, 1901 and 1905.

Flood of 1896. The most disastrous flood which has occurred within the memory of the present inhabitants of Gayā is that which visited the eastern portion of the Nawāda subdivision on the 16th September 1896. For two days there had been exceptionally heavy rain, which filled up all the water-courses and reservoirs, and at midday the river Sakrī, which takes its rise in the hills to the south-east, came down in flood, sweeping cattle, houses and trees before it, and covering the country for miles round with a sheet of water some two to twelve feet deep. There was but little loss of life, as the inundation was of short duration and the people were forewarned of its approach; and only 34 persons were drowned in the Gobindpur outpost, and 15 in the Kauwākol outpost, where the Natah and Baghail streams rose in flood. The damage to property was, however, very great, over 2,000 houses being completely demolished or seriously damaged, and large numbers were left homeless. The village of Gobindpur suffered especially severely, as out of 540 houses only 40 were left standing, and the houseless people had to take shelter in three masonry houses which escaped and in the office of the police outpost. The latter had been removed from another site 20 years previously, in order that it might be beyond the reach of floods, but the site to which it had been transferred proved equally unsafe, as the office was the only portion of the buildings which remained uninjured. Many of the roads were breached, and long stretches, especially on the Nawāda-Pakrībarāwān Road, were swept away. The damage done to cultivation was scarcely less serious. The mouths of several *pains* were silted up, many *āhars* and other reservoirs were damaged or destroyed, and large areas were filled with sand, the crops being destroyed and the land rendered unculturable. The damage caused in this way was especially great in Dariyāpur. In South Dariyāpur only 12 out of 125 houses were left standing; and in the northern portion of the village some 50 houses were demolished, and the seventy houses which were left standing were all more or less damaged. Of the total cultivated area of 1,600 *bīghas*, about 700 *bīghas* were filled up with sand, and in place of a *pian*, which used to be only 18 cubits broad, the Sakrī threw off three wide branches extending over an area of one-sixth of a mile. In all nearly 100 villages were affected, and the total loss of property was very great.

Flood of 1901.

The inundation of 1901 was due to a simultaneous rise of both the Son and the Ganges. On the 1st September the level of the Son at the Koelwār bridge was only 9 feet, but by the morning of the 3rd idem it had reached the height of 17·6 feet; and the river continuing to rise throughout the night and all through the next day, the gauge showed the unprecedented flood-level of 22 feet by 2 A.M. on the 5th September. At the same time owing to a high Himalayan flood, the Ganges was rising abnormally high, and on the morning of the 5th September the flood-level of that river also was higher than any previously recorded, the gauge at Dīgha reading 35·10 feet in the early morning and 35·60 at midday. The Son, being thus unable to discharge the volume of its waters into the Ganges, forced its way over its western bank and poured over the low-lying lands towards Arwal.

The flood rapidly subsided, and to this must be attributed the small amount of damage done. No loss of life occurred, and the number of cattle drowned was inconsiderable. House property, however, suffered seriously, and some 520 houses were wrecked in the Arwal thāna. The damage to the crops was inappreciable, and the only serious loss was that of the houses and of the grain stored in them, which deprived their owners of their means of livelihood. In the event, it was found only necessary to relieve some of the poorer classes whose houses and stocks of grain had been swept away, and for this purpose a grant of Rs. 1,000 was given by Government and Rs. 600 was raised by public subscription.

The immediate cause of the flood of 1905 was the exceptionally heavy rainfall which took place on the 14th, 15th and 16th September. On these three days there was heavy rain all over the district, but it was especially heavy in the southern portion of the Aurangābād subdivision and at Jahānābād, the fall ranging from 11 inches at the latter place to $16\frac{1}{2}$ inches at Nabīnagar. Owing to this excessive precipitation, the rivers Pūnpūn, Dardhā and Jamunā rose to a great height and soon began to overflow their banks and flood the country. The drainage slope being from south to north, the water was held up by the two main embankments running east and west, viz., the Mughalsarai-Gayā Railway line and the Arwal-Jahānābād Road. The water rose to a considerable height on the southern side of these embankments on the 16th September, and the waterway provided proving insufficient, they both gave way. The railway line was breached in several places near Jākhim; and though the bridges on the Arwal-Jahānābād Road fortunately stood, long lengths of the road were swept away. The Grand Trunk Road was also breached in two places, and many minor roads suffered severely. At Jahānābād the Court compound was under water to the depth of about a foot, and this too at a distance of over 200 yards from the ordinary bed of the river. The flood was of short duration: indeed in one place it was seen to rise 3 feet and again go down 2 feet within 10 hours on the 16th. It had entirely subsided in the Aurangābād subdivision by the morning of the 17th, though it went down somewhat more slowly in the Jahānābād subdivision.

Flood of 1905.

As in the flood of 1901, little serious damage was caused by the inundation. The people had time to escape to the high lands near their homes, and 7 persons only were killed by being buried under falling houses. Many *āhars* were breached, but the crops were on the whole benefited, owing to the fertilizing silt deposited by the receding water. But few cattle were drowned, and the only loss sustained by the people was the destruction of their houses, which were washed down in large numbers.

FAMINES. Owing to the protection afforded by the canals in the western portion of the district and the indigenous system of irrigation in other parts, the district as a whole is practically safe from famine. It suffered to some extent in 1866, but passed through the scarcity of 1874 without receiving more than the modicum of relief insisted upon by Government, and in the great famine of 1897 no relief was required. In 1866 there was undoubtedly great suffering in outlying parts to the south and south-west, but the more fertile portions of the district were not seriously affected in spite of the failure of the rains, and during the period of greatest distress the average daily number of persons receiving relief was only 1,167. The great famine of 1874 made but little impression on Gayā, the largest number of persons on relief works being 2,756 and the average number gratuitously relieved for 7½ months being only 977. Even in the famine of 1897, which was so terrible a calamity elsewhere, Gayā did not suffer. Test-relief works were opened but were not attended, and out of the 50,000 persons who received gratuitous relief only 1,000 were inhabitants of the district.

Famine of 1866. The district suffered severely during the famine of 1866, but no standard exists by which to gauge the actual pressure. The Collector reported that the price of common cleaned rice rose to Rs. 6-10-8 a maund, but prices in this district are an uncertain index to the pressure of want. Market rates apply only to a small fraction of the population; and in a time of scarcity, when people are unwilling to sell, they indicate far greater hardship than really exists. The distress was most severe in the vicinity of Gayā town, and to the south-west and south of the district within the Aurangābād and head-quarters subdivisions, the distressed tract extending over an area of 1,300 square miles. The rice crop, in the greater part of this area, may be said to have failed completely in 1864; and from that time prices rose considerably and general distress began to be felt. The *rabi* or spring crops of 1865 were also much below the average, as the area under those crops was much contracted, owing to want of sufficient moisture in the ground and the difficulty experienced in obtaining seed, while the outturn was still further diminished by heavy hailstorms in the spring of 1865. From these causes the distress became so acute that in May and June the poorer classes were reduced to living upon the seeds of the *mahuā*-tree, berries, grass and herbs.

This extreme destitution abated on the setting in of the rains, prices fell, and as field labour was obtainable, special relief measures were not deemed necessary. The condition of the people, however, did not improve, and the general distress reached its climax in October 1865, when only 7 seers of rice could be purchased for the rupee. The Collector commenced a daily distribution of grain, subscriptions were raised to defray the cost of maintaining the starving people, and a daily average of about 1,000 persons were fed at Gayā town from the 12th October to the 17th December. In the latter month, when the rice harvest afforded means of employment, and the market again fell, relief was suspended. But there was a renewal of the distress in March 1866. Severe hailstorms and a heavy rainfall in February, with the premature arrival of the hot winds, caused much injury to the spring crops. The stocks in the hands of dealers became exhausted, and the local supplies were mainly dependent on importations from Patna, the land-owners, who are large holders of grain under the *bhāoli* system, withholding their stocks from the market, in the expectation of still greater scarcity. Still no special measures were adopted till June, when relief centres were opened at Gayā town, and at Sherghāti, Nawāda and Aurangābād; subsequently in August and September, additional centres were established at Konch and Fatehpur.

The sufferings of the starving people were still further aggravated by cholera, which made its appearance in the town of Gayā, about the middle of July, and thence spread over the interior of the district: the severe character of the outbreak is sufficiently illustrated by the fact that out of 927 pauper recipients of relief admitted to the Gayā hospital between June and November 1866, 447 died within an average period of two days after admission. During the period of the greatest distress, the average daily number of persons receiving relief ranged from 1,167 in the beginning of July to 934 in the first week of September. The mortality reported by the police, who probably underrated the actual loss of life, established the fact of 3,387 persons having died, or more than double the number of those relieved. This lamentable disproportion can only be attributed to the fact that the relief depôts were practically inaccessible owing to their distance from the mass of the starving population.

Famine of 1873-74.

The course of events in Gayā during 1873 strikingly demonstrated the principle that the seasonable distribution of the rainfall is of more importance, within certain limits, than its actual quantity. The fall was below the average only in the headquarters and Aurangābād subdivisions, and in each of these tracts the deficiency was not more than 4 inches. Judging of the harvests from the quantity of rain which fell in 1873, it is difficult to believe that there could have been an extensive failure of the crops in Gayā in that year. Only 3 inches of rain fell in the first six months of the year, and even June, which is ordinarily classed as a portion of the monsoon period, was almost rainless; but in July there was an excessive precipitation amounting to double that of average years and varying from 20 inches in the west to 27 inches in the east of the district. In August the fall was slightly under the normal, but still it was sufficient to maintain the inundations caused in the preceding month. The autumn crops were seriously injured, and many reservoirs, on which the winter rice depends in dry years, were burst. The September rains, which are perhaps the most important for these crops, were however markedly deficient, the consequence being a failure of varying degrees of intensity in different portions of the district. It is difficult to gather from the official reports and narratives a distinct idea of the outturn of the autumn crops, but it was probably not less than half of an average crop. The reports on the winter rice crop which, in the end of 1873, were very gloomy, assumed, as the harvest progressed, a much more hopeful tone; and in February 1874, when it had been gathered on the threshing floors, the outturn all over the district was estimated to have been three-eighths of an average crop, the yield in parts of Aurangābād and Nawāda subdivisions being even characterized as particularly fine. Towards March the district was providentially favoured with an abundant fall of rain which, combined with the judicious utilization of the canal water in the west of the district, secured to it an average spring food-crop and a good outturn of opium. The price of rice did not rise above 10 seers to the rupee; from June to August 12 seers were obtainable, and it was much cheaper later on.

Private trade was active throughout the year, and one of the chief causes of the distress in 1866, viz., the impassable condition of the Patna and Gayā Road, no longer existed to hinder the transport of grain. Government grain, however, was stored throughout the district, relief works were instituted, and a comparatively small number of the poorest classes were charitably relieved. But these special measures were simply precautionary. In charitable relief 220 tons of rice were distributed, 2,433 tons sold for cash, 85 tons advanced on loan, and 117 tons paid in wages. In all Rs. 11,522 were distributed in charitable relief, Rs. 40,648 paid as wages, and Rs. 40,503 advanced on recoverable loans. The daily average number of persons chaaitably relieved in the whole district rose from 480 in the beginning of May to 2,120 in the beginning of August, and fell in the beginning of October to 542. There were 454 labourers employed on relief works in February; 1,334 in April; 2,756 in June, and 377 in August.

The irregularity of the monsoon of 1888, marked by a late commencement and early cessation, together with excessive rainfall in August, resulted in the partial destruction of the autumn rice crop and in the diminution through drought of the yield of the winter harvest. The total rainfall was plentiful, amounting to 55·78 inches, but it was very unevenly distributed, being enormously excessive in August, when over 7½ inches fell in one day, and far below the requirements of September and October. Eventually, the outturn of both the *bhadoi* and *rabi* crops was under 40 per cent., and that of the *aghani* crop only 50 per cent. of a normal crop. Scarcity ensued, but there was not much distress, except in a tract near Sherghāti. Some relief works were started, but the expenditure only amounted to Rs. 4,300, the largest average daily attendance being 4,500 in June. Scarcity of 1888-89.

The history of the famine of 1896-97 showed clearly how great is the protection secured to Gayā by the system of *pains* and *āhars* in a year of unequally distributed rainfall. The rains of 1896-97 began late, not commencing till late in June, when there was a heavy fall amounting to 8⅓ inches. There was another downpour of 10½ inches early in July, and then a long drought succeeded, which was followed by nearly 11 inches of rain in August. Another long break next ensued till the middle of September, when the rainfall was nearly 4 inches. After this there was no more rain, and by the end of October the deficiency was 7⅓ inches or 17·8 per cent. The season was thus characterized by heavy falls alternating with long periods of drought, which would have resulted in scarcity elsewhere, as the *bhadoi* would have withered, the seed-beds of rice dried up, and the rice-fields remained unplanted. In Gayā, however, the evil effects of these vagaries of the rainfall were counteracted by the system of irrigation by which the water is conserved in reservoirs and thence distributed over the fields, for, as each burst of rain occurred, the water was carefully stored and used as required. In the event, the outturn of *aghani*, which is the most important crop in the district, was 50 per cent. and that of *bhadoi* 75 per cent. of a normal crop, while the *rabi* crop was nearly up to the average. Prices here as elsewhere ruled very high, rising to 8·4 seers to the rupee at the end of October 1896, but considerable stocks were held by the cultivators. Exportation was stopped, and the reserve stores of grain which the people keep were Famine of 1896-97.

everywhere held up, partly for consumption and partly for sale when prices rose still higher. Work was plentiful in the fields, and as this is always paid chiefly in grain, the labourer did not feel the high prices any more than the agriculturists who lived on their own stocks; while there was plenty of additional employment on the Mughalsarai-Gayā and South Bihār Railway lines, which were then under construction. Grave apprehensions were entertained at one time for some tracts, viz., the northern part of the Jahānābād subdivision, the portion of the Sherghāti thāna south of the Grand Trunk Road, and a tract in the north-east of the Aurangābād subdivision between Aurangābād and Goh. In these tracts the people were not so well off as elsewhere, because the rainfall was more scanty; and the system of reservoirs being incomplete, there had been a more or less complete failure of the *aghani* crop. Eventually, however, even these tracts did not suffer, the *rabi* crop being far better than had been expected; and, as in 1873-74, the stocks of the people enabled them to maintain themselves until the *rabi* was reaped, and again till the *bhadoi* harvest came in. The district, in fact, passed scatheless through the famine, no relief being required except what was given in kitchens and poor-houses along the Grand Trunk Road to pilgrims and travellers, and, late in 1897, to beggars and paupers in the town of Gayā. The only expenditure incurred by Government was in the shape of advances to landlords and tenants, Rs. 1,06,000 being given out under the Land Improvement Loans Act, and Rs. 23,600 under the Agriculturists' Loans Act. The expenditure on gratuitous relief was met out of charitable funds, Rs. 9,900 being spent in the distribution of grain and money, while the maintenance of kitchens cost Rs. 7,700. In this way about 50,000 persons were relieved, but, as already stated, only 1,000 of these were natives of the district.

Since that time the district has been entirely free from famine or scarcity of any kind, though scarcity was apprehended in a limited area in the west and south of the Aurangābād subdivision in 1902. This tract is unfertile, the soil is poor, and there is practically no irrigation, so that the crops are scanty at the best of times. There had been bad harvests in the two preceding years, the last rice crop had been almost a complete failure owing to a failure of the rains, and the outlook for the *rabi* crop was very poor. The ordinary cold-weather rains however fortunately fell, and this crop turned out a fair one; the population is scanty and inured to bad harvests and hard living; and labour being available in the neighbouring areas of greater prosperity, as well as on works specially opened by the District Board in the tract affected, the people were enabled to hold out, and there was but little real distress.

When the district has been affected so slightly by one of the greater famines on record and has suffered so little from similar visitations in previous years, an immunity from general famine can reasonably be claimed for it. The reasons for this immunity are not far to seek. The district is cultivated almost entirely by artificial cultivation, canal irrigation renders one-fifth of the area independent of the vicissitudes of the seasons, and, though the rainfall is light, the system which obtains elsewhere is devised so as to utilize all the water available, whether that brought down by the hill-streams or the surface drainage of the country. The cultivators themselves are protected from the distress consequent on scarcity and the rising price of food by the reserve stocks of grain which they keep, in accordance with immemorial custom, both for their own consumption and to afford seed for the ensuing harvest. The effect of high prices is moreover discounted in the case of landless labourers by the fact that they are paid in kind, while the lowest and most destitute of them, the *kamiyās*, are entitled to be fed by their masters in virtue of their position as bond-servants. The district is covered with a network of roads, and the railway has now penetrated in all directions, with the result that even the more remote parts are within easy reach of the markets. The development of communications has had the effect of levelling prices over larger and larger areas, and at the same time there has been a great advance in the material prosperity of the people. On the other hand, isolated tracts, where the soil is unfertile and where there is practically no system of irrigation, are always exposed to the danger of scarcity; and according to the official returns for 1905-06, it is estimated that 2,061 square miles, with a population of 772,000, is liable to famine, and that 49,000 persons are likely to require relief in the event of serious famine.

CHAPTER X.

IRRIGATION.

SYSTEMS OF IRRIGATION.

THE agricultural prosperity of Gayā depends in an unique degree on an extensive system of artificial irrigation. To the north-east the cultivators have the benefit of the Son Canals and are thus certain of an ample and regular supply of water, but elsewhere the people are dependent on methods of irrigation which have been practised from time immemorial. This indigenous system is the outcome of the natural conditions and physical configuration of the country, and has been evolved to meet the obstacles which they place in the way of cultivation. The district is characterized by a scanty rainfall, a rapid slope off which the water quickly runs, and a soil which is either a stiff clay or a loose sand equally unretentive of moisture. To a ryot of Eastern Bengal the country would seem utterly unsuited for rice cultivation, both from the nature of the surface and the comparative scantiness of the rainfall. But both difficulties have been overcome by the ingenuity and industry of its inhabitants, who have devised a system by which the natural drainage is blocked and the water impounded for use, and have also brought the rivers into their service by diverting the water they bring down.

The district is bounded on the south by the high lands of the Chotā Nāgpur plateau and the spurs which project from it, and along the northern boundary it marches with the low-lying plains of the Patna district. The general slope is accordingly from south to north towards the Gangetic valley, and it is comparatively rapid, the average fall northwards being about six to four feet in the mile. A number of wide rivers debouch from these southern hills and intersect the district as they flow across it from south to north. They are swollen torrents after heavy rainfall in the hills, but the slope of the country is so great and their beds are so sandy, that the water is rapidly carried through the district or it percolates down through the sand. In order therefore to prevent the water being wasted in this way, long narrow artificial canals, called *pains*, are led off from the rivers, by means of which the river water is conveyed to the fields. The same rapid slope would also prevent the land from gaining the full benefit of the rain water, were it allowed to flow unchecked; and the cultivation of the rice crop, on which the people almost entirely depend, would be impossible, if the water were not impounded in extensive reservoirs, called *āhars*, which are formed by constructing a series of retaining embankments across the line of drainage. The whole forms a most remarkable and ingenious system of artificial irrigation, which is admirably supplemented by the manner in which the water is distributed from field to field and retained in them by a network of low banks. In the cold weather, again, when the *āhars* have dried up and the *pains* no longer contain water, the people can fall back on their wells; and thus the crops are protected from failure throughout the year.

INDIGENOUS SYSTEM. *Pains.*

The rainfall being often scanty and untimely, the system of *pains* has been devised in order to make the most of the scanty supply, by utilizing the rivers for the purposes of cultivation. The rivers of Gayā have only a fitful flow; they may fill for a few days and be almost empty for the next fortnight, and then fill again with a day or two's rainfall; but by means of these artificial channels the cultivators secure all the water they bring down. Roughly one-third of the total irrigation of the district may be said to be derived from *pains*.

They are led off from a point facing the current of the river, some way upstream above the level of the land they are intended to irrigate; and it is often 2 or 3 miles before the water of the *pain* reaches the level of the cultivation. Some are large with many distributaries and some small with few or no distributaries. They are sometimes as much as 10, 12 or even 20 miles in length, and some of them irrigate hundreds of villages. The largest *pains* that feed a number of distributaries and irrigate many thousand acres are known as *dasiain pains*, *i.e.*, literally *pains* with 10 branches. The main channels are known as *pains*, and the smaller channels taking off from them are called *bhoklās*, while the smallest channels that lead immediately into the fields are known as *karhās*. Where the level of the country permits, the water is led into the fields from these *pains* and *bhoklās* by means of the *karhās*, but where the level of the water in the *pain* or *bhoklā* is below that of the fields on either side, the water is raised by some of the artificial means in use in this part of the country, such as the *lāth kunri* or lever and bucket, the water-basket called *chānr* or *sair*, and the *karīn* or wooden canoe-shaped lift.

During the rainy season from July to September, the *pains* are full and flow well, but as the rains cease and the rivers dry up, the water has to be led into the *pain* by means of training works, known as *derhiain* or *baluain*. In a year of scanty rainfall or when the rain has been untimely, these *pains* are of the greatest importance for the rice crop and the sowing of the *rabi*. Should there be no rain at the time of the *Hathiyā nakshatra*—that most critical period of the year when water is absolutely essential to fill out the ripening grain, a sudden activity is at once seen in the rivers. Training works are vigorously pushed on at the heads of the *pains* to try and lead into them every drop of water left in the beds of the rivers; and the more wealthy landlords cause *bāndhs* to be erected at customary places to block up what water there is and thus give it a head into some *pain*.

These channels have been constructed by the landlords, who are also responsible for their maintenance—a work which entails considerable expense, as the *pains* quickly silt up, owing to the sandy nature of the river-beds, and have to be cleared out every year or two. Ordinary petty maintenance, however, such as the periodical clearance of silt, the repair of small breaches, etc., is done by the cultivators themselves under the *goām* system. At the order of the landlord or his local agent or servant, the cultivators have to supply one man per plough to turn out on these occasions and carry out the work; the peasants come in a body, and this is called a *goām*.

The *pains* are essentially private canals, and in the case of the more important which serve many villages, each village has its fixed turn of so many days and hours to use the water, these turns being assigned by mutual agreement or ancient custom. This distribution of the right of irrigation by turns (*pārā*) is known as *pārābandi*. In the case of the principal *pains* there is a celebrated register of the distribution—the *Lāl Bahi*—prepared by the former owners of the Tekāri Rāj; and the entries in this book are still accepted as evidence of the rights of the villages specified in it. Disputes, however, frequently occur. One village often tries to get more water than it should, or else when the rainfall is scarce, villages lower down seek to get water before their proper turn; and the disputes sometimes terminate in blows, and occasionally in bloodshed. Quarrels are also common in regard to *bāndhs* or *garāndis*, erected across the *pains* or *bhoklās* to steal or divert the water, thus depriving lands further down of all supply; but considering the number of these channels and the vital importance of water in years of unfavourable rainfall, and considering the fact that they are all under the private control of the zamīndārs and tenants, it is surprising how few cases end seriously.

Ahars. Side by side with the *pain* system is that of *āhars*, the latter being constructed essentially for the irrigation of the high lands between the rivers which the *pains* cannot serve, though some are also constructed on the lower levels where *pains* are practicable. An *āhar* is an artificial catchment basin formed by blocking the drainage of the surface water, or even by blocking a small drainage rivulet, and thus locking up the water. These catchment basins are nearly always of a more or less rectangular shape, embankments being raised on three sides of the rectangle, while the fourth side is left open for the drainage water to enter. Owing to the slope of the land, the highest embankment is usually on the north, and this embankment generally runs east and west. From either side of it other embankments project southwards, diminishing in height as they proceed, according as the level of the ground rises. In this way a three-sided catchment basin is formed, deepest at the northern side, where there is always some arrangement to let out the water for the purposes of irrigation at the spot where the drainage of the catchment would naturally issue if there were no embankments.

If the *āhar* is built on a drainage rivulet, and thus receives the drainage of a larger area than its own, there is a spill or weir to pass off surplus water, which may perhaps flow to another *āhar* further north. In small *āhars* where the quantity of water banked up is not great, it is generally sufficient to cut a narrow passage through the earthen bank at the deepest spot to draw off the water as required. If the mass of water is greater, a half pipe, formed out of the trunk of a palm-tree and known as a *dongā*, is let into the bank to protect it from excessive erosion; and if the *āhar* is a very big one, a masonry outlet is often built into the bottom of the bank, which goes by the name of *bhāo* or *bhāoāri*. The different parts of an *āhar* also have distinctive names. The bed inside the embankments is the *pet* or belly, the banks are called *pind*, the side banks being known as *ālang*, and the main bank at the lowest side of the *āhar* as the *pīth* or back—a name which is also frequently given to the portion behind the main embankment.

When the water is wanted to irrigate, not the lands to the north, which are on a lower level, but the lands to the east or west on the same or a higher level, it is lifted by one of the methods for raising water mentioned above. One or other of these lifts is erected on the edge of the *āhar*, and the water is raised into a channel on a higher level, through which it flows to the field where it is required. If the water in the *āhar*, is low and does not reach the bank, a depression (*kandari*) is dug by the side of the bank, and a small channel is cut from the deep part of the *āhar* leading into this depression. Sometimes when the level of the water is very low, it is necessary to employ a series of two or even three lifts to raise it to the level required.

The prime value of these catchment reservoirs is that they store up the water that would otherwise be carried away by the naturally rapid drainage of the country. They are in fact indispensable on the higher tracts that lie between the river-basins, firstly for irrigating the paddy as it grows up, and secondly for the sowing and germination of all the *rabi* crops. On these high lands *pains* are not practicable; and if it were not for the *āhars*, there would be no water available for the purposes of irrigation after the month of September. Almost half the irrigation in the district is effected by the *āhar* system, which is quite distinct from that of *genrābandi* mentioned below and also from that of *pain* irrigation. A *pain* may eventually lead into an *āhar* after it has almost spent itself, but, as already stated, *pain* irrigation is not possible on the highest lands, for which the *āhars* have been specially devised. They are in fact usually constructed on high lands in the parallel strips lying between the rivers, where the clay is comparatively hard and little silt accumulates, whereas the *pains* take off from the sand-laden rivers and irrigate the lands situated in the river-basins. These *āhars* are often of great size, the largest irrigating about 1,000 acres. They are usually kept in good repair, by digging a layer of soil from the bed of the *āhar* and heaping the soil on the banks. As in the case of *pains*, small repairs are done by the tenants, and large repairs requiring considerable expenditure are carried out by the landlords.

Genrā-bandi.

The system of *āhars* and *pains*, which prevents the water escaping and makes it available for cultivation, is further supplemented by that known as *genrābandi*. It has already been remarked that the country slopes gradually to the north and that the rivers and hill-streams, issuing from the hills and flowing northwards, intersect it and cut it up into a number of parallel strips. Each of these watersheds again has a strong slope east and west from the centre down to the river-beds, and much of the land is too high for artificial irrigation and depends for its moisture on the rainfall. A series of low retaining banks are therefore built across the line of drainage, which are connected by other banks running north and south. The main outer embankment (*gherawā*), which is about 4 feet high, encloses a considerable area; this is split up by minor embankments called *genrā*; and within these again are low banks (*āl*) round the fields. This series of banks, which has aptly been described as resembling an enormous chess-board, is admirably adapted for retaining the surface water, as not a drop is allowed to flow beyond their limits and the stiff soil is given time to absorb the moisture. This system is known as *genrābandi*, and is followed not only on the high lands, but also in the irrigated area, in order to ensure the fullest possible use being made of all the water available.

Wells. As water does not remain in the rivers for more than a few months, and the *pains* usually dry up before the end of the year, irrigation must be carried on from *āhars* or wells when this source of supply fails. In a very dry season the *āhars* also dry up by the end of the year, and from January to June recourse must be had to wells, except when rain falls. Well irrigation is almost entirely confined to the immediate vicinity of the villages, where poppy, market and garden produce, *maruā*, barley and similar crops are grown, and where the produce is much better and more valuable than in the lands further from the village, which are irrigated from *pains* and *āhars*. Perhaps 90 per cent. of the wells in the district are in lands immediately adjoining the village, and they are hardly ever used for the *kharīf* or the larger portion of the *rabi* crops. Temporary wells are also commonly used in tracts where the soil is sandy or along water-courses. Such wells afford considerable protection against drought to the poppy which is so largely grown in the district, and also to other dry crops. It has been estimated that 12 or 13 per cent. of the total irrigation is effected from wells.

Water-lifts. The methods of drawing and distributing water are those common to the whole of Bihār, and here, as elsewhere, the most usual contrivance for lifting it is the *lāth* or lever. This consists of a long beam working on an upright forked post, which serves as a fulcrum ; at one end the beam is weighted with a log, stone or mass of dried mud, and at the other is a rope with a bucket attached, which when not in use rests above the well. When water is required, the cultivator pulls down the rope till the bucket is immersed ; as soon as the tension is relaxed, the weight attached to the lever raises the bucket of itself ; and the water is then emptied and led by narrow channels into the fields. Irrigation by means of the *mot* (leather bucket) is much rarer. When this method is employed, water is raised by a large leather bucket secured to a rope, which passes over a rude wooden pulley supported by a forked post, and is fastened to the yoke of a pair of bullocks. These supply the motive power, for as soon as the bucket has been filled, they descend an inclined plane, varying in length with the depth of the well, and thus bring it to the surface. One man is required to look after the bullocks and another is stationed on the well to let down the *mot* and empty it when it comes to the surface.

Two other water-lifts commonly used are the *karīn* and *sair*. The *karīn* is a long wooden scoop, made out of a single piece of wood, hollowed out and shaped like one-half of a canoe. The broad open end of this scoop rests on the water-channel leading to the field, and the pointed closed end is dipped into the water, which is then raised by means of a lever overhead with a weight at the end of it. This machine is used for lifting water either from the reservoirs (*āhars*) which are so numerous in the district, or from a lower to a higher channel where water is plentiful and the elevation small. The *sair or chānr* is used when the quantity of water remaining is small; it is a triangular basket made of bamboo with the edges raised on two sides; cords are attached to each side, and these are held by two men, one standing on either side of the ditch from which the water has to be raised. Holding the ropes attached to either side, they swing it backwards, and bringing it down sharply into the water, carry the forward motion of the swing through until the basket, now full of water, is raised to the level of the water-channel, when the contents are poured out.

Canals. The north-western portion of the district is not dependent on the methods of irrigation mentioned above, as it is served by a portion of the Son canal system. This system derives its supply from an anicut across the Son at Bārun, which was begun in 1869 and completed in 1875 at a total cost of 15 lakhs of rupees. The anicut or weir, which is 12,469 feet long, consists of a mass of rubble stone laid to a uniform slope and stiffened by walls of masonry founded on shallow wells. Scouring sluices are provided at either flank; and these are fitted with gates which can be opened or closed at any state of the river other than high flood. By means of these gates the level of the water in the pool above the weir can be kept at the height required to feed the canals. Here the Main Eastern canal branches off and runs as far as the Pūnpūn river, 8 miles to the east. It was originally intended to carry this canal as far as the Monghyr district, but after being cut as far as the Pūnpūn, the project was abandoned. The Patna canal leaves the Main Eastern canal 4 miles from the Son, and, running north through the *pargana* of Arwal almost parallel to the western boundary of Gayā, eventually joins the Ganges at Dīgha between Bankipore and Dinapore. Its total length is 79 miles, of which 43 miles lie within this district, where it irrigates parts of the *parganas* of Siris, Dādar, and Goh, and the greater part of Arwal. The total area commanded by these two canals and their distributaries is 170,000 acres, being bounded on the north by the Patna district, on the south by the Grand Trunk

Road, on the east by the river Pūnpūn, and on the west by the Son. It is estimated that 166,000 acres are annually irrigable, but the area actually irrigated has never been anything like this figure. In 1904-05 it was 56,400 acres, of which 48,700 acres were under rice. Though the area actually under irrigation is even now only one-third of that irrigable, it has been expanding speedily, and it is now 50 per cent. greater than in 1893-94.

Canal administration.

The whole system is under the control of a Superintending Engineer, who is assisted by an Executive Engineer and an Assistant Engineer. The latter are responsible for the maintenance of the canals and the conduct of irrigation operations, and a separate establishment is entertained for the collection of the revenue. The irrigated area is divided into blocks, the lease of all the lands in each block being arranged so as to lapse in the same year; and in fixing the period of the leases efforts are made to see that leases for an equal area expire each year. Water is supplied to the cultivators on application on a prescribed form, the year being divided into three seasons, that is, hot weather, *kharīf* and *rabi*. A date is fixed for each season, and the lease or permit granted for that season is only in force for that particular period.

Besides the season leases, there are long-term leases, or leases for a period of seven years, which are granted at a somewhat reduced rate. These long-term leases are only granted for compact blocks defined by well-marked boundaries of such a nature that the leased lands can be clearly distinguished from the adjoining unleased lands, and also so situated that unleased lands will not be ordinarily irrigated by water supplied for the land included in the block. These boundaries are mentioned in the application for the lease, on receipt of which a special report is submitted to the Subdivisional Canal Officer. If the lease is likely to be approved, he issues orders for the block to be measured, and a detailed *khasrā*, or measurement of each cultivator's holding is then made. The lease is finally approved by the Divisional Canal Officer who issues the permit, but before this can be done, every cultivator, who has fields within the block, must sign his name against the area which has been measured, and which will be assessed in his name. In order to admit of a lease getting water for the season, a provisional permit is granted for the season on the area originally applied for; this permit is cancelled when the long-lease permit is finally granted. Fields which cannot be ordinarily irrigated, or for which canal water is not ordinarily required can be excluded from the block, such fields being duly noted in the *khasrā* or measurement paper.

In these long-term leases water-rates are charged for the area measured and accepted by the cultivators, whether water is required or not; and the channel by which the area is irrigated must be registered as well as the name of its owner. In *rabi* and hot-weather leases water is supplied on application, and water-rates are levied on the actual areas irrigated, and not necessarily on those specified in the application. In order to assist the Canal Department as far as possible in regulating and distributing the water to the different cultivators named in the leases, *lambardārs* or headmen are appointed; these are influential men of the village, who are appointed on the approval of the majority of the cultivators concerned. Their duty is to assist in measurements, to give in the names of the cultivators of the different holdings, and to see that water is properly distributed over the leased area. For these duties they are paid a commission of 3 per cent. on the total assessment on long leases and of 2 per cent. on season leases.

Water-rates.

There are five rates charged for the water supplied, viz., (1) *rabi* season leases from the 15th October to the 25th March at Rs. 2-8 an acre; (2) hot-weather leases from the 25th March to the 25th June at Rs. 4-8 an acre; (3) leases during the same period at Rs. 2 for each watering; (4) *kharīf* season leases between the 25th June and the 25th October at Rs. 4 an acre; and (5) seven years' leases for block areas for any kind of crop between the 25th June and the 25th March in the next year at Rs. 3 an acre.

In the case of *bhāoli* lands, where the produce is divided between landlord and tenant, the duty of paying the water-rate falls primarily on the tenant, but usually he prevails on the landlord to pay half or such proportion as the latter receives of the produce. In the case of *nagdi* lands for which rent is paid in cash, it has become a recognized custom that the landlord should pay half the water-rate, and in practice this is done by deducting half the rate from the demand leviable from the ryot.

When the long-lease system was inaugurated, it was calculated that water would be given for 50 per cent. of the whole area of a village; and this portion was marked off into one or more well-defined blocks, for the irrigation of which a charge was made at a reduced rate. The cultivator is supplied with water enough for his own block, but he may not use it beyond these limits; and it is, therefore, laid down that there must be a well-defined village channel to conduct the water from the distributary, and that it is not to be allowed to escape to an *āhar*. The landlords generally bear the expense of constructing these channels, but occasionally it is met by the tenants when the land is held under occupancy right. Of all the leases the most popular are the long leases, which are given only for the areas for which protection can be assured even in the driest years. The rates for this class of lease were originally fixed at a low figure, owing to the backwardness of the cultivators in resorting to canal irrigation and to the fact that the use of canal water is not indispensable in years of ordinary rainfall; the holders of these leases have preferential claims to water during periods of high demand such as occur in dry seasons; and, as the cultivators have been quick to recognize the advantages of the system, the area under long leases has steadily expanded, until at the present day by far the greater part of the whole irrigated area receives water on long lease, and the demand for such leases cannot be fully met.

WORKING OF THE INDIGENOUS SYSTEM.

Canal irrigation has turned a most infertile tract, a large part of which was sandy and unproductive, into a region of rich fertility. It serves, however, but a comparatively small portion of the district, and the remainder is dependent on the indigenous methods of irrigation mentioned above. There can be no doubt that the latter system is absolutely indispensable, and that without it a large portion of Gayā would be converted into barren waste. The construction and maintenance of these irrigation works is consequently a matter of supreme importance, but unfortunately there is a tendency to let them fall into disrepair. Owing to the general prevalence of produce-rents and the physical and climatic conditions that necessitate the upkeep of artificial works of irrigation, the duty of inaugurating and maintaining them lies to a peculiar extent upon the landlords. The ryots could not or would not combine of their own accord to keep them up. Individually, they have not the capital necessary to undertake expensive works of such magnitude, and collectively they have not yet acquired sufficient self-reliance to unite among themselves for the purpose of constructing them. The result is that it is the customary obligation of the landlords to construct and maintain these works of public utility; but the latter are not always alive to the necessity and advantage of doing so. This is particularly the case with *pains*, which are apt to be neglected, while there is a more serious danger in the fact that no new *pains* of any considerable size are being constructed. The largest of these irrigation channels, and those that serve the greatest number of villages, were made many years ago, when larger areas were under the control of single zamīndārs, and the local authority of these zamīndārs to enforce their orders and wishes was more absolute than it has been, or can be, under the restrictions imposed by the legislation of more recent times. As a general rule, no large *pain* is now excavated, and many of the largest of former times have fallen into disrepair and even disuse. This result is due to the gradual disintegration of property, that *parcellement* of proprietary rights which has been encouraged by modern legislation. Where formerly there was a single zamīndār in more or less absolute authority, there are now perhaps fifty petty landholders, whose interests conflict or whose relations are so strained that they can never combine to carry out a work of mutual benefit. As an instance of this, it will be sufficient to cite the case of a *pain* now in almost complete disuse, which is reported to have served a hundred villages in its day. This *pain* passed through a tract of country, where, owing to three successive years of scanty rainfall, scarcity was apprehended, and the Collector endeavoured to persuade all the landholders through whose properties the channel passed to combine and repair it, as a certain remedy against scarcity in the future. These efforts were unsuccessful; many of the zamīndārs were quarrelling and engaged in litigation *inter se;* and nothing would induce them to carry out the work.

Not only are *pains* liable to be neglected owing to the subdivision of proprietary rights, but their number is apt to diminish owing to the want of a proper headwork to control the inflow, as well as to regulate the water-level of the channel at its entrance. Much damage is caused by *pains* scouring out at the head, and sometimes such widening and deepening results in the channel of the *pain* becoming ultimately the course of the river. In this way, the original bed of the river becomes silted up; the tract of country formerly irrigated from it by other *pains* taking off lower down are left without means of irrigation, and cultivated lands are converted into waste; while the main stream, having adopted the artificial channel of the *pain*, cuts away the adjoining land, and floods and depreciates other lands by a deposit of sand.

CHAPTER XI.

SYSTEMS OF RENT PAYMENT.

THE *Bhāoli* SYSTEM.

THE system of rent payment prevalent in Gayā is that known as *bhāoli*, *i.e.*, the payment of rents in kind. Some 70 to 75 per cent. of the cultivation is held under this system, which is a necessary result of the physical configuration of the country and is intimately connected with the system of irrigation in vogue. It has already been explained that Gayā owes not only its fertility, but almost its very existence as an agricultural country to artificial irrigation, and that extensive irrigation works are necessary to render rice cultivation possible. Their construction requires a large expenditure which the ryots themselves would be unable to afford and an amount of combination which they have not yet attained. The whole of the tenants in one village may depend upon the water obtained from one *āhar* or *pain*; one reservoir or channel again may serve several villages some distance apart; and it is quite beyond the means of the cultivators to construct and keep up such extensive works or maintain their rights in them against the encroachment of others. The landlord is the only person who can supply the capital for their construction or fight for the villagers' rights; and for this again ample means are necessary, as the bulk of the litigation of the district arises out of irrigation disputes. Without *pains* and *āhars*, the tenant in many parts would get no rice crops; and on the other hand, if he paid a fixed cash rent to his landlord, the latter would be in a position to spend the money in other ways and to neglect the duty of laying out channels and embankments and of keeping them in order. Custom has therefore decreed that these works shall be made and maintained by the landlord, each tenant paying his quota of the expense by giving a certain proportion of the harvest as rent; and the result of this arrangement is that the amount of the landlord's rent depends entirely on the extent to which he provides facilities for irrigating the land. Splendid rice crops are obtained wherever the embankments and water-channels are kept in proper working order; and, on the other hand, where they are neglected, the yield falls off enormously in a year of capricious rainfall. The actual produce of the land, therefore, varies in proportion with the extent to which the zamīndār incurs expenditure on irrigation; and this consideration has induced the cultivators, so far as the memory of man or tradition runs, to secure the active partnership of their landlords by giving them a share of the actual crops in lieu of a regular money rent. Rents are accordingly paid in kind for lands benefited by irrigation works constructed at the zamīndār's expense; the profits of the latter are directly affected by the outturn; and an assurance is thus afforded that he will not neglect to spend money on their upkeep. In this way, if the landlord does not bear what are called *gilandāzi* charges, *i.e.*, does not maintain the reservoirs properly, the crop is a failure, and he gets little or nothing; while if he spends an adequate amount on such works, a good harvest is reaped and he gets a fair outturn for his outlay.

This *gilandāzi* is an excellent form of investment, as the capital spent on it returns a dividend of 40 to 50 per cent. in the first year; in some cases, it is said, it has been found to yield a profit of cent. per cent. If landlords even received only half the produce of the land irrigated by these works, they would get a very good return on their capital outlay. The ideal rule of the *bhāoli* system is that the produce should be divided half and half between the landlords and tenants, but, as a matter of fact, such a division is very rare, and the landlords constantly take $\frac{9}{16}$ths and often $\frac{10}{16}$ths of the produce. In exceptional cases, it is true, they may take less than a half share of the produce, *e. g.*, when waste land has been brought under cultivation, or, in special cases, when the cultivation requires unusual labour on the part of the tenant; but these cases are not frequent, and the ordinary practice is for the landlord to take a little more than half.

Batāi.

The share of the produce which the landlord receives is determined either by *batāi*, *i.e.*, the actual division of the crops on the threshing floor, or by *dānābandi*, *i.e.*, appraisement of the crop before it is reaped. Under the *batāi* system, or the *agorbatāi* system, as it is called, because the landlord's men have to watch (*agornā*) the crop carefully to prevent their masters being robbed, the grain is harvested by the cultivator and carried by him to the threshing floor, where it is divided between the landlord and tenant, after the payment of the allowances given to the harvesters and others.

Dānā-bandi.

Under the *dānābandi* system the division of the produce has passed into an estimate of its quantity or value before the crop is cut. The produce of each field is appraised before the harvest, and the ryot is allowed to take the whole away, being debited with the landlord's share or its value. When the crops are nearly ripe, the landlord, or his agent, and the cultivator repair to the field, accompanied by the *patwārī* or village accountant, an *amīn* or assessor, a *jarībkash* or measurer, a *sālis* or arbitrator, a *navisinda* or writer, and the village headman. The measurer having measured the field with the local pole, the arbitrator goes round it, and, after a consultation with the assessor and the village officials, estimates the quantity of grain in the crop. If the tenant accepts the estimate, the quantity is entered in the *patwārī's* field-book (*khasrā*), and the matter is considered settled. If the tenant objects, or if the assessor and the arbitrator cannot agree, the fellow-tenants are called in as mediators; and if they fail to convince either party, a test crop-cutting (*partāl*) takes place, the landlord selecting a portion of the best part of the field, and the tenant an equal part of the worst part. The produce of both is reaped and threshed, and the grain having been weighed, the whole produce of the field is calculated from the amount weighed, and is entered in the field-book. The tenant is then at liberty to reap the crop and harvest it whenever it suits his convenience. The total share of the landlord, which is entered in a statement called *behrī*, is appraised according to the market value of the grain, and is paid by the tenant either in grain or money according to the agreement made between them.

There is no regular custom as to the method of realizing produce-rents. It is not the case that one village has a permanent custom of always paying rent by the *batāi* system, and that in another village it is the invariable practice to pay rent by the *dānābandi* system. The method is settled at each crop by mutual agreement, though naturally custom has a considerable part in determining which method shall be adopted. When the two parties quarrel, the tenants hold out for the *batāi* system, because it gives them opportunities for misappropriating the grain in the field before it is divided; and, on the other hand, the landlord strives for the *dānābandi* system, both because he is better protected against peculation, and because he can try to secure an excessive appraisement.

Customary allowances.

Whether the *dānābandi* or the *batāi* system prevails, a number of customary allowances have to be made out of the grain before the landlord's and tenant's share is determined, the only difference being that in the case of appraisement the amounts given in the form of allowances are calculated instead of being actually weighed. These allowances vary greatly, as almost every village has its own custom or *lagan*, and in some villages more, and in some less, is given or allowed to the landlords, tenants and labourers. When the crops are cut and the sheaves are being harvested each day, the first deduction made is that of *mazdūrī* or the labourers' share, those belonging to the village being paid at a higher rate than outside labourers. In some villages the rate allowed is 1 sheaf in 21 for outside labour, and 1 in 16 for the regular village servants; in other villages the rate is as high as 1 out of every 11 or 12 sheaves for village servants. In addition to this, they are allowed a daily diet allowance (called *lohrā chhakautī*) of grain in the ear, which is made over to the tenant to disburse as he likes. This allowance also varies greatly in quantity. In some cases, it amounts to 5 seers per day for an outsider and 16 seers per day for a village servant; but elsewhere each cooly gets 2 seers per day, or sometimes 10 seers for each 21 sheaves cut, and in other places about 6 seers per day. In some villages, again, outside coolies get only half the allowance. After the labourers' share has been deducted, the blacksmith, carpenter, village washerman, etc., get their shares from each tenant. The *barhi* (carpenter) and *lohār* (blacksmith) generally get 1 *bojhā* or sheaf, and the *chamār* (cobbler), *hajjām* (barber), *dhobī* (washerman), *bhāt* (village bard) each half a *bojhā*, while even the beggars are given an allowance, called *bhichchhā*, at the rate of ½ seer or one seer each.

After this the remaining sheaves are threshed and the grain is collected into one heap and weighed; and then the village officials are allowed their shares (*rasūm*) out of the undivided grain, the *patwārī* (accountant) receiving 4 chittacks (8 oz.), in each maund, the *gorait* (watchman) and *barāhil* (peon) 2 chittacks each, and the *kumhār* (potter) and *tahalu* (office servant) 1 chittack each. In some villages, however, the *patwārī* and *gumāshta* or landlord's agent get 8 chittacks between them, and the *barāhil*, *gorait*, *tahalu*, *kumhār*, and *hatwā* (weighman) each get 2 chittacks; sometimes too the *badhwār* or field-watcher, gets 2 chittacks, and the weighman has a perquisite of 4 chittacks called *partāl*.

The customary concessions are then made to the tenants; sometimes, under the name of *chārserī* or *doserī*, 4 seers in one maund are allowed to high castes and 2 seers to low castes, or 2 seers only are given to the higher and 1 seer to the lower castes; sometimes, under the name of *bishunprit*, a portion of the heap, estimated at about 2 seers to each maund, is portioned off for the tenant. Then the remaining grain is divided between the tenant and landlord according to the proportion customary in the village; and finally a further concession, called *neg*, is made to the landlord, $1\frac{1}{4}$ seer per maund for each high-caste and $2\frac{1}{2}$ seers for each low-caste tenant being deducted from the cultivator's heap and transferred to that belonging to the proprietor. These rates differ in each village; and there are often three or four classes of tenants in receipt of allowances, the *jeth raiyats* or headmen being the most favoured and the lower castes the least. In some villages Goālās, who supply milk and *ghī*, are charged a lower rate, in others a toll, called *chungī*, is levied at the rate of $2\frac{1}{2}$ seers for every 21 sheaves cut by outside coolies; and a charge called *paserā* is also sometimes made, *i.e.*, in the case of each tenant whose grain exceeds 5 or, in some cases, 10 maunds, 5 seers are made over to the proprietor's heap. Finally, the *gorait* gets a *pabbī* of 4 chittacks per maund, and the village priest another 4 chittacks from the proprietor's heap.

These archaic customs appear to be survivals of the primitive village organization. The *patwārī*, who takes the largest share, is practically the village solicitor, as he writes any deeds that are required in the village, and acts as scribe generally to the community. The result is that the tenants, being illiterate men, are as a rule dependent upon him for their titles to any land they possess. The *gumāshta* has the responsibility of the irrigation of the crops, he has to settle disputes between the different tenants as to water, etc., and he also heads them when they have to protect their rights by a *levee en masse*, as well as in the litigation which inevitably ensues. The *barāhils* and *goraits* are expected by the tenants to watch the crops and prevent grazing, and the artisans such as the carpenter, blacksmith, etc., are similarly indispensable members of the village community, who by old custom and tradition are bound to serve the villagers in the needs of every-day life.

THE *Nagdi* SYSTEM.

Side by side with the *bhāoli* system is that known as *nagdi*, *i.e.*, the payment of rents in cash. These systems are not localized or confined to particular tracts, but co-exist all over the district, and almost every cultivator holds some land under both systems. Certain crops however are nearly always cultivated under the *bhāoli* system, such as rice; and cash rents are invariably paid for other crops, such as poppy, sugarcane, and garden produce. Money rents are, in fact, paid for all land growing crops which require special care and expense; and this is generally the case with homestead land, as it is peculiarly adapted for the growth of special crops, and the cultivator can cultivate it entirely by his own means.

***Nagdi* tenures.**

In the case of cash rents there are two special kinds of tenures, called *shikmī* and *chakath*. A *shikmī* holding is one held on a cash rent in perpetuity, and the term is said to be derived from the fact that a former Mahārājā of Tekāri introduced the system and fixed his tenants' rents for ever in sicca rupees. Another theory is that the word is derived from *shikam*, the Persian for belly, a term applied to the rich land held under this tenure, because it is generally the best in the village, usually yields two crops, and is the main source from which the cultivator obtains his livelihood. *Chakath* lands are those temporarily settled at cash rents for a period of years. The term is specially applied to temporary settlements of waste or uncultivated lands, made for a limited number of years, with the object of reclaiming them or bringing them under cultivation. Such settlements, however, are made not only of waste lands, but also of lands which are unpopular and will not be taken on any other terms, owing to the difficulties of irrigation or natural unfertility. The landlord reserves to himself the right of demanding a produce-rent on the expiry of the settlement, but in practice this right is seldom enforced.

Paran tenures.

Another tenure peculiar to Gayā is that called *paran*, which appears to occupy an intermediate position between the *bhāoli* and *nagdi* systems. The *paran* or *paran pheri* tenure is one under which paddy land, held on the *bhāoli* system, and suited to the growth of sugarcane or poppy, is settled at a specially high rate of rent for growing either of these crops. When the sugarcane or poppy is harvested, the land reverts to the *bhāoli* system and is sown with paddy. Thus the land held under this tenure grows two crops, sugarcane and poppy, during the first two years, the former being on the ground for 14, and the latter for three months, and in the third year rice is grown. Each block is accordingly sown in turn with sugarcane, poppy and rice, the rent being paid in cash while the land is under the first two crops, and in kind when it is under rice. The *raison d'être* of this arrangement is simply that in Gayā cash rents are invariably paid for land growing sugarcane and poppy, while produce-rents are nearly always paid for land growing rice.

MERITS OF THE *Bhāoli* SYSTEM.

There can be little doubt that, under present conditions, the *bhāoli* system is absolutely indispensable for the greater part of the cultivation. On it depends the system of indigenous irrigation which is essential to the prosperity of the country and to its protection against famine; and it is not too much to say that, if it were abolished, *pains* and *āhars* would not be constructed and the existing works would fall into disrepair. It is true that the landowner now-a-days does not do his duty in keeping the *pains* clear of silt and in maintaining the *āhars* properly; but he would do it still less if it were not that he shares in the produce of the land. On the other hand, the system has grave defects, not the least of which is that it engenders slovenly cultivation. The incentives to industry are not so strong as in the case of *nagdi* lands; for the tenant, receiving only half the produce, has only half the usual motives for exertion and will not devote the same time and trouble to improving the land. The result is that while the *nagdi* lands are cultivated almost like gardens, the *bhāoli* lands are comparatively neglected. This is no new feature, as 100 years ago it was so noticeable that Buchanan Hamilton remarked:—"This system of levying the rent by a division of crops has produced a slovenly and careless cultivation. The tenant is not pushed for his rent; and his great object, in place of cultivating well, is to diminish the expense of cultivation. From this a very great loss arises to the landlord and still more to the public. Almost every tenant, however, has some land for which he pays a money rent, and on this is bestowed all his care, by rearing on it rich crops, by manuring, and by frequently repeated ploughing and hoeing. The rent is much higher than the share which the landlord receives on the division of crops, and the farmers who have the largest proportion of this kind of land are in the easiest circumstances." The superior cultivation of cash-paying lands is as apparent at the present day; all produce above what suffices to pay the rent is pure profit, and the result is that they receive the cultivator's best care and labour, and all his available manure.

It is obvious, moreover, that the complicated method of appraisement and division must result in a vast amount of peculation and mutual friction. Endless disputes are the rule, and the apportionment of the crop furnishes many opportunities for fraud and oppression. In a small estate, where the petty zamīndār can look after his own fields and see the crops divided or check the appraisement personally, the system is not so open to objection. The small proprietor is often a resident of the village and therefore amenable to public opinion; he is so directly dependent on his tenants that he has to keep on good terms with them; and his income is so vitally affected by the irrigation works that in his own interests he is bound to keep them up. The defects of the system are more apparent in large estates. If the method of *batāi* is followed, the opportunities for fraud are very great, and if the *dānābandi*, both landlords and tenants are at the mercy of the underlings whom the former has to maintain. The estimates they make cannot very well be checked; if the *gumāshtas* side with the ryots, it is easy for them to cheat the proprietor; if they are not on good terms with the ryots, they can grossly over-estimate, and they can always bring pressure to bear by neglecting to appraise until the crops are ruined by the delay. The result is that the subordinates can enrich themselves at the expense of both parties, and the landlord is often forced to introduce the middleman, as a preferable alternative to entertaining a great staff of servants, who are an expense to himself and a fruitful source of oppression to the tenants. Here again the estate suffers. The farmer has no permanent interest in the property, he endeavours to squeeze out of it as much as he can during the period of his lease, and the tenants are oppressed. The injury done to the interests of the proprietors themselves is scarcely less; and the state of the 9 annas share of the Tekāri Rāj, when the Court of Wards assumed charge of it in 1886, shows how great this injury is and how strong is the tendency to lease out villages in this way. No less than 638 villages were leased out temporarily, and only 65 were under direct management; the irrigation works on which the crops almost entirely depended had been much neglected and were ineffective; and the productive power of the lands held by the *thīkādārs* or lessees had greatly deteriorated. Similar results were witnessed at the beginning of last century by Buchanan Hamilton, who wrote of this same splendid property:—"Perhaps 15 annas of the estates are let by an actual division of the crop. As it would be impossible for the Rājā to superintend such a collection, without suffering the most enormous losses, he has farmed out the greater part of his rents, and this has given rise to considerable complaints of oppression; nor is the cultivation on his estates so good as might have been expected from the money he has expended in constructing reservoirs, canals and roads. Had his estate been let for a money rent, it might, with his prudence, have been managed by his stewards entirely without loss, and the tenants would have had no cause for complaint, while the rents would have been a stimulus to industry."

In any case, the system gives tremendous power to the landlords over their ryots. The control of the irrigation works places the peasantry in more or less complete subjection to the landlord, who can, and very often does, exact most unfair terms from them. The result is that even where the landlords maintain irrigation works, they do not always do so at their own cost; that they often make their tenants labour without charge, or else appropriate a larger share of the produce than they should according to the strict principles of the system, and that the tenants are markedly subservient to them. There is however a steady tendency to convert produce-rents to cash rents—a change noted by Buchanan Hamilton 100 years ago, which has been accelerated by the policy of the Court of Wards in the Tekāri Rāj during the last 20 years. In some cases the produce-rents were commuted in whole villages, and in others small plots were settled on cash rents (called *chakath*); altogether the rents of 29,314 *bīghas* were so converted during the term of the Court's management. It was decided, however, that such commutation was not to be carried out except where the irrigation system was complete, as in the area irrigated from the canals, or where no further improvements were possible in that dependent on indigenous irrigation. The process is slow, but it is developing as the tenantry and the more enlightened landlords begin to see the disadvantages of such a complicated method of rent recovery. The Son canal system, which affords the ryot a certain supply of water independent of the zamīndārs, has done much in this direction; and the tendency is for the ryot to pay produce rents only for those lands in which cultivation depends entirely on large works of irrigation constructed and kept up by their landlords. Here the system is justified by necessity, and is appropriate, if fairly worked; but where cultivation depends on large irrigation works which the landlords do not maintain, it is an anomaly which fortunately is gradually disappearing.

In concluding this sketch of the *bhāoli* system, the following remarks of a former Collector of Gayā may be quoted:—"Considerable misapprehension appears to exist in regard to the system of payment of produce-rents prevalent in this district, known as the *bhāoli* system, which is chiefly due, as far as I can judge from what I have seen written on the subject, to the fact that the actual working of the system in practice on the spot has not been sufficiently known or distinguished from the theoretical working of the system in its general and broad lines. Although the peculiar system has, no doubt, lasted in this district by reason of the necessity which underlies it, viz., the necessity of the landlord, (or the *capitalist*) keeping up the comparatively expensive works of irrigation, without which cultivation could not be successfully carried on throughout a great part of the district, it is not now, it will be found from actual observation, the custom of every landlord to make new works of irrigation, or to maintain the old ones in good order entirely at their own expense. It may be the traditional custom; and the Wards' estates in the district, and Government, in respect of their own estates held under direct management. have adopted this custom, and have thus done much to keep it alive. The fact, too, that the custom is observed in these estates, the administration of which comes so prominently before the officers of Government has done much to make it conspicuous. But, as a result of this, much that has been written in regard to the *bhāoli* system in this district has emanated from a perhaps too exclusive experience of these classes of estates.

"The system is advantageous to a powerful and unscrupulous landlord, as against a poor and weak tenantry, and keeps up, or fosters the existence of, so many middlemen and encourages so much dispute, peculation and dishonesty on all sides as to stamp it unmistakably as bad. I have never heard an educated or a sensible native of high or low class praise it *in se*. It is the fact that it favours the rich and powerful that has caused it to maintain its position so long; and I have no doubt that the poverty and serf-like status of many of the tenantry in this district, that have been noticed from time to time, are the result in great measure of this system."

CHAPTER XII.

RENTS, WAGES AND PRICES.

THERE are no statistics available showing the rates of rent prevalent throughout the whole district, but the rates ascertained during the years 1893—98 in the course of the survey and settlement of the Tekāri Ward's estate, the Government estates and the Belkhara Mahāl may be regarded as applicable to the district as a whole. The area cadastrally surveyed was 582 square miles containing over 660,000 plots and 65,800 tenancies, and the rents and status of 59,334 tenants were attested. This area is equal in extent to about one-eighth of the total area of the district, and as the villages concerned are scattered over all parts of Gayā, the statistics obtained are fairly representative of the whole of the district. At the same time, it should be remembered that the statistics showing the incidence of rent per acre of cash-paying land are rendered of less value by the fact that so much of the settled area is held on produce rents, and that cash rents are paid only for the most fertile lands, to which the ryot devotes special attention. RENTS.

It was ascertained that the rate paid by ryots at fixed rates in the Tekāri estate was as high as Rs. 4-9, while in the other two estates it varied between Re. 1-8 and Re. 1-12 per acre. The rate payable by occupancy ryots was found to be Rs. 3-8 per acre in the Government estates, Rs. 4-6 in the Tekāri estate, and Rs. 5-14 in the Belkhara Mahāl, this variation being a measure of the relative productiveness of the three estates. Non-occupancy ryots pay the highest rents in the Belkhara Mahāl, viz., Rs. 5-15 per acre, while the rate is only Re. 1-10 to Rs. 2-8 in the other two estates, where only the worst land or land of inferior quality is settled with new and non-resident tenants. The average rent paid by under-ryots was found to be Re. 1-15-11 in the Tekāri estate, Rs. 3-10-11 in the Government estates and Rs. 6-1-10 in the Belkhara Mahāl. In the Tekāri estate the area held on cash rents is small (22 per cent.), and no inference can be drawn from the low rate of rent; but in the other two estates the rates are very little above the rates paid by occupancy ryots—a fact which supports the conclusion that there is very little competition for available land in this district.

Taking the *parganas* according to their fertility, it was found that in the most fertile tract the average rate of rent paid by settled ryots possessing occupancy rights, who form a large proportion of the tenantry, was Rs. 5-12 per acre; in the second of the tracts mentioned in Chapter VIII it was Rs. 4-7; in the third tract it was Rs. 3-2-3; and in the fourth tract of fertility it was Rs. 2-7-1. In the case of non-occupancy ryots, the rent rates bore little relation to the general fertility of the *pargana*, as the area of the land held by these ryots is so small that the rate depends entirely on the quality of a few isolated plots.

The rents paid vary very largely according to the class of soil cultivated and the crops grown, and the following rates of rent per acre may be regarded as fairly general; paddy lands, if fit for only a single crop, Re. 1-8 to Rs. 8, and those yielding a double crop, Rs. 3 to Rs. 10; lands on which wheat, barley, gram, pulses and oil-seeds are grown, Rs. 2 to Rs. 8; sugarcane and poppy lands, Rs. 3 to Rs. 16; lands growing *bhadoi* crops, such as maize, *maruā* or *jowār*, Re. 1-8 to Rs. 5; and lands growing potatoes, Rs. 4 to Rs. 16.

Dr. Buchanan Hamilton estimated the average rate of rent at the beginning of last century at from Re. 1 to Rs. 2 per acre, and there can be no doubt that the increase during the last 100 years has been very large. On the other hand, the price of grain has risen even more during the last 30 years, but cash rents have not risen to a corresponding extent; and the rise in the value of the produce has outstripped whatever enhancement may have been made in the cash rents.

WAGES. Statistics of the wages paid for certain selected classes of labour and the rates current during the decade 1893—1902 will be found in the Statistical Appendix. It is interesting to compare these figures with those of 100 years ago given by Dr. Buchanan Hamilton. At that time the usual daily allowance for a labourer engaged in ploughing was 3 seers of grain, or in some places from $1\frac{1}{2}$ to 2 pice, with half a seer of the unboiled porridge called *sattu*. This wage, representing in English money about one penny, was earned by nine hours' work. The annual wages earned by a poor family of three persons were Rs. 26-8; and though one rupee represented 156 lbs. of maize, or other coarse but wholesome grain, the whole living expenses of the family, including clothes, had to be met from this sum. An estimate of the earnings of a family from Nawāda, where wages were still lower, gave as the annual gain, represented in money, Rs. 22-1-6.

The rise in the rate of wages has apparently not kept pace with the general rise in the price of food-grains, especially for the lower classes of labour, and the village craftsman earns about the same year after year. In the towns, however, where there is a special demand for it, skilled labour undoubtedly commands a higher price than formerly, and the carpenter or smith, who earned only 4½ annas a day, now gets a wage of 8 annas per diem. Among masons, carpenters and blacksmiths the wage shows an upward tendency; the silversmith charges a higher rate for his workmanship; the shoe-maker and the tailor have raised their tariff; and there is a similar tendency among domestic servants. The rise is small and gradual, but is observable all the same; and it appears to be due to the opening of new lines of railway and the resultant communication with large centres of industry.

Outside urban areas the wages of labour maintain much the same level from year to year; and in the case of unskilled labour their measure is usually the minimum amount required to afford means of subsistence. Fortunately, however, wages in the villages are usually paid wholly or partly in kind; even the village artisan receives grain for the services he renders; and the field-labourer generally gets the whole of his wage in one or other of the inferior grains. The rates of the wages thus paid in kind vary in different localities, but the following are said to be the general rates. At harvest time the village labourers get 1 out of every 16 sheaves cut, and outside labourers 1 out of every 21 sheaves, in addition to a diet allowance known as *lohrā* and *chhakautī*, while ploughmen receive 1 out of every 16 sheaves cut, besides the daily wages paid to him at ploughing time. Among the village artisans, the carpenter and blacksmith each get 5 local seers of the *rabi* crop and 1 *bojhā* or sheaf of paddy per *har* (a holding measuring about 10 *bīghas*), at the time of harvesting; the cobbler (*chamār*) receives one *bojhā* per *har;* the barber 5 seers of *rabi* and 5 seers of paddy per head shaved; and the washerman (*dhobī*) half a *bojhā* per head in a tenant's family. The Māli and Tamoli (betel-leaf seller) each get one *bojhā* per tenant; the Goālā, or cowherd, one local maund of rice and an equal quantity of *rabi* plus one *bojhā* per *har;* the Badhwār, or crop-watcher, a quarter seer per local maund of grain produced ; and the Bhāt, or village bard, half a *bojhā* per tenant. This system is particularly suited to an agricultural country like Gayā, as it has the advantage of being unaffected by any rise in the price of food-grains. Whatever the fluctuations in the price of these in the market, the labourer's wage remains the same.

PRICES. A statement of the prices current in each subdivision during the years 1893-1902 is given in the Statistical Appendix. They show an extraordinary advance on those obtaining a little more than a century* before, when even the finest kind of rice sold at 31 to 44 seers and paddy at 95 to 129 seers per rupee, while the price of wheat ranged from 55 to 64 seers and of gram from 72 to 104 seers per rupee. The prices of grain have risen enormously during the last hundred years; but on the other hand there has been a very great growth in the income of all classes, and during the last generation the development of communications has had the effect of levelling prices over larger and larger areas. Ten years ago there was only one line of railway running through the north of the district, but within the last few years three more lines have been added, which tap the district in all directions, and the network of main roads and feeder roads admirably supplement the work of the railway. There is consequently less variation in prices between various parts of the district than formerly, when the railway only traversed the north of the district and the prices of food-grains varied directly with the distance of the markets from it. Besides this, the vast majority of labour is of an agricultural character and is paid in kind, and immemorial custom has fixed the amount thereof, so that the high prices of grain affect a large section of the community less than would otherwise be the case. To this it should be added that the rural population keep large stores of grain, and are, therefore, to a certain extent protected from the distress consequent on scarcity and the rising price of food.

MATERIAL CONDITION OF THE PEOPLE. The subject of the material condition of the people of Gayā has attracted a considerable amount of attention owing to the somewhat startling picture of their poverty presented by Dr. Grierson in his Notes on the District of Gayā. This account formed the subject of a question in Parliament, and advantage was taken of the survey and settlement operations then in progress in the district to institute a special enquiry into the economic condition of the poorer classes. A detailed criticism of the conclusions arrived at by Dr. Grierson will be found in Mr. Stevenson-Moore's Report on the Material Condition of Small Agriculturists and Labourers in Gayā, and it will be sufficient here to summarize the results of his exhaustive investigations.

According to Dr. Grierson, 70 per cent. of the agricultural holdings, unaided by supplemental sources of income, do not

* For a list of the prices current in 1781 and 1782, two average years, see Early English Administration of Bihar, by J. R. Hand, pp. 61-62.

support their cultivators, *i.e.*, the net profit does not give a family of six persons sufficient clothing and two full meals a day; while all persons of the labouring classes and 10 per cent. of the cultivating and artizan classes may be considered as insufficiently clothed or insufficiently fed, or both. "It is not suggested," he added, "that this large number of human beings is as a rule in actual want of food, or has never more than one meal a day. In the majority of cases two meals a day form the rule, but they have often to curtail the number of their meals for a few days at a time to enable them to tide over difficulties." The results obtained by Mr. Stevenson-Moore disclose a very different state of affairs. He found that the conditions depicted by Dr. Grierson, namely, that 70 per cent. of the holdings do not support the cultivators, might perhaps apply to the most unfertile tract in Gayā, or to 8 per cent. of the cultivated area of the district; but that approximately only 25 per cent. of the holdings in the entire district were insufficient to support their cultivators in comfort without supplementary sources of income. Generally speaking, the cultivating labourers were found to be well off, the average income per head falling under Rs. 15 only in the most infertile tract, where it was Rs. 14·6. Among landless labourers the average income per head ranged from Rs. 14 to Rs. 18·2, assuming that they worked full time throughout the year. If steady, industrious and fully employed, they can earn nearly Rs. 15 a head, which would amply cover the cost of living in comfort. This however is a maximum, for though they are supposed to get work for nine months in the year, it is doubtful whether they get it for so long a period. On the other hand, a large portion of them are *kamiyās* or bond servants, and as such are supported by their masters even in times of adversity.

The general conclusion at which Mr. Stevenson-Moore arrives is as follows:—"Dr. Grierson's finding that the labouring classes are insufficiently nourished can be accepted so far as it concerns landless labourers. That 10 per cent. of the artisans are similarly situated is little better than conjecture, but I am not prepared to deny it. There is no reason whatever to believe that 10 per cent. of pure cultivators suffer from want, but it is possible 10 per cent. of cultivating labourers are in that condition. From these premises the result is obtained that 20·86 per cent. of the entire population, or about 425,000 people, as against Dr. Grierson's estimate of 45 per cent. of the population amounting to one million people, are so circumstanced that periods occur during the year when they are not able to take two full meals a day." These statistics were based on enquiries conducted by a trained staff, which had means of attaining accuracy which Dr. Grierson had not; and they may be accepted as more reliable than those obtained by him. The result, however, is to show how large a proportion of the population do not possess an income of Rs. 15 a year, which, as Dr. Grierson subsequently explained, may be regarded as "the sum required to give a well-to-do native of the lower classes, with a fairly high standard of comfort, plenty to eat and drink and a sufficient supply of clothing and the usual luxuries."

Indebtedness.

The indebtedness of the cultivating classes is however small; and Mr. Stevenson-Moore found that the incidence of debts per head varied from Rs. 6·6 in the case of families holding under 10 *bīghas* to Rs. 11 in the case of those holding over 10 *bīghas*. The extent of the cultivator's indebtedness in Gayā is, in fact, in direct proportion to his prosperity; the bigger the cultivator, the greater his credit, and the higher his expenditure on marriages and other ceremonies. The ryot generally keeps a certain amount of grain in store, but he is often improvident, and the general custom of the country makes heavy expenditure on social ceremonies obligatory. For these reasons, agriculture, like other industries, is supported on credit, and the *mahājan* is as essential to the village as the ploughman. Some of the ryot's debt is owed to the shopkeeper who sells grain, or to the *mahājan* or landlord for advances to purchase food while the harvest is ripening, and such accounts are usually closed when the harvest is reaped; some is contracted, more particularly if the harvest promises to be a bumper one, for the purpose of marriages; and some debts are business transactions closely connected with agriculture, *e.g.*, for the purchase of seed, ploughs or cattle, or for extending cultivation or making agricultural improvements. As Dr. Grierson says:—"So far as Gayā is concerned, the much-abused *mahājan* is much more of a banker than money-lender, and advances grain during the hot weather and rains to be repaid at harvest time. He is the Eastern substitute for occidental thrift. He saves the ryot the trouble of saving for himself, and makes him pay highly for it;—that is all. Debts are, of course, contracted for marriages and the like, but these are rarely large in amount, and the debtors are generally able to pay off the principal besides paying the heavy rate of interest."

Agricultural classes.

Not only have the cultivators better credit than the labouring classes, but being in the habit of keeping grain for home consumption, they are in a better position than the non-agricultural class when grain is scarce and prices are high. The greater portion of the land is held on the *bhāoli* system, and the tenant has not therefore suffered from enhancement of rents, as the proportion of produce taken by the landlord does not alter; while the price obtained for the surplus of his own share which is available for sale has considerably increased. Many parts of the district are moreover capable of greater agricultural development, and the incidence of population (437 per square mile) is the lowest in the Patna Division. In the south of the district it is very much lower than this, and there is much waste land which could be brought under the plough if only people to cultivate it were available. Many of the cultivators are even now in possession of more land than they can cultivate, and owing to the absence of competition they have generally not been disturbed in the enjoyment of their rights. On the whole, they have more resources than any other class, and are probably more comfortably off than the cultivators in the densely inhabited districts of North Bihār.

Labouring classes.

As regards the labouring classes, the village artizans who never go out of the village form a recognized part of the village community and are indirectly supported by agriculture. As in other parts of Bihār, the lot of unskilled landless labourers is a hard one. They own no land, grow no crops, and depend entirely on the wages of labour. Spending what they earn from day to day, they have very little to pawn or sell, and they are the first to feel the pinch of scarcity when any failure of the crops occurs. On the whole, however, they are better off than formerly, to judge from the greater number of utensils and ornaments they possess. This improvement of condition may probably be ascribed to the fact that large numbers of labourers migrate year after year at the beginning of the cold season, for temporary employment on roads, tanks and railways, in the harvest field, and in other miscellaneous employments, returning again at the end of hot weather in time for the agricultural operations which commence with the bursting of the monsoon.

Kamiyās.

Side by side with this class of free labourers there is a section of the community known as *kamiyās*, *i.e.*, labourers who sell themselves to a master and whose position is that of mere serfs. The *kamiyā* probably dates back to the time when the Aryans overran the country and found the district inhabited by low castes of aboriginal cultivators, suitable labourers for a military aristocracy, to whom it would have been a severe degradation to handle the plough. Formerly the *kamiyā* used to sell both himself and his heirs into bondage for a lump sum down; but this practice having been declared illegal, he now hires himself, in consideration of an advance or loan to serve for 100 years or more till the money is repaid. They are not allowed to work for any one but their master, except with his permission, and have their food supplied by him. Their position is in many ways little, if at all, worse than that of the free labourers, as they are not in want of food even in lean years, whereas the ordinary labourer is the first to suffer in times of distress. Their master is bound to feed them whatever the price of food-grains may be, and if he neglects this duty, the *kamiyā* is released from his bond and is at liberty to leave his service. On the other hand, their degradation is extreme and the disadvantages of their lot are very heavy, as shewn in the following description written by Mr. Stevenson-Moore:—"This is the one class in Gayā that is entitled to the sympathies of the philanthropist. The members of the landless labouring class, other than *kamiyās*, wander from village to village in search of work. They are free, and if they get the opportunity for bettering their condition, can seize it, but the *kamiyā* can never have such an opportunity. He is attached to a master who does not give him more than sufficient to keep him in good working order. If he deserts, he is driven back by public opinion. He is ill-fed and of poor physique. When not required by his master, he is allowed to earn what he can by *pālki*-carrying, wood-cutting and other extraneous means; but so degraded is his nature that he usually dissipates one-fourth of his income in drink. The only compensation he derives is that in times of famine his master cannot allow him to die of starvation. He can neither profit by his industry nor suffer from his indolence. This system of serfdom is no innovation. It is as old as the history of Gayā, and I should imagine that it is on the decrease."

General aspects.

We have then at the bottom of the social scale the landless labourers, who are miserably poor and are often pinched for food. The more degraded members of this class are condemned by immemorial custom to a state of serfdom; and though the demand for labour is very considerable and the supply is not excessive, they seem to have little desire for emancipation. Higher in the social grade come the cultivating and landholding classes, whose income has increased considerably of late years. The great bulk of the ryots enjoy a fixity of tenure which leaves them a fair share in the produce, and the cultivators of small holdings, a class but little superior to the labourer, have benefited greatly by the general rise in prices. The railways and roads place every part within easy reach of the markets and enable them to dispose of their surplus produce with ease, while irrigation renders a large portion of the population independent of the seasons. Since 1866 famine has never taken a real hold on the district, and even the famine of 1897, which was probably the most severe famine in Bihār since 1770, did not affect the people much. The cultivating class have, moreover, a resource unknown to the ryots in Bengal proper in the cultivation of poppy, which plays an important part in the rural economy of Gayā. Those who undertake to grow it receive allowances in cash proportionate to the area which they undertake to plant, and these advances are made at a time when money is most coveted. By this means, large sums find their way into the hands of the people; in the famine of 1896-97 over 25½ lakhs was paid to the cultivators; and though the area under poppy has shrunk of late years, no less than 12½ lakhs was paid as advances in 1903-04. Besides this, emigration is more active than elsewhere; large numbers emigrate annually in search of work on the roads, railways and fields in the eastern districts, and many thousands of the adult males of Gayā are to be found spread over other parts of India in quasi-permanent employ. All these persons make remittances to their homes, while those who migrate for a time bring back with them the balance of their savings; in this way, large sums of money are sent and brought into the district every year, and are expended in the support of their families. In the famine year 1896-97 over 16½ lakhs was paid by money-order in the district, and from the fact that the money-orders were almost all for sums below Rs. 10, the average being about half that sum, it may be concluded a large proportion represented remittances sent by emigrants to their homes. Since that time this means of remitting money has grown in popularity; and in 1904-05 the amount paid by money-order exceeded 30 lakhs—a fact which may reasonably be taken as an indication of the increased prosperity of the people.

CHAPTER XIII.

OCCUPATIONS, MANUFACTURES AND TRADE.

OCCUPATIONS. In Gayā, as in other Bengal districts, a large majority of the people are engaged in agricultural pursuits, no less than 65·1 per cent. of the whole population deriving their livelihood from cultivation. Of these, 48 per cent. are actual workers, among whom are included 395,000 rent-payers, 214,000 labourers, and 15,000 rent-receivers. Of the remainder, 14 per cent. are supported by industries; the professional classes account for 1·9 per cent., of whom 40 per cent. are actual workers, including 7,000 priests and 1,500 teachers; and the commercial class is even smaller, amounting to only 0·6 per cent. Of the industrial population, 46 per cent. are actual workers, including 16,000 cotton-weavers, 11,000 oil-pressers and sellers, 9,000 sellers of firewood, 8,000 dealers in pulse and grain, the same number of grocers and of potters, 7,000 toddy-sellers, 6,000 carpenters, 5,000 cow-keepers and milk-sellers, besides numerous tailors, shoe-makers, blacksmiths, basket-makers, and workers in gold and silver. Among those engaged in other occupations are 116,000 general labourers, 13,000 herdsmen, 7,000 earth-workers and 6,000 beggars.

Though not so large as in the adjoining districts of Shāhābād and Patna, the proportion of persons engaged in industrial occupations is very much greater than in the North Bihār districts, where native handicrafts are of far less importance. It has been suggested that the reason of this is that, after the murder of Alamgīr and the fall of Delhi in 1759 A. D., some members of the Muhammadan nobility attached to the Mughal court retired to the *jāgīrs* that had been given them in the Patna, Gayā, and Shāhābād districts, bringing in their train large numbers of artificers and traders who settled down in these three districts; while the districts to the north of the Ganges were still in an unsettled state, sparsely populated and only partially cultivated.

MANUFACTURES. Gayā contains no manufacturing towns or important trade centres, and, as might be expected in a district where the great majority of the people are engaged in agricultural and pastoral pursuits and where the urban population is small, the bulk of the industrial community are employed in supplying the simple needs of a rural people. The people require very little that cannot be supplied by the village artisan beyond the common commodities imported everywhere in Bengal, such as Manchester piece-goods and kerosine-oil; and the various articles manufactured for local consumption, such as brass utensils, bell-metal ornaments, earthenware pots, woollen blankets, etc., meet most of their wants. Manufactures in the proper sense of the word are few in number and of little ignificance, and scarcely any of the industries produce anything for export. A short account of the principal industries is given below.

The lac industry in this district is confined to the area comprised within the jurisdiction of the Imāmganj and Dumaria police-stations and the town of Dāūdnagar in the west. The cultivation of lac is carried on chiefly by the Bhuiyās and other low castes, who take out leases of the trees on which the insect (*Coccus lacca*) is reared, at a rental of some four or five rupees for each hundred trees. Lac merchants also take leases at similar rates from the zamīndārs and employ labourers to rear the insects. The tree most commonly used in this district is the *palās* (*Butea frondosa*), which grows in large numbers to the south, but the *pīpal* (*Ficus religiosa*) is also sometimes used. The insects take six months to complete the secretion of lac, and the lac harvest is thus reaped twice annually, about the months of November and May. When the secretion is complete, the twigs, on the bark of which the lac incrustation has been formed, are cut off, and the crude material is removed and ground in heavy stone mills. When they have been thoroughly ground, they are sifted in a coarse sieve, and the fragments of twigs which still remain are removed. The grains of lac which are left are next washed several times, by being loaded in big tubs and worked by the labourers' feet, and all particles of wood and other foreign substances are strained off; they are then strained through a cloth, and after being dried in the sun, are again passed through a sieve; and the refuse having been removed, the finer product is mixed with arsenic and placed in long cloth bags. The latter are twisted round and round before a fire, the heat of which causes the grains to melt and ooze out; the liquid lac is then scraped off the bag and placed on a stone slab below it. It is generally gathered up again and replaced in the bag till the lac is thoroughly melted and the proper consistency is obtained; and it is then pressed out into thin sheets. It is now ready for ordinary rough work, and is made into bangles, bracelets, rings, beads and other trinkets. It is also employed by turners for the colouring of wooden toys, by Lac.

goldsmiths for the colouring of metals, and for lacquered ware generally. Nearly all the lac produced in the district is exported, and the industry is in a flourishing condition, there being 32 factories with an annual outturn of about 50,000 maunds.

Sugar.

Raw sugar, including molasses, jaggery and other crude saccharine produce, is one of the most important manufactures in the district, large quantities being sent out every year to Eastern Bengal, the Central Provinces, Rājputāna and Central India; over 200,000 maunds of crude sugar are exported annually. The process of manufacture may be seen in every village; it is extremely simple; and the apparatus required is far from elaborate. To extract the juice (*ras*), the sugarcane is pressed in a mill worked by bullocks. Formerly the mills used were primitive wooden or stone machines, but in recent years the iron roller mills, known as the Bihiā mills, have come into universal use. The juice extracted is poured into shallow iron pans, called *karāhis*, and boiled, the only fuel used being the cane-leaves and the dried stalks from which the juice has been extracted. When the juice thickens, it is poured into small pots and exposed to the air to harden, the molasses thus produced being known as *gur*.

The manufacture of refined sugar is carried on only on a very small scale, and the condition of the industry is in striking contrast with that just mentioned. With the development of communications and the growth of trade, the sugar-refining industry has been less and less able to compete with the imports of cheap Mauritius and Cossipore sugar. Large quantities of these and other foreign sugars are sold at rates lower than those obtained for the local product; the crystalline sugar thus imported is purer and of a superior quality to that made in the district; and the manufacture of the latter has consequently declined and is now almost extinct.

Brass.

One of the few industries which has not yet suffered from the competition of foreign or machine-made articles, and which is still in a prosperous condition, is the manufacture of brass utensils. These are made in the town of Gayā at Mārufganj, Gayāwālbigha, and Buniādganj, and at Kenār in the head-quarters subdivision; at Hasuā and Kauwākol in the Nawāda subdivision; and at Dāūdnagar and Nabīnagar in the Aurangābād subdivision. A large number of elegant brass vessels are made at the latter place, and some of those turned out at Gayā are chased with some skill. The braziers of the town also manufacture figures of Hindu deities, which are taken away by pilgrims in considerable quantities. Except at these localities, the village workers confine themselves almost exclusively to the manufacture of bracelets and anklets of bell-metal, which the lower classes use instead of more costly ornaments.

Cotton weaving was formerly a large and prosperous industry, which was of such importance 100 years ago that, in addition to the central depôt at Patna, the old East India Company had three cloth factories in the district of Bihār, situated at Jahānābād, Maghra and Bigha, besides five subordinate factories and 22 houses for the purchase of cloth. According to Buchanan Hamilton, the agent of the Company "entered into engagements with 2,200 of the best weavers in the country round Jahanabad, including that division, Holasgunj, Sahebgunj, and a few perhaps in Vikram, Arwal, Daudnagar and the corner of Ramgar, next to that town. Each man on becoming bound (Assami) to the Company received two rupees, and engaged not to work for any person until he had made as much as the Company required; and no other advance has ever been made by the commercial residents. The agent orders each man to make a certain number of pieces of such or such goods, and he is paid for each on its delivery, according to the price stated in the tables." This extensive industry is now a thing of the past, and as in other parts of the Province, the hand-made article has been driven out of the market by imported piece-goods. Though the product of the local looms lasts longer, the advantage thus gained is counterbalanced by its higher cost. The preference for *mārkin*, as the Manchester article is called, can be readily understood, as a piece of country cloth costs Re. 1-4 and will last 8 or 9 months, whereas a piece of *mārkin* of the same size will last 6 months, but will be only half the price. Cotton fabrics.

The well-to-do have now discarded the coarse cotton cloth of the district, but weaving is still carried on to some extent, as the poorer classes prefer it on account of its strength, durability and greater warmth. This *motia* or *gāzi* cloth is still used in the winter, the men wearing it in the shape of *dhotīs*, *mirzāis* (jackets) and *dohars* or *dulāis*, which take the place of quilts, while women of the labouring, artizan and shop-keeper classes use it in the shape of *sārīs* and *kurtas* (bodices or chemisettes). It is woven in all parts of the district, the weavers being mostly Jolāhās, though some Patwas in Gayāwālbigha and Buniādganj also sometimes produce it instead of tusser silk. The profits of manufacture are very small, being, it is said, about 2 pice for every yard of a breadth of 27 inches; a cloth 18 yards in length takes 3 days to finish, and the profits would therefore be about 9 annas for every 3 days, or about Rs. 5-10 a month, assuming that the weaver is always fully employed. This however is not the case, and if all the numbers of the Jolāhā caste had to depend on the produce of their looms, they would have disappeared long ago. Many of them have now forsaken their hereditary calling for more profitable occupations, and others who still work their looms eke out their slender earnings by agriculture and labour of various kinds. Every year large numbers of them seek service in the jute mills on the Hooghly or work as menials in Calcutta, and those that still ply the trade have seldom more than one loom at work at a time, whereas formerly the number was only limited by that of the members of the family who could work.

Woollen fabrics.

The woollen fabric industry may be divided roughly into two branches, the manufacture of the country blankets of rough texture ordinarily used by the poorer classes, and the manufacture of carpets, called indiscriminately *kālins* and *gāñchas* in this district, which are of a superior texture and require more skilled workmanship. The manufacture of coarse blankets is confined to one class of people, the Gareris or shepherd caste, who keep sheep, shear them, make the wool into cloth, and sell the blankets. The price of a blanket thus produced is so low as to barely cover the value of the material, but as the wool is the produce of the sheep which the Gareris themselves rear, the whole price of the cloth they weave is pure gain, for the cost of the loom and other instruments used in weaving is practically nothing. Part of the plant is home-made, and the rest is bought from the village blacksmiths and carpenters, the total value of a complete woollen weaving outfit being less than 8 annas, including the home-made instruments. The only places now noted for the manufacture of blankets are Ambā and Chilki in the jurisdiction of the Kutumbā outpost, where blankets of superior finish and greater thickness are made, ornamental designs being occasionally introduced. These blankets are generally made to order for the richer classes, as they are much more expensive than those of the ordinary type. The latter are exported in small quantities, but are mostly made for local use, a coarse blanket being the only protection against the cold that the poorer classes can afford.

Carpet-weaving is practically confined to the villages of Obrā and Koraipur and the town of Dāūdnagar in the Aurangābād subdivision, where some Muhammadan (Kālinbāf) families monopolize the trade. The carpets they produce are generally made of cotton, but frequently wool is mixed with the cotton, or else wool only is used. They vary in size, colour, texture and design according to the demand or to such special orders as may be received. The price varies from about Rs. 3 to upwards of Rs. 500, according to the size and quality, the annual value of the total outturn being about Rs. 5,000 or Rs. 6,000. The carpets are exported to a small extent to Calcutta, and may often be seen in the booths at the various fairs held in Gayā and the neighbouring districts.

Silk weaving is carried on at Mānpur and Buniādganj on the outskirts of Gayā, to a small extent in the Gayāwālbigha *mahalla* in the town itself, and at Chākand some 5 miles to the north; at Kādirganj and Akbarpur in the Nawāda subdivision; and at Dāūdnagar in the Aurangābād subdivision. The silk produced is that known as tusser (*tasar*); it is generally of a coarse description, and much of it is remarkable neither for durability nor beauty. The class rich enough to buy expensive silk is necessarily somewhat small, and is generally able to purchase silk of a better quality, such as that of Murshidābād, which the cheapness of carriage afforded by the railway puts on the market at a low rate. Such competition naturally tells against the home-made article, and the result is that the cloth woven tends to deteriorate in quality. The best kinds are now rarely woven, and the quantity of coarse *bāfta* (mixed tusser and cotton) turned out by the local looms is on the increase. Silk fabrics.

On the whole, however, the industry is in a fairly flourishing condition, and so far the weavers have been able to hold their own, largely owing to the fact that silk is used by Hindus for religious purposes. From Vedic times the use of silk fabrics on ceremonial occasions has been enjoined on Hindus; those who can afford it regard it as incumbent on them to wear silk daily at the time of worship; and foreign silks or silks containing an admixture of other fibres are prohibited for such ceremonial purposes. The silk-manufacturing industry has thus a peculiar vitality of its own, which is not shared by the cotton-weaving industry; and consequently the weavers, who have the advantage of living close to a pilgrim city, manage to earn a competence by weaving alone: some of them indeed are in easy circumstances and have considerable incomes. Most of them have only one loom, but some have as many as four or five, the industry giving employment to all the members of a family, as the men weave, the women spin, and the children set the warp. The cocoons have not to be got from any great distance, as they are imported from the jungles in Palāmau and Hazāribāgh to the south; and there is a sufficient demand for the finished product locally. Gayā itself offers a good market for its sale, owing to the number of priests who officiate there and of pilgrims who are glad to take away with them a piece of the local silk, and besides this a considerable quantity is exported to Azīmgarh and elsewhere. Most of the cloth is used for *sārīs*, *chadars*, *kurtas*, etc., but a great deal is woven and exported for use as shrouds in which to wind the dead. The weavers are most numerous in Mānpur and Buniādganj; but even here they form a small community. Their profits have, however, increased considerably of recent years, the value of the total annual outturn rising, in the decade ending in 1901, from Rs. 25,000 to Rs. 80,000; and as the number of families engaged in weaving has also grown, there appears no reason to apprehend that the industry is declining.

Stone-carving.

Gayā is one of the few districts in Bengal in which stone-carving is carried on. The principal seat of the industry is at Pathalkati, a village some 19 miles north-east of Gayā, but there are also some workmen at Dhanmahuā and Sapneri, 3 and 4 miles respectively west of that place, and at the foot of the Manglagaurī Hill in Gayā itself. The art is said to have been introduced by some workmen of Jaipur, who were brought to Gayā to build the Vishnupad temple some 140 years ago, and, their attention having been attracted by the possibilities of the quarry at Pathalkati, eventually gave up the idea of returning to their homes and settled there. The present race of stone-carvers say that their forefathers were skilled sculptors, and point to the image of the Sun god in the local temple as a specimen of their proficiency, but the art has now fallen to a low state. With a few exceptions, only plain vases, cups, bowls, dishes and cups of a stereotyped pattern are manufactured, but some of the carvers produce ornamental vases, figures of gods, human beings, animals, etc., carved with a certain amount of taste and skill. The equipment of the workshop is primitive, and the implements used consist merely of a chisel, hammer, compasses, a roller which serves the purposes of a lathe, and a *narhani* or thin piece of iron used to apply lac, cement broken pieces, or place the rough article on the lathe to be polished. The process is a simple one, as after the stone has been carved and polished, it is only necessary to blacken it, which is done by means of soot either alone or mixed with the juice of *sim* leaves (*Dolichos Lablab*). These articles find a ready sale in Gayā, where they are in great request among the pilgrims; while some serve a useful purpose locally, such as the *kharals* or mortars used by native medical practitioners for compounding medicines.

Wood-carving.

The following account of the wood-carving of Gayā is taken from the Monograph on Wood-carving in Bengal, by Chevalier O. Ghilardi (1903):—"In this old city the wood-carving industry must have reached the apex of the beautiful as shewn in the examples which belong to the earliest periods of this art. Unhappily this excellence has not been maintained in the pieces of latter date. I went through the remotest recesses of the extensive native quarter and had the opportunity of admiring some really beautiful wood-carving, which must have originated from the splendid examples of old carved stone on the Buddhist and Hindu temples which seem so gloriously to defy the ravages of the centuries. I visited the house of Rai Behari Lall Barrick Bahadur, where the best specimen of ancient carving can be admired and profitably studied. Here I found a door with its pillars, architrave and friezes so admirably carved that they might well be exhibited in a museum. Near this house is the corner of a very narrow lane, at which there is a small house evidently old, and displaying some beautiful carvings of the more minute style, almost resembling chased silver or filigree work. The natives themselves have great veneration for this building, owing to the beautiful construction of its verandah, beams, pillars, and friezes. Many other fine examples here are injured by several coats of tar having been laid over them in such a way as almost to obliterate the ancient carving, of which little or no trace is now visible. * * * There is now no wood-carver in Gaya able to do any work similar to these splendid remains. The mistries are mere carpenters, and very seldom receive orders for even common carving. * * * All the mistries, when not engaged on simple carpenter's constructive work, employ themselves making boxes of different sizes, inlaid with brass—a very common work indeed in this locality, for which there is always a demand, and from which they can earn from 8 to 12 annas per day."

From the preceding account it will be seen that the art of wood-carving is almost extinct in this district; and it is noticeable that the fine work referred to above is only found in the old town of Gayā, and not in the modern quarter. With a few exceptions, this carving possesses all the characteristics of the Burmese manner, and there is now no demand for good work of this kind.

Other manufactures.

The other manufactures are of little importance, with the exception of tobacco curing, which is an important local industry, although the leaf itself has to be imported, chiefly from Tirhut. The principal centres of manufacture are Gayā, Guruā and Paibīgha, the brand manufactured in the latter place being held in much esteem all over India; 30,000 maunds are exported annually. The other industries are those common all over the country, such as the manufacture of tiles and pottery by the village Kumhārs, of gold and silver ornaments by the Sonārs, and of oil by the Telis. The latter industry has however been seriously affected by competition; and though mustard and linseed continue to be pressed in the old-fashioned country mills, the manufacture of vegetable oils is everywhere suffering from the increasing use of mineral oils. Of these regular village artisans practically the only class which exports anything consists of the Chamārs, as hides are cured in many places for export, though there is no large tannery in the district.

MINES.

Mica.

The south-east corner of the district forms part of the mica-producing area of Bengal, which coincides with a great belt of schists and associated gneissose granite, some 12 miles broad and 60 miles long, stretching from Hazāribāgh through the south of the Nawāda subdivision into Monghyr. In this portion of the district there are 6 mica mines, situated at Singar, Sapahī, Basauni, and Belam, and in the Government estates of Chatkarī and Dubaur; but the mineral is also found in small quantities in other localities among the hills in the south on the border of Hazāribāgh. During the last 15 years the production of mica in Bengal has undergone a phenomenal development, in which this district has shared very fully. In 1891 the industry was almost non-existent, the total production in the whole Province being only valued at Rs. 87,000; whereas in 1904-05 the outturn in Gayā alone was 246 tons, valued at over 1½ lakh of rupees; of this amount, the Singar and Chatkarī mines produced 84 and 98 tons respectively. The methods of working are very simple. The seams are reached by blasting, and the sheets of mica are dug out with spade and pick, after which they are separated, clipped and sorted; they are then packed according to sizes and despatched to Calcutta for export to Europe and America. The industry gives employment to an average daily number of 1,269 persons, of whom 984 work below and 285 above ground; the labourers are drawn from the ordinary labouring classes and are paid a wage varying from two to six annas, according to age, sex and skill.

Iron ore is found in considerable quantities at Pachambā in the Nawāda subdivision and Lodhwe in the head-quarters subdivision, but is not worked there. It also exists in the Barābar Hills, where there were formerly smelting works under European management; it is now being worked again to a small extent. Granite, syenite and laterite are also quarried in many of the hills for building purposes and road metalling. The so-called Gayā black stone, of which ornaments, bowls and figures are carved, is, as already stated, quarried at Pathalkati in the Atrī thāna. Pottery clay exists in many places and nodules of limestone are found in scattered localities. Saltpetre is manufactured in the Jahānābād subdivision from efflorescence in the clay of village sites, but elsewhere the manufacture is merely nominal, owing to the fact that the soil is not saliferous.

TRADE. The district being almost purely agricultural, the chief trade consists of the various products of cultivation. The principal exports are cereals, pulses, oil-seeds, raw sugar, crude opium, *mahuā* fruit, saltpetre, mica, lac, blankets, carpets, stone and brass utensils, hides and manufactured tobacco. The principal imports are salt, coal and coke, piece-goods and shawls, kerosine-oil, tea, cotton, timber, tobacco (unmanufactured dry leaves), iron, spices of all kinds, dried and fresh fruits, refined sugar, paper and various articles of European manufacture.

Exports. According to the returns showing the export and import traffic, by far the most important articles of export are linseed, raw sugar, gram and pulse, these commodities accounting for seven-eighths for the total export trade. The quantity of linseed sent out of the district forms more than a third of the total exports, and nearly the whole of this finds its way to Calcutta and Howrah. The metropolitan districts, in fact, receive by far the greater part of the products exported, with the exception of rice, which is distributed among the other Bihār districts, and of raw sugar, which is consigned in large quantities to the Central Provinces, Central India, Eastern Bengal and the adjoining district of Monghyr. Among other exports, crude opium is taken to Patna, where it is manufactured in the Government factory; hides, mica and saltpetre to Calcutta; and blankets to Howrah and the districts of the Chotā Nāgpur Division. Lac is chiefly exported to Calcutta, Patna and Mirzāpur, manufactured tobacco to Patna and Howrah, and wood and *mahuā* flowers to Patna and Monghyr. Stoneware is taken to all parts of India by pilgrims, who visit Gayā in large numbers.

Imperial. Salt, piece-goods and other articles of European manufacture, tea, iron, spices and refined sugar are imported from Calcutta; coke and coal from the districts of Hazāribāgh and Mānbhum; kerosine-oil from the 24-Parganas; gunny-bags from Calcutta and Patna; shawls from Kashmīr and Rājputāna; cotton from the United Provinces; timber from Patna and Nepāl; bamboos from Patna; unmanufactured tobacco and fresh fruit from Patna and Muzaffarpur; and paper from Serampore, Bally and Calcutta.

Trade centres. The chief centres of trade are Gayā, Tekāri, Guruā, Rānīganj and Imāmganj in the head-quarters subdivision; Rajaulī and Akbarpur in the Nawāda subdivision; Jahānābād and Arwal in the Jahānabād subdivision, and Dāūdnagar, Deo, Mahārājganj, Khiriāwān, Rafiganj and Jamhor in the Aurangābād subdivision. Owing to the opening of new railways, which now tap most of the trade routes in the district, several other places are rising in importance, the most noticeable being Nawāda. Feeder roads have been constructed by the District Board wherever required, and trade tends to converge upon the railway stations. For the conveyance of produce, bullock carts are generally used, but pack-bullocks are also very largely employed, especially in the hilly parts.

Fairs.

There are a large number of fairs held in different parts of the year throughout the district, but most are only religious gatherings and of little importance from a commercial point of view. The greatest of these fairs are the Bisuā and Kārtik Purnamāshi fairs held at Salempur near Gayā, the Bisuā *melā* held at Rafiganj and the Sivarātri *melā* held at Deokund, at which a busy trade is driven in cattle, piece-goods, brassware, earthenware, and a variety of articles of country manufacture. The Bisuā fair at Salempur, which is held in the month of Chait (March-April), attracts about 15,000 people, and the fair held at the same time at Rafiganj attracts as many more; these are the largest cattle fairs in the district, and great numbers of cattle and horses are brought to them for sale. At the same time, there are smaller gatherings at Guruā to the south-west of Gayā, at Machendra in the Nawāda subdivision, and at the falls of Kakolat. The other great fair at Salempur, the Kārtik Purnamāshi, is strictly a bathing festival held in November on the last day of Kārtik, when about 10,000 people assemble to bathe in the Phalgu. Similar gatherings take place on the same day at Guruā, at Bharāri and Jahānābād in the subdivision of that name, and at Jamhor in the Aurangābād subdivision. The Sivarātri fairs at Deokund are held in commemoration of the marriage of Siva, and take place twice in the year, once in the month of Phāgun (February-March) and again in Baisākh (April-May); the number assembling on each occasion is estimated to amount to 20,000 or 30,000. Similar fairs are also held in Phāgun at Wazīrganj, Dumaria, Bārāchatti and Fatehpur in the head-quarters subdivision, and at Barāwān in Aurangābād.

Among other fairs there are two of considerable local importance. A large concourse of people, numbering about 4,000 or 5,000 persons, meet at the fair known as *Chhath* which is held at Deo twice a year, in October on the 22nd Kārtik and again in April on the 22nd Chait, in honour of the Sun god; and some 10,000 to 15,000 people assemble at the Aghani *melā* at Sītāmarhi which is held in December on the last day of Aghan in honour of Sīta, the wife of Rāma, who is said to have spent some time there during her exile. The only other fairs which call for separate mention are the Sankrānti *melā* held in the month of Māgh (January-February) on the Makara Sankrānti (the passage of the sun from Sagittarius to Capricornus) at the town of Gayā, at the hot springs of Tapoban near Wazīrganj, and at Jamhor and Umgā; and the *Anantchaudas*, celebrated in the month of Bhādo (August-September) in honour of Siva, when about 15,000 people gather at the Barābar Hills. The duration of these fairs varies from one to seven days, except those held at Umgā and Rafiganj, which last for two weeks.

Weights and Measures.

There is no uniform system of weights and measures in the Gayā district, as though the maund is recognized as equivalent to 8 *paserī* or 40 seers, both the *paserī* and the seer vary in different places. The *paserī*, though literally meaning 5 seers, ranges from 6 to 7½ seers according to local custom, and the seer again varies from 42 to 84 *tolās*. The standard seer of 80 *tolās* is universally recognized for the weighment of *gānja*, *bhāng*, opium and precious metals, but different localities give a different value to the seer in weighing other articles. The various values of the seer are reported to be as follows; in Aurangābād town, Gayā town and the Nawāda subdivision 42 and 72 *tolās*; in the Arwal thāna 44 *tolās*; in Tekāri, Rajaulī, Kauwākol and the head-quarters subdivision, 48 *tolās*; in Hasuā, 52 *tolās*; in the Pakrībarāwān thāna, 56 *tolās*; in Dāūdnagar, 80 *tolās*; in Nawāda town, 84 *tolās*; while in the case of wholesale goods the weight observed in Gayā is 82 *tolās*. On the other hand, the standard seer of 80 *tolās* is generally recognized for measures of capacity, and is held to be equivalent to 1·142 quarts. For measures of length the Government yard of 36 inches (called the *nambari gaz*) is used for cloth, side by side with various local yards, *e. g.*, the Gayā yard is 41 inches, that used in Nawāda and Hasuā towns is 40 inches, and elsewhere in the Nawāda subdivision it is 39 inches. For measuring lands and houses the *hāth*, or cubit, is in universal use, but its length varies from 16 to 20 inches; for measuring lands, the *bāns*, which generally is equivalent to six cubits or 108 inches, is employed; and for measuring walls house-builders have a yard, called the *Sikandari gaz*, equal to 33 inches.

CHAPTER XIV.

MEANS OF COMMUNICATION.

The account of the Gayā roads given by Buchanan Hamilton nearly 100 years ago presents a vivid picture of the deficiency of communications at that time. "During the rainy season," he says, "all internal commerce is at a complete standstill, as the roads are then so bad as not to admit of even cattle travelling with back loads. I have seen no country, that could be called at all civilized, where so little attention has been paid to this important subject, and even in the vicinity of the jails, where many convicts sentenced to labour are confined, very little has been done. The cross roads from market to market are those which are chiefly wanted, and no one who has not seen the condition of these could believe that a country so extremely populous and rich, and having such occasion for land conveyance, could be so ill provided. The object in such roads is not to enable gentlemen to drive their curricles, but to enable cattle carrying back loads to pass at all seasons from one market to another, and in the fair season to enable carts to do the same." This is not a very high standard of efficiency; but it is clear from the absence of local carts for the carriage of supplies during the Mutiny that there was but little improvement in the succeeding half century, though the Grand Trunk Road and the Patna-Gayā Road were important trade routes. The Collector, in his account of the events of 1857, speaks of the difficulty he had in supplying the indents made on him for carriage: all transport, he said, was carried on by means of small pack-bullocks, useless, on account of their size, for military purposes; he could hire no carts, and so had to make them. Altogether 85 carts were supplied in this way, and the fact that it was found impossible to hire such a small number of carts is a striking proof of the absence of good roads in the interior. This wretched condition of inaccessibility has long since passed away, and Gayā is now wonderfully well served with different means of communication. The Patna-Gayā canal passes along its western boundary for over 40 miles, the Grand Trunk Road runs along through the southern portion for nearly 70 miles, the interior is covered by a network of roads, and the map of the district is now intersected from north to south and from east to west with railway lines.

The present system of roads is a creation of the last half century. Fifty years ago the only road by which a traveller could go to Calcutta was the Grand Trunk Road, the only means of conveyance were the relays of carriages provided by various contractors, and the state of the country was so unsettled that constables had to be stationed in stage-huts built at short intervals. To the north the principal route open to traffic was the Patna-Gayā Road along which the railway now passes, but this was unmetalled, and in the rainy season communication with Patna was almost entirely interrupted. During the famine of 1866, when it was the one channel through which food could be brought in to feed the starving people, it was impassable, the population was cut off from supplies, and the severity of the famine was consequently aggravated. By 1875 this road had been metalled throughout its length, and there were but two other metalled roads, the Grand Trunk Road and the Bihār-Rajaulī Road. Three other roads only were considered of sufficient importance to deserve separate mention, viz., those from Gayā to Daūdnagar, to Sherghāti, and to Nawāda, and of the 97 miles they covered only 16 were metalled. Besides these, there were 8 other unmetalled roads of less importance with a total length of 163 miles, and most of these had been constructed or put into working order during the famine of 1874. ROADS.

At the present time, the district is intersected by a number of excellent roads which place every part of it within easy reach of the markets. The expenditure on original works during the quinquennium 1900—04 has been Rs. 3,19,000 and on repairs Rs. 3,64,000; and Gayā is now richer in metalled roads than any district in the Patna Division except Shāhābād. The District Board maintains 30 metalled roads, 69 unmetalled roads and 193 village roads with a length of 163, 715 and 628 miles, respectively, and in addition to these there are 67 miles of metalled and 168 miles of unmetalled roads in the charge of the Public Works Department. The most important of these roads is the Grand Trunk Road, maintained from Provincial funds, which passes through the south of the district for a distance of 65 miles. It enters Gayā from the Hazāribāgh district near Bhalua, and leaves it by a great causeway in the bed of the Son at Bārun, crossing on its way the broad streams of the Mohāna, Morhar, Batāne and Pūnpūn, and passing the trade centres of Bārāchatti, Sherghāti and Aurangābād. The other roads of greatest importance are those running from Gayā to various parts of the district, such as that joining the Grand Trunk Road at Dobhī, and the roads to Dāūdnagar and to Sherghāti, the latter and its continuation to Imāmganj and Dumaria being the chief line connecting Gayā and Palāmau before the opening of the new line of railway from Bārun to Daltonganj. Some roads leading from Gayā, which were formerly the principal trade routes, such as those to Aurangābād, Jahānābād and Nawāda, have now lost much of their importance owing to the railway lines which run parallel to or alongside them, though they still serve a useful purpose as feeder roads. In the interior traffic is heaviest along the road from Jahānābād to Arwal (21 miles) and that running for 24 miles from Rajaulī to Nawāda and thence across the border at Kharhāt to Bihār, which brings down the produce of the hills.

Much of the internal trade of the district is still carried very largely by pack-bullocks, as the villages off the roads are not accessible to carts in all months of the year. The irrigation channels spread out in all directions, and the nature of the soil, which, being largely composed of clay, becomes very heavy when wet, precludes bullock carts from travelling about with the same ease and freedom as in North Bihār. It is not until the cold weather that the interior of the country is opened out to them, and during the rains pack-bullocks ply to and from the villages. They are also largely in request in the broken hilly country to the south, where the only carts in use are low, strong carts with solid wooden wheels suitable for the rough country which they have to cross. Elsewhere the carts in use are similar to those used in other parts of Bihār. The light springless carts known as *ekkās* are common, and along a few roads away from the railway there are camel carts carrying passengers and goods, Gayā being one of the districts furthest south in which camels thrive and can be usefully employed.

Roadside arboriculture. Great activity has been shown in recent years in planting roadside avenues along the principal roads. In the quinquennium ending in 1904-05 the expenditure on the planting of trees and the establishment of nurseries was greater than in any other district in the Division. It is estimated that 138 miles of roads require to be planted, though it is doubtful if any road can be said to have been completely planted, as the avenues are seldom continuous for a complete mile, and there are many gaps where the trees have died out. A programme has been prepared, under which 69 miles are to be planted by the end of 1907-08, and this programme is being worked up to.

The district is singularly well served by railways, which have made the head-quarters station the centre of a number of radiating lines and of a busy railway system. It has for many years been the terminus of the Patna-Gayā Railway, but within the last few years no less than 3 new lines have been opened, and one more is now under construction. To the north, the Patna-Gayā Railway connects it with the main line of the East Indian Railway at Bankipore, 34½ miles of it and 6 stations besides Gayā lying within the district. To the east the South Bihār Railway runs east from Gayā to Lakhisarai through the Nawāda subdivision, 58 miles of the line and 9 stations falling within the district. To the east is the Mughalsarai-Gayā Railway running from Gayā through the Aurangābād subdivision to Mughalsarai, 51 miles of the line and 7 stations lying within Gayā; and to the south-west the Bārun-Daltonganj Railway takes off at Bārun on the Son, and, passing by Nabīnagar, runs a distance of 23¼ miles before it enters the Palāmau district. A fifth line running through the south-east of the district from Gayā to Katrāsgarh is now under construction, of which 34 miles will fall within Gayā district. When completed, this line will, with the Mughalsarai-Gayā line, form the Grand Chord line to Calcutta. RAILWAYS.

None of the rivers, except the Son, are navigable, and navigation on that river is intermittent and of little commercial importance. In the dry season the small depth of water prevents boats of more than 20 maunds proceeding up-stream, while the violent floods in the rains equally deter large boats, though boats of 500 or 600 maunds occasionally sail up it. Except one or two streams which retain a little water in the dry season, the rivers are only filled during the rains, and even then the water passes off in a few days. When they are in flood, they quickly become unfordable, and, as a rule, no boats are obtainable, except at the ferries which are few and far between. The country people however provide a ready substitute in the shape of light rafts, called *gharnais*, made of a light framework of bamboos supported on inverted earthenware pots (*gharā*). Besides this, the District Board maintains ferries across the larger rivers, where they are not bridged. The most important ferry is that across the Son from Dāūdnagar to Nāsriganj in Shāhābād. On the Patna-Gayā canal a small steamer plies weekly, but there is not much traffic. WATER COMMUNICATIONS.

There are altogether 712 miles of postal communication and 76 post-offices in the district. The number of postal articles delivered in 1904-05 was 1,095,648, including letters, post-cards, packets, newspapers and parcels; the value of the money-orders issued was over 15 lakhs, and of those paid nearly 24 lakhs, and POSTAL COMMUNICATIONS.

the total amount of Savings Bank deposits was Rs. 2,10,000. There are also 8 telegraph offices, from which 21,800 messages were issued in the year; these offices are situated at Gayā, Arwal, Aurangābād, Bārun, Dāūdnagar, Jahānābād, Nawāda and Tekāri.

CHAPTER XV.

LAND REVENUE ADMINISTRATION.

EARLY ENGLISH ADMINISTRATION.

WHEN the *Dīwāni* or fiscal administration of the three Provinces of Bihār, Bengal, and Orissa was granted to the East India Company in 1765 by the Emperor Shāh Alam, a dual system of government was inaugurated, by which the English received the revenues and undertook to maintain the army, while the criminal jurisdiction, or Nizāmat, was vested in the Nawāb. But, though the civil and military power of the country and the resources for maintaining it were assumed on the part of the Company, it was not thought prudent to vest the direct management of the revenue in the hands of Europeans whose previous training in mercantile affairs had not qualified them to deal with the intricacies of the revenue system. Accordingly, they continued the existing system of administration, and until 1769 a native *Naib* or Deputy *Dīwān* conducted the collection of the revenue under the nominal control of the European Chief at Patna. In 1769 Supervisors were appointed in subordination to the Chief to superintend the native officers employed in collecting the revenue and administering justice, and in the succeeding year a Revenue Council of Control was established at Patna. When, however, the Court of Directors sent out orders in 1771 "to stand forth as *Dīwān* and by the agency of the Company's servants to take upon themselves the entire care and management of the revenues," the *Naib Dīwān* at Patna was removed, and it was decided to substitute European for native agency. The Supervisors were now designated Collectors, and a native officer styled *Dīwān* was associated with each in the "superintendency of the revenues." In the following year, it was determined to make a five years' settlement of Bihār, and the zamīndārs having declined to accept a farm of the revenues of their districts, the system of putting them up to public competition was attempted. A body of speculators, called renters, accordingly sprang up, and farmed the revenue till 1777, the zamīndārs themselves receiving an annuity of 10 per cent. (*mālikānā*) on their collections. The experiment proved a failure, as these speculators, ignorant of the real capabilities of the country and incited by the hopes of profit, readily agreed for sums which they were utterly unable to pay; and on the expiry of the settlement it was determined to introduce the system of yearly farms. This arrangement only intensified the mischief; the renters had no assurance that they would hold the farm another year or even have time to collect the current demand; they exacted as much as they could extort in the shortest time possible; and knowing that they would be imprisoned for any arrears, they made every endeavour to amass a fortune as soon as they could.

The *Dīwān* of the Company, Rājā Kalyān Singh, exercised arbitrary powers over the zamīndārs, confining them and confiscating their estates practically at his pleasure, and the authority of his *Naib Dīwān*, Rājā Kheāli Rām Singh, was almost as extensive. Rājā Mitrājīt Singh of Tekāri was placed under close arrest by the latter, who sent a Government agent to manage his estate; Rājā Narāyan Singh, the zamīndār of Siris and Kutumbā, was imprisoned and ousted from his property; and Rājā Akbar Alī Khān of Narhat and Samai was put under arrest at Patna. Such being the state of affairs, the zamīndārs being liable to be imprisoned and dispossessed of their estates at any moment for arrears of revenue, it is not surprising that when Chait Singh's rebellion broke out in 1781, some of the discontented chiefs took sides against the English, to whose mismanagement they naturally attributed their misfortunes. As soon as the rebellion started, Akbar Alī Khān made his escape from Patna, and going to Nawāda, raised a force of 4,000 or 5,000 matchlockmen, with which he proceeded to plunder the country. A small expedition was sent out to quell the insurrection and capture the rebel, but it was not till large reinforcements had arrived that he was driven out to the Kharagpur hills in Monghyr. Narāyan Singh also took advantage of the confusion to raise the standard of revolt, and took the field with a body of 1,500 troops against Major Crawfurd, who was then on the march to Bijaigarh. The English commander avoided him and got through to the Kaimur hills, but next year he received orders to seize the traitor, and shutting up every road and *ghāt* on the river Son by which Narāyan Singh could retreat, left him only the alternative of surrendering to him or delivering himself at Patna. The rebel chief adopted the latter course, and was finally sent as a State prisoner to Dacca.

In the meantime, the whole of Bihār had been settled with Kalyān Singh, who proceeded to divide the settlement with Kheāli

Rām Singh. Neither of them, however, was in a position to manage such a large extent of country, and they were forced to let out the *parganas* to farmers or sub-renters called *āmils*. In many cases the ancient families of zamīndārs secured the farms, but in others the *āmils* were strangers and speculators, with no local influence or prestige, and utterly ignorant of the people and their rights. Sepoys had to be sent to assist them in enforcing payment; they collected the rents at the point of the bayonet, wrangled with the local zamīndārs on the one hand, oppressed the ryots on the other, and embezzled as much as they could. The *āmils* had to be constantly changed, no less than six being employed one after the other in Siris and Kutumbā in 1783; and the practical result of this system may be gathered from a report of the Revenue Chief in 1782, in which he stated that he could get no one to accept the farm of Narhat and Samai, as "the confusion occasioned by the variety of *aumils* sent into these *parganas* has lessened the number of ryots very considerably, and cultivation is entirely neglected."

ADMINISTRATIVE CHANGES.

These disastrous experiments in revenue administration were not finally ended till the decennial settlement was concluded in 1790 and declared to be permanent in 1793. In justice, however, to the officers responsible for the administration, it should be said that proper supervision was practically impossible owing to the smallness of the staff and the vast territory under their control. Till 1774 the European Collectors controlled the revenue administration, and also exercised a general superintendence over the Criminal and Civil Courts; but in that year they were withdrawn, and their duties were transferred to a Revenue Council established at Patna, while the administration of justice was entrusted to native officers. This Council again was abolished in 1781, and its President or Revenue Chief was appointed Collector under the orders of the Committee of Revenue in Calcutta. His jurisdiction was enormous, as it included Tirhut, Shāhābād and Bihār, *i. e.*, the modern district of Patna and the northern portion of Gayā; but for judicial purposes Bihār was now formed into a district, a covenanted Judge-Magistrate being placed in charge of the civil and criminal jurisdiction. Five years afterwards the powers of the Collector, Civil Judge and Magistrate were vested in the same person, but for criminal cases the real power was left with the native Judges till 1793. The offices of Judge and Collector were then again separated, and the district of Bihār had one civilian as Civil Judge and Magistrate, and a second as Collector under the Board of Revenue. At the same time, native Munsifs were appointed to hear and decide, in the first instance, suits relating to personal property not exceeding the value of Rs. 100, appeals from their decisions lying to the Civil Judge.

Formation of the district.

The whole of the south of Gayā was included in Rāmgarh, a huge amorphous district, including practically the whole of Chotā Nāgpur and stretching on the south to Jashpur, Gāngpur and Singhbhūm. This district, we are told,* was "long distinguished for the numerous crimes and devastation which occasioned annually the loss of many good soldiers from the unhealthiness of the country. The residence of the Magistrate was usually above the ghauts or passes into the mountains, and circumstances frequently rendered his visiting places also within the ghauts necessary. In this predicament it became difficult for him to exercise an effectual control over the territory adjoining to Bahar proper, which state of things would naturally suggest the expediency of transferring all such places to the latter district. But here obstacles presented themselves, the jurisdiction of Bahar being already so extensive, that the management of any addition of magnitude would be utterly beyond the natural powers of any single Judge and Magistrate. To obviate this objection as far as practicable, it was recommended that a Joint-Magistrate should be stationed at Sherighautty." This proposal was sanctioned, and in 1814 a special Joint-Magistrate was stationed at Sherghāti with jurisdiction over the southern portion of Gayā, the remainder being still included in the district of Bihār.

For revenue purposes, the Collector was subordinate to the Board of Commissioners in Bihār and Benares, and for judicial purposes there were native Munsifs under a Judge-Magistrate from whom again an appeal lay to the Provincial Civil Court at Patna; this Court and also the Board were abolished in 1829, and their powers were vested in a Commissioner at Patna acting under the orders of the Board in Calcutta. It was not till 1825 that Bihār was constituted a separate Collectorate, and in 1831 the Judge-Magistrate of Gayā was given increased powers as a Sessions Judge; and his magisterial powers being made over to the Collector, the present unit of administration, the Magistrate-Collector, was created. In 1845 the offices of Magistrate and Collector were separated, to be again reunited in 1859 by the orders of the Secretary of State. Finally, the district of Gayā was created in 1865 out of parts of the old districts of Bihār and Rāmgarh, the subdivision of Bihār with an area of nearly 800 square miles being transferred to the Patna district; six years later the *parganas* of Japlā and Belaunjā, containing 650 square miles, were annexed to Lohārdagā (now Palāmau); and in 1875 an area of 6 square miles was transferred to Hazāribāgh.

* Description of Hindostan, by Walter Hamilton, 1820.

In 1789 the demand of land revenue for the district of Bihār was Rs. 10,41,700, payable by 744 estates with 1,160 proprietors; but the area of the district did not correspond with that of the present district of Gayā, and of the 41 *parganas* which were included in it, 16 have since been transferred to Patna, two (Japlā and Belaunjā) to Palāmau, and one (Amarthu) to Monghyr. In 1870-71, when the district was practically the same as at present, the total demand of land revenue was Rs. 13,80,320, payable by 4,411 estates owned by 20,453 proprietors. Since that time the demand has increased but little, but on the other hand the number of estates and proprietors has grown very largely, owing to the extraordinary rapidity with which proprietary rights have been subdivided under the operation of the law of succession, and of modern legislation regarding partition and land registration which causes such minute subdivisions to be recorded. In 1881-82 the current demand had risen to Rs. 14,36,900, payable by 5,614 estates and 59,172 proprietors, and in 1900-01 to Rs. 14,80,700 due from 7,514 estates owned by 72,404 proprietors. The average payment from each estate has thus fallen during the three decades ending in that year from Rs. 313 to Rs. 256 and Rs. 197, and the payment from each proprietor from Rs. 37-8 to Rs. 24-4, and finally to Rs. 20-8. In 1904-05 the demand amounted to Rs. 14,85,300 payable by 8,044 estates, of which 7,996 with a demand of Rs. 13,39,700 were permanently settled, 14 with a demand of Rs. 41,200 were temporarily settled, the remainder being held direct by Government. **GROWTH OF LAND REVENUE.**

Roughly speaking, the land-owners of Gayā pay a land revenue of 8 annas and receive from their ryots Rs. 3 an acre. Thus the land revenue demand is 16 per cent. of the total rent demand, or over 80 per cent. is profit. The amount of profit even in 1812 attracted Buchanan Hamilton's attention, and we find him writing: "Although the people of this district are very cautious in speaking of their affairs, it is very generally admitted, even by themselves, that the owners of the assessed lands have very considerable profits; nor do they scruple to admit that it far exceeds the estimate of the one-tenth of the revenue, which was supposed to be the profit that they were to have by the settlement." **Incidence of land revenue.**

The Government estates mentioned above extend over an area of 102 square miles and comprise 118 villages. They may be roughly divided into three groups, the escheated property of Ekbāl Bahādur, the Sarwa Mahāl, and the Nawāda group. **GOVERNMENT ESTATES.**

The first group passed to Government in 1879 by escheat, in consequence of the death without heirs of Ekbāl Bahādur, the son of a Muhammadan mistress of Mod Narāyan, the Rājā of Tekāri. It is composed of 28 villages, called the Dakhner Mahāl, in which Government has $8\frac{1}{2}$ annas interest; of a group of six villages, of which five are near Tekāri and one is in the Belā thāna; of nine villages constituting the Ghenjan Mahāl, situated 7 miles west of Makhdumpur; and of three villages some 5 miles west of Jahānābād.

The large and extensive tract called the Sarwa Mahāl comprises 47 villages, with an area of 31,284 acres, to the south of Gayā; most of them are at a distance of 11 miles from the town, but a few are situated on the southern border of the district. These villages came into the possession of Government about the year 1842, owing to the refusal of the former proprietors to take settlement of them.

The third group of estates contains 25 villages in the Nawāda subdivision, comprising an area of 16,282 acres. The history of fifteen only is traceable; three were escheated to Government in 1820 on the death of the proprietor, a descendant of Kāmgār Khān, a military adventurer of the 18th century, to whom they once belonged; and twelve were confiscated in 1841, on account of the part taken in a daring dacoity by their former proprietor, a zamīndār of Hazāribāgh. The latter villages, which are known as the Dubaur Mahāl, are situated in the extreme south of the Nawāda subdivision; they are mostly jungle and hills, but contain valuable mica mines. Produce-rents prevail in altogether 64 of these villages, and cash-rents are paid in the remainder, the total annual average income derived from them being Rs. 1,35,100.

SURVEYS AND SETTLEMENTS.

These estates were cadastrally surveyed, and a record of rights was prepared during the years 1893 to 1898; and at the same time the Belkhara Mahāl in the north-west of the district and the property belonging to the 9 annas share of the Tekāri Rāj, then in the charge of the Court of Wards, were brought under survey and settlement. The whole tract thus dealt with included 758 villages extending over an area of 582 square miles, and the cost of the operations was $2\frac{1}{2}$ lakhs.

In 1838 a demarcation survey of the district was carried out, in which the boundaries of villages and estates were defined and a compass and chain survey was made. This was followed by the professional village survey of 1838-44, which Government undertook with the object of making a scientific survey of the village boundaries and of preparing a map showing the geographical and topographical features of the country. The area commanded by the Son Canals in the north-west of the district was cadastrally surveyed in connection with the survey made for irrigation purposes in 1876-77; and recently survey and settlement operations have been extended to the Deo and Maksudpur estates. The former estate, which covers an area of 92 square miles, mostly in the Aurangābād subdivision, was settled in the years 1900—03. The latter includes 160 villages, covering 130 square miles; about 50 square miles are in the Atrī thāna, forming a fairly compact block, and another 60 square miles are to be found in and about Rajaulī. In this estate the proceedings commenced in 1900 and were concluded in 1904 at a net expenditure of Rs. 75,000, or Rs. 577 per square mile.

LAND TENURES.

In Gayā, as elsewhere in Bengal, a longer or shorter chain of intermediate landholders is generally to be found. At one end of the chain stands the proprietor or *mālik*, who holds the estate from Government under the Permanent Settlement, and pays his land-tax direct to the Government Treasury. At the other end is the actual cultivator, called the *jotdār* or *kāshtkār*. There are a number of intermediate tenures between the *mālik* and the actual cultivator, the majority of which partake of a *zar-i-peshgī* nature, *i.e.*, they have been granted by the zamīndār in consideration of a money advance or mortgage on loan, *e.g.*, the *mukararī*, which is a lease from the *mālik* at a fixed rental, after the payment of an installation fee called *nazarāna*. This lease is either permanent, in which case it is called *istimrārī* or *barfarzandān* (from generation to generation), or it is only granted for the life of the lease-holder, in which case it is called *hinhiyātī*. In addition to the *nazarāna*, the lease-holder has sometimes to pay an advance (*zar-i-peshgī*) as security for the payment of the rent. *Dar mukararī* is an exactly similar lease to the above, granted by the *mukararīdār* to a third party. The holder of any of the preceding permanent tenures may either cultivate the land with his own labour, in which case the holding is called *nij-jot;* or with hired labour, in which case it is called *sir;* or he may make over the land to another for a fixed term, which gives rise to a number of subordinate tenures. *Thīkā* or *ijārā* is the common term for a sub-lease for a definite term. The holder of a *thīkā* obtains the estate either from the *mālik* or *mukararīdār* and has to pay an advance, on getting possession, and afterwards a fixed rent till the expiration of the term for which the lease has been taken. The *thīkādār* or *ijārādār* takes the place of the proprietor, who can only interfere on the ground that his ultimate rights are being prejudiced, or on the lease-holder failing to pay the fixed rent. The sub-lessee holding a lease from the *thīkādār* is called a *katkanādār*, and the tenure held by him a *katkanā;* and lower down still in the chain of sub-infeudation is the *darkatkanādār* who has a subordinate tenure under the *katkanādār*.

Thīkādārī system.

The *thīkādārī* system is an important feature in the system of land tenure prevalent in Gayā. In most cases it owes its origin to the large number of *bhāoli* tenures and the constant and detailed supervision on the part of the landlord which the tenure entails. This he is unable to give himself, and he prefers the certain income from the *thīkādār* to the fluctuating one dependent on the peculations of unchecked servants. As stated in Chapter XI, this system of letting out estates on lease is, as a rule, objectionable in many respects and detrimental to the interests of both landlords and tenants. It is, how ver, justified in some cases, *e.g.*, where the *thīkādār* is the *bonâ fide* representative of the ryots, and is amenable to public opinion in the village ; or where he is a better and less oppressive landlord than the proprietor, and is strong enough to obtain his lease on fair terms ; or where, on the contrary, the proprietor is a good and strong landlord, and is able to retain a firm hold on his village even during the course of the lease, and to prevent any alteration in the rents of the ryots or any modification of their rights in their lands. In such cases, there are advantages in the *thīkādārī* system. Its disadvantages are, however, very numerous, and it has been abandoned in the Government estates, where it has been proved that the direct management of a large property paying *bhāoli* rents is perfectly feasible. Direct management necessitates the upkeep of a highly-paid local agency, but even this is more economical than the middleman ; and the experiment has met with fair success from the proprietor's point of view, while it is in every respect desirable in the tenants' interests.

The peculiar tenures which exist under the *bhāoli* and *nagdi* systems obtaining in this district have been already described in Chapter XI, and the only other tenures calling for special mention are the rent-free or *lākhirāj* tenures. These were once very numerous, and Buchanan Hamilton estimated that over one-third of the tenures in Bihār were free of revenue. Most of these have been resumed, but some still exist of a special nature, such as *altamghā* grants (from *āl*, red, and *tamghā*, a seal) or lands given in perpetuity as a reward for conspicuous military service, *madadmāsh* grants (from *madad*, assistance, and *māsh*, livelihood) or lands granted to favourites and others for their personal expenses, and *digwār* (*i.e.*, warder) lands assigned for the maintenance of guard and patrol on roads and passes.

CHAPTER XVI.

GENERAL ADMINISTRATION.

THE revenue administration of the district is in charge of the Collector under the Commissioner of the Patna Division; and for general administrative purposes it is divided into four subdivisions with head-quarters at Gayā, Aurangābād, Jahānābād and Nawāda. The bulk of the revenue work is done at the head-quarters station, where there is a staff consisting generally of three or four Deputy Collectors, besides some officers employed on special branches of work, such as a special Excise Deputy Collector and a Deputy Collector in charge of partition work. A Joint-Magistrate is usually deputed to the district for the cold-weather months, and occasionally also an Assistant Collector and one or two Sub-Deputy Collectors. The other subdivisions are in charge of Deputy Collectors, designated Subdivisional Officers, who are sometimes assisted by Sub-Deputy Collectors. The oldest of these subdivisions is the Nawāda subdivision, which was created in 1845; the Aurangābād subdivision was constituted in 1865; and the Jahānābād subdivision was established in 1872, when the old Sherghāti subdivision was abolished. ADMINISTRATIVE CHARGES AND STAFF.

The revenue of the district was Rs. 24,91,228 in 1880-81 (when the tncome-tax had not been imposed), Rs. 24,81,768 in 1890-91, and Rs. 28,51,857 in 1900-01. In 1904-05 it amounted to Rs. 31,96,444, of which nearly half (Rs. 14,71,294) was derived from land revenue, the other main heads of income being excise (Rs. 7,10,573), cesses (Rs. 5,60,940), stamps (Rs. 3,71,567) and income-tax (Rs. 82,070). REVENUE.

The excise revenue is, as usual, derived from imported liquors, country spirits, *tāri*, opium, and the duty and license fees on hemp drugs. A statement of the various exciseable articles and of the sums realized from them in the decade 1893—1902 is given in the Statistical Appendix, from which it will be apparent that the income from this source has been fairly constant, except for the three lean years 1896—99, when it fell below 6 lakhs. It has now risen to over 7 lakhs, and the revenue thus derived is greater Excise.

than in any other Bengal district, except the adjoining district of Patna.

Drinking in Bengal is largely indulged in by Hindī-speaking races, aborigines and mixed tribes, and consumption also varies inversely with the proportion of Muhammadans in the population. Gayā is a Hindī-speaking district; a large portion of the inhabitants are of aboriginal descent, and the number of Musalmāns is small. It is not surprising therefore that the natives of the district are on the whole hard drinkers, over six-sevenths of the whole excise income being derived from the country spirit prepared by distillation from the flower of the *mahuā*-tree (*Bassia latifolia*) and molasses, and from the fermented palm juice called *tāri*. The consumption of the latter is indeed greater than in any other Bengal district, and the gross receipts from this liquor and country spirit aggregate over Rs. 3,000 for every 10,000 of the population, as compared with the Divisional average of Rs. 1,778. The manufacture and sale of country spirit are carried on under what is known as the dual system, *i.e.*, there is a central distillery at the head-quarters station, which serves the town of Gayā and a certain area round it, and outstills for the supply of the rest of the district; the average consumption of outstill liquor is 98, and of distillery liquor 325 proof gallons per mille, the incidence of taxation per head of the population being annas 3-3 and 12-7 respectively. There are 19 shops for the sale of distillery liquor and 178 outstills selling outstill liquor, *i.e.*, one retail shop for the sale of country spirit to every 10,456 persons; and besides these, there are 2,295 shops licensed to sell *tāri* or one shop to every 897 persons. Imported liquors have found no favour with the mass of the population, both because they are unable to afford them and because they prefer the country spirit and *tāri* they have drunk for generations past; and the receipts from the license fees only amount to Rs. 1,476, as compared with nearly 5 lakhs derived from country spirit and Rs. 1,36,000 obtained from fermented *tāri*. The receipts from hemp drugs are comparatively insignificant, amounting to only Rs. 72,260, and are less than in any other Bihār district. Of this sum, over Rs. 63,000 is obtained from the duty and license fees on *gānja*, *i.e.*, the dried flowering tops of the cultivated female hemp plant (*Cannabis sativa*), and the resinous exudation on them. Less than Rs. 10,000 is obtained from the consumption of opium; and though the use of *bhāng*, *i.e.*, the dried leaves of the hemp plant, is more common than in any other Bengal district, the income derived from it is under Rs. 9,000.

Cesses.

The road and public works cesses are, as usual, levied at the maximum rate of one anna in the rupee, and the current demand in 1904-05 was Rs. 5,43,481, the greater part of which (Rs. 5,16,614) was payable by 17,492 revenue-paying estates, while the remainder was payable by 307 revenue-free estates, 6,073 rent-free lands and 15 mines and railways; the total collection of both current and arrear demand was Rs. 5,60,940. The number of tenures assessed to cesses was 9,699, while the number of recorded shareholders of estates and of tenures was 68,219 and 33,035 respectively. A revaluation of the entire district was undertaken in 1901 and was completed in two batches. The revised assessment in the first batch took effect from the 1st April 1903, and that in the second batch from the 1st April 1904. The operations cost Rs. 17,768, and the increase of the cess due to this revaluation was Rs. 53,000.

Stamps.

The revenue from stamps ranks next in importance as a source of income to that derived from cesses. During the ten years ending in 1904-05 it rose from Rs. 2,66,000 (1894-95) to Rs. 3,71,000, the increase being mainly due to the growing demand for judicial stamps which brought in Rs. 2,89,000, as compared with Rs. 1,97,000 ten years previously. The increase in their sale has been steadily progressive, and has presumably been caused by the growth of litigation, as the proceeds from the sale of court-fee stamps alone have grown by over Rs. 85,000 and now amount to Rs. 2,64,000. The revenue derived from non-judicial stamps has stood practically still during the same period, and has risen only from Rs. 69,000 to Rs. 82,000.

Income-tax.

From the Statistical Appendix it will be observed that in 1901-02 the income-tax yielded altogether Rs. 77,211, paid by 2,471 assessees, of whom 1,622 paying Rs. 18,243 had incomes of Rs. 500 to Rs. 1,000. At that time the minimum income assessable was Rs. 500, but this was raised in 1903 to Rs. 1,000 per annum; and the number of assessees consequently fell in 1903-04 to 1,015 and the net collections to Rs. 76,067. In 1904-05 the amount of the tax increased to Rs. 82,070 paid by 1,078 assessees, a sum larger than in any of the districts of the Patna Division except Patna (Rs. 84,006). Of the assessees, 429 are inhabitants of Gayā town, and they pay over half the total amount, but the incidence of taxation is only three-fifths of an anna per head. The realizations are chiefly on account of grain and money-lending, the renting of houses, and trade.

Registration.

There are six offices for the registration of assurances under Act III of 1877, viz., Gayā, Aurangābād, Jahānābād, Nawāda, Sherghāti and Tekāri. At the head-quarters station the Special Sub-Registrar deals, as usual, with the documents presented there, and assists the District Magistrate, who is *ex-officio* Registrar, in supervising the proceedings of the Rural Sub-Registrars who are in charge of the other registration offices. The marginal statement shows the number of documents registered and the receipts and expenditure at each office in 1904. The number of registrations has increased but little since 1894, when 7,726 documents were registered. It is, in fact, far less than in any other Bihār district, the reason apparently being that the prevalence of the *bhāoli* system results in a paucity of formal transactions in the transfer and leasing of holdings.

NAME.	Documents registered.	Receipts.	Expenditure.
		Rs.	Rs.
Gayā ...	3,658	19,282	4,360
Aurangābād ...	1,302	2,901	1,055
Jahānābād ...	1,288	3,506	1,140
Nawāda ...	866	2,448	830
Sherghāti ...	391	1,341	610
Tekāri ...	967	1,830	868
TOTAL ...	8,472	31,308	8,863

ADMINISTRATION OF JUSTICE.

Civil Justice.

The judicial staff entertained for the purposes of civil justice consists of the District Judge, two Sub-Judges and four Munsifs; all of these officers are stationed at the head-quarters station, except one Munsif who holds his court at Aurangābād and has a separate jurisdiction. Statistics of the civil work will be found in the Statistical Appendix, and it will be sufficient to state that the classes of cases most common in the district are suits for the partition of revenue-paying estates, suits involving questions of easements regarding the irrigation of land, and rent suits relating to land held under the *bhāoli* system of cultivation.

Criminal Justice.

Criminal justice is administered by the District and Sessions Judge, the District Magistrate and the various Deputy and Sub-Deputy Magistrates at the head-quarters and subdivisional stations. The sanctioned staff at Gayā consists, in addition to the District Magistrate, of four Deputy Magistrates of the first class and one Deputy Magistrate of the second or third class. Besides these officers, an Assistant Magistrate and a Sub-Deputy Magistrate exercising second or third class powers are sometimes posted to the head-quarters station, and a special Magistrate is authorized, under section 14 of the Criminal Procedure Code, to try cases connected with breaches of the Irrigation laws. The Subdivisional Officers at Aurangābād, Jahānābād and Nawāda are almost invariably officers vested with first-class powers, and they are sometimes assisted by Sub-Deputy Magistrates of the second class. There are also Benches of Honorary Magistrates at Gayā (27 members), Aurangābād (6 members), Dāūdnagar (5 members), Jahānābād (9 members), Nawāda (7 members) and Tekāri (6 members), all of which exercise second-class powers, except those at Jahānābād and Tekāri, which have third-class powers only.

In all there are 60 Honorary Magistrates, of whom six are authorized to sit singly. Statistics showing the work of the criminal courts will be found in the Statistical Appendix.

Gayā was formerly notorious for the prevalence of crime, specially in the southern portion included in Rāmgarh. Here we are told,* the destruction of many old forts had to be "recommended by the Magistrate at an early period of the British domination, as they afforded protection to the refractory zamindars and hordes of irregular banditti. Theft is common throughout Rāmgarh, but murder more prevalent among a particular class, which are the slaves possessed by persons inhabiting the mountainous and inaccessible interior, and of savage and ferocious habits. When petty disputes occur, these slaves are compelled by their masters to perpetrate any enormity, and are more especially employed for the purposes of assassination. Any hesitation or repugnance on the part of the slave is attended with immediate death, which is equally his fate should he fail in the attempt. On the other hand, if he succeed, he is sought out by the officers of Government and executed as a murderer. The usual police have hitherto been unable to seize the cowardly instigator, and if recourse be had to a military force, he retires into the jungle. On the occurrence of such an event, the whole country is thrown into confusion and rebellion, during which many unoffending persons lose their lives; and the troops, after many ineffectual efforts to execute the Magistrate's orders, return to their stations, worn out with fatigue, and their numbers thinned by the pestilential atmosphere of the jungles." Crime.

Dacoities were extremely common, the gangs of dacoits being sometimes led by zamīndārs; highway robberies were even more frequent, and the generally unruly state of this tract finally made it necessary to appoint a special Joint-Magistrate at Sherghāti in order to cope more effectually with the elements of disorder. The north of the district was more settled, but even here there was little real security of person and property. In 1789 a gang of 200 robbers,† armed with swords, spears and bows, were able to make a raid into the town of Gayā itself; and having stationed guards to prevent the communication of intelligence to the European Magistrate, they surrounded and plundered the houses of two bankers, and after murdering upwards of 20 persons made off with their booty. Even at a later period, it is stated:*—"The number of crimes originating in the Bahar district, of which Gaya is the capital, may in great measure be attributed to the

* Description of Hindostan, by Walter Hamilton, 1820.

† Memoir of the Ghazeepoor District, by Wilton Oldham, 1876.

vast crowd of pious and superstitious pilgrims. The wealth these persons possess generally consists of money, jewels and other articles, which excite the cupidity of the unprincipled, while the defenceless position of the greater number of these stragglers exhibits it to them as a prey of easy acquisition."

This state of affairs has now passed away; and though dacoities are still sometimes committed, the most general offences are ordinary housebreaking and cattle theft, and riots caused by disputes about irrigation. Here, as elsewhere in Bihār, housebreaking is one of the commonest and easiest forms of crime. The soft mud walls of the houses, the weary sleep of the inmates, the negligence (or often the acquiescence) of the *chaukīdārs* combine with the adroitness of the burglar to render his trade easy and his arrest a rare occurrence. Further, the property stolen generally consists of brass utensils, trumpery ornaments, clothing, cash, or grain; and when the same pattern prevails throughout the district, the identification of the property is as difficult as the concealment of it is easy. Cattle-lifting is another common form of crime, practised chiefly by Goālās, and this district has long been notorious for its prevalence; it is more frequent than would appear from the statistics of convictions both because of the difficulty of tracing the offenders, who remove the stolen cattle to great distances, and also because it is usual for the thieves to restore them for a consideration. Cattle-theft is in fact recognized by the people as part of an organized system of levying blackmail (called in this case *panhā*); they frequently know to whom to apply, and hence a considerable portion of the cases which actually occur are not reported. Disputes about land and irrigation are a fruitful source of offences against the public tranquillity; and violent breaches of the peace are common when the crops are on the ground or the reservoirs are full of water. Two known cases of *satī* occurred in the years 1901 and 1903 in the Aurangābād subdivision.

Criminal classes.

There are three classes in Gayā district who may be considered habitual criminals, viz., Goālās, Dosādhs, and aboriginal tribes, such as the Bhuiyās, Rajwārs and Musahars. Cattle-lifting and grain-thefts are the special crimes of the first class; lurking house-trespass and burglary of the second; and thefts of the third. The Goālās are continually engaged in that most exasperating form of theft which consists of petty thefts of crops from granaries and fields, and they seldom lose an opportunity of grazing their cattle on a neighbour's crops. They are even more notorious for cattle-lifting, which they practise with equal boldness and success. The Dosādhs are a more contemptible class than the Goālās. With the same predilection for crime, they want the daring, the insolence and the physique which make the Goālā such a dangerous ruffian. Their crimes, therefore, are of a meaner description, such as petty thefts and skulking burglary. The low aboriginal tribes have also an evil reputation as criminals, but in their case crime is due as much to poverty as to anything else. They indulge mostly in petty thefts or burglary, but they also frequently join in highway robberies and dacoities. Here, however, they are generally merely the employés of the bolder spirits who organize these outrages and whose orders they obey for the sake of a petty share of the plunder.

The Bābhan class supply the leading spirits in a gang-robbery, riot or any other mischief. When the crops are on the ground, or the reservoirs full of water, the Bābhan's opportunity comes, and violent breaches of the peace occur in twenty villages at once. Besides this taste for rioting, they are remarkable for their litigiousness, and are ever ready to contest to the last halfpenny a neighbour's claim, or seize upon a poorer man's right. Their crookedness of mind has passed into a proverb, "*Bābhan bahut sidhā ho, to hasuā ke aisā*," *i.e.*, "The straightest Bābhan is as crooked as a sickle."

For police purposes, the district of Gayā is divided into 14 police circles (thānas):—viz., (1) Gayā Town or Kotwāli, (2) Gayā Mofussil, (3) Atrī, (4) Tekāri, (5) Bārāchatti and (6) Sherghāti in the head-quarters subdivision; (7) Nawāda, (8) Rajaulī and (9) Pakrībarāwān in the Nawāda subdivision; (10) Jahānābād, and (11) Arwal in the Jahānābād subdivision; (12) Dāūdnagar, (13) Nabīnagar, and (14) Aurangābād in the Aurangābād subdivision. Subordinate to the thānas are 22 outposts and beat-houses, of which a list will be found in the Statistical Appendix; and there are therefore 36 centres in all for the investigation of crime. The force engaged in the prevention and detection of crime consisted in 1904 of the District Superintendent of Police, an Assistant District Superintendent of Police, 6 Inspectors, 49 Sub-Inspectors, 56 head-constables and 659 constables; and the rural force for the watch and ward of villages in the interior had a strength of 304 *dafadārs* and 4,119 *chaukīdārs*. The cost of the regular force was nearly Rs. 1,45,000, and there was one policeman to every $9\frac{1}{2}$ square miles and to every 4,153 persons, as compared with the average of $9\frac{4}{5}$ square miles and 5,386 persons for the whole of Bihār. In addition to the rural and regular police, there is a small force of town police employed in the municipalities under head-constables drawn from the regular force. POLICE.

JAILS. Besides the three subsidiary jails at the head-quarters station in each of the three subdivisions of Aurangābād, Jahānābād and Nawāda, there is a District Jail at Gayā. Statistics will be found in the Statistical Appendix. The subsidiary jails at Aurangābād, Jahānābād and Nawāda are merely lock-ups, in which prisoners sentenced to imprisonment for a fortnight or less are confined; in 1904 the daily average of prisoners was only 13, 7 and 9 respectively. In the Gayā jail, on the average, 422 prisoners were confined daily in 1904, and the death-rate was extraordinarily low, being only 2·5 per mille of its average strength, a smaller percentage than in any other jail in the Province. Accommodation is provided for 542 prisoners; there are cells for 16 male convicts and 5 Europeans; the hospital holds 33 patients; and there are barracks with separate sleeping accommodation for 14 juvenile convicts, and without separate sleeping accommodation for 6 civil prisoners, 22 under-trial prisoners, 15 female convicts and 431 male convicts. In the subsidiary jails the convicts are employed in oil-pressing, wheat-grinding and the manufacture of *sābe* grass string. The industries carried on in the district jail are oil-pressing, breaking of stone for road metal, weaving of carpets and *newār*, and the manufacture of bamboo-baskets, *sābe* grass string and mats, jute twine, cotton string and money-bags for the Government treasuries.

CHAPTER XVII.

LOCAL SELF-GOVERNMENT.

OUTSIDE municipal areas, local affairs are managed by the District Board which has jurisdiction over the whole district, and by the Local Boards which have been constituted for each of the outlying subdivisions. The District Board is responsible for the maintenance of roads, bridges and roadside rest-houses, and has the general superintendence of primary and middle schools. It is also entrusted with the management of pounds and public ferries, the control over dispensaries, the provision of a proper water-supply and village sanitation. To the Local Boards, which work in subordination to it, have been delegated the administration of small sums allotted for the construction and repair of village roads and the discharge of certain functions which will be mentioned later.

DISTRICT BOARD.

The District Board was established in the year 1887, and consists of 21 members. The District Magistrate is an *ex-officio* member of the Board and is invariably its Chairman; there are 4 other *ex-officio* members, 7 members are nominated by Government, and 9 are elected. The Statistical Appendix shows, for the 10 years 1892-93 to 1901-02, the principal sources from which this body derives its income, and the objects on which it is spent; and it will suffice here to say that its average annual income during this period was Rs. 2,84,000, of which Rs. 2,07,000 were derived from Provincial rates, and the average expenditure was Rs. 2,87,000, of which nearly two lakhs were spent on civil works, Rs. 27,000 on education, and Rs. 20,000 on medical relief. In 1904-05 the Board had an opening balance of Rs. 1,16,141, and its income was Rs. 3,34,600, or annas 3-2 per head of the population; the expenditure in the same year was Rs. 2,78,500. Here, as elsewhere, the Provincial rates form the chief source of income, bringing in over 2½ lakhs of rupees. The incidence of taxation is annas 2-1 per head of the population, a figure higher than in any other district of the Patna Division, except Patna (annas 2-5) and Shāhābād (annas 3-6).

By far the largest portion of the income of the District Board is spent on civil works, *i.e.*, the extension and maintenance of communications, the upkeep of staging bungalows, the construction of buildings and the provision of a proper water-supply. Altogether Rs. 1,72,000 were expended on these works in 1904-05, over two-thirds of this sum being spent on the construction, improvement, and repairs of roads. The Board maintains altogether 163 miles of metalled and 715 miles of unmetalled roads, besides 628 miles of village roads, the cost per mile being Rs. 571, Rs. 31 and Rs. 10-4 respectively. The immediate administration of the roads is vested in the District Engineer, who is also responsible for the management and repair of 23 inspection houses and 2 dâk bungalows kept up by the Board. That body also controls 40 ferries and 73 pounds; the latter are generally leased out, and the average income derived from them was Rs. 10,700 during the 16 years ending in 1903-04.

After civil works, education constitutes the heaviest charge upon the District Board, the amount expended upon it being over Rs. 45,000 in 1904-05. It maintains 5 middle schools, and aids six others, besides 43 upper primary and 684 lower primary schools, and, for the supervision of education, it employs an inspecting staff of 5 Sub-Inspectors and 14 Inspecting Pandits. Besides this, it awards a scholarship tenable at the Bihār School of Engineering, and pays the stipend of a student at the Bengal Veterinary College at Belgāchia. For the relief of sickness, it maintains two dispensaries and aids ten others, and it has recently taken in hand the construction of dispensary buildings at Rafiganj and Nabīnagar. The proportion of its available income, *i.e.*, of the income derived from sources other than road cess, which is spent on hospitals and dispensaries is particularly high; and in the five years 1898-99 to 1902-03 the percentage (18·11) thus expended was higher than in any other Bengal district, except Backergunge (20·57) and Patna (18·12). The sanitary work done by the Board is of a somewhat varied character. It includes preventive measures against plague, cholera and other epidemic diseases, sanitary arrangements at fairs and *melās*, the construction, repair and improvement of wells, and experiments in village sanitation, such as the clearance of jungle, the excavation of roadside drains, and the filling up of hollows containing stagnant water. Altogether 9·3 per cent. of its ordinary income was expended on medical relief and sanitation in 1904-05.

LOCAL BOARDS.

In subordination to the District Board are the Local Boards of Nawāda, Jahānābād and Aurangābād, the jurisdiction of each corresponding with that of the subdivisional charge of the same name. There was formerly a Local Board for the head-quarters subdivision, but as it did no useful work, it was abolished a few years ago. The system of election which obtains in most of the districts in Bengal has not been introduced, and the members are appointed by Government, the Subdivisional Magistrates holding the office of Chairman. These bodies were established at the same time as the District Board, and receive annual allotments from its funds; the functions with which they are entrusted being the maintenance of village roads, the supervision of some local dispensaries, the control of a certain number of pounds, and certain other minor works such as village sanitation and the upkeep of wells.

MUNICIPALITIES.

There are three municipalities in this district, viz., Gayā, Tekāri and Dāūdnagar. The number of rate-payers is 15,757 out of a total population of 87,469, the ratio being 18 per cent. as compared with the Divisional average of 17·7 per cent. Taxation takes the form in the two municipalities first named of a rate on holdings, and in Dāūdnagar of a tax on persons residing in municipal areas according to their circumstances and property; besides this, there is a latrine-tax in Gayā. The incidence of taxation varies between Re. 1-2-10 in Gayā and 5 annas at Dāūdnagar, the former being, next to Muzaffarpur, the most heavily-taxed, and the latter the most lightly-taxed municipality in the Division, the average taxation in which is 12 annas 7 pies per head. Statistics of the annual income and expenditure of each municipality during the 10 years 1892-93 to 1901-02 will be found in the Statistical Appendix.

GAYĀ.

The Gayā Municipality, which was constituted in 1865, is administered by a Municipal Board consisting of 25 members, of whom 3 are *ex-officio* members, 16 are elected and 6 are nominated. The area within municipal limits is 8 square miles, and is divided into 10 wards; the number of rate-payers is 13,285, or 18·6 per cent. of the population. The average annual income for the decade ending in 1901-02 was Rs. 87,800, and the expenditure Rs. 82,600. In 1904-05, they were Rs. 1,16,388 and Rs. 1,01,169, respectively, the incidence of taxation per head of the population being Re. 1-2-10. The main heads of income are a tax on holdings at 7½ per cent. of their annual value, which yielded Rs. 50,200 in 1904-05, a conservancy rate (Rs. 23,500), and a tax on animals and vehicles (Rs. 8,850). The principal items of expenditure are conservancy, medical relief and public works, which accounted, respectively, for 46·9, 15·1 and 16·8 per cent. of the expenditure.

The two great needs of the municipality are an effective system of drainage and a filtered water-supply, but at present its finances are insufficient to carry out such expensive schemes.

The present drainage system comprises 18 miles of masonry, cement or brick drains, and 12 miles of other drains, nearly all the outlets leading into the Phalgu river; the natural drainage of the town is principally from south to north, but in a few cases the fall is from east to west. In three wards the night-soil is removed to a trenching-ground near the Rāmsilā Hill in iron trucks by a steam-tramway, which was procured from England at a cost of Rs. 43,450, and which costs over Rs. 12,000 a year to maintain. The old town of Gayā has a complete underground sewerage system linked up with the houses along the course of the drains. It is plentifully supplied with man-holes, and as this part of the town is on high ground, the gradients are good. The drains are free from objection during the rains, when the sewers are thoroughly flushed; but, during the dry months of the year, the contents stagnate a great deal and give rise to offensive odours. The new part of the town has a system of surface drainage only, and many of the drains have an inadequate fall and are badly designed; some of them in the crowded portions of the towns are indeed little less than a succession of cess-pools filled with black festering liquid. The drainage of the town is thus still far from satisfactory, though the municipality are doing and have done much during the last few years to improve the present state of affairs; large sums have been spent from the Lodging-House Fund on the construction of new drains and the improvement of existing ones, the town has been surveyed and levels have been taken for an improved drainage scheme. The resources of the municipality have, however, been severely strained by repeated visitations of plague, and the want of funds at present prevents the execution of this most necessary improvement.

The same difficulty stands in the way of a pure water-supply. The present sources of supply are the river Phalgu and the wells scattered about the town, but the Phalgu dries up in the hot weather, and at the same time the wells also contain insufficient water for the requirements of the large number of inhabitants. To remedy this state of affairs, a scheme has been proposed for pumping water from the Phalgu to filtering tanks on a hill in the old town and thence distributing it. Endeavours were made to raise a sufficient sum from donations to enable the municipality to carry out the scheme with the additional aid of a loan; but adequate support was not forthcoming and the scheme is in abeyance. In other respects, the requirements of the citizens are well provided for, and there is a very extensive network of roads, streets and lanes, the metalled roads alone having a total length of 43 miles.

The Tekāri Municipality was constituted in 1885, and is administered by a Municipal Board of 12 Commissioners, of whom 3 are *ex-officio* members and 9 are nominated. The area within municipal limits is a lttile over a square mile, and is divided into 9 wards. There are in all 1,149 tax-payers, or 17·9 per cent. of the population. In 1904-05, the total income was Rs. 7,530, of which Rs. 5,660 were realized from the tax on houses and lands, the incidence of taxation being annas 15-9 per head. The expenditure was Rs. 6,385, of which more than a third was spent on conservancy. The town contains a municipal market, and there is a good system of drainage well planned and arranged. The total length of the drains is already over 7 miles, of which 2 miles have masonry drains, and the efficient drainage of the whole area appears to be only a question of time. Tekāri.

The municipality of Dāūdnagar was constituted in 1885, and has a Municipal Board consisting of 13 members, of whom one is a member *ex officio* and 12 are nominated. The area within municipal limits is 5 square miles, and the number of rate-payers is 1,323 or 13·5 per cent. of the population, an extremely low proportion for this Division. In 1904-05, the total income was Rs. 4,040, of which Rs. 1,750 was realized from a tax on persons according to their circumstances and property; the average rate at which this tax is levied does not exceed 2 per cent. of the income of the assessees, and the incidence of taxation of all kinds is only 5 annas per head of the population. Of the expenditure, 27·2 per cent. was devoted to conservancy and 23·8 to medical relief, while the expenditure on education reached the unusually high figure of 9·9 per cent. The total length of the roads maintained by the municipality is 4 miles, one mile of which is metalled, and the length of the drains is 8 miles, but the masonry drains extend over only one mile; the natural drainage lines tend in two directions, the drainage of the old town falling into the river Son, and that of the new town, or Ahmadganj, into the old moat surrounding the town. The people obtain their water-supply from the Patna-Gayā canal, from the Son river and from wells; but the people are almost entirely dependent upon the latter for their drinking-water. Dāūdnagar.

CHAPTER XVIII.

EDUCATION.

PROGRESS OF EDUCATION.

In no respect has the advance of the people of Gayā under British rule been more clearly shown than in the progress of education. A century ago education was almost an unknown factor, and the people were in a state of terrible ignorance and backwardness. The state of affairs at that time may be gathered from the description given by Buchanan Hamilton. Speaking of the district in the year 1812, he writes:—"There are no public schools, and there is no *guru* or teacher who is not a servant to some wealthy man. The *gurus*, however, are generally allowed to instruct the children of the neighbours, and a hut is built for a school-house without the village, lest the *guru* should have too frequent opportunities of seeing the women. These school-houses are called *pindās*, a name applicable to several things considered sacred. In parts of the country where sugar-cane grows, the boiling-house usually serves for a school. The profit of the teachers is very small. Many children are taught by their parents." Persian was the language used in the courts, and many Hindus were taught to read and write the Persian character before they began Hindī; but the greater part of them proceeded little further than understanding and writing a revenue account, and were not able either to fully understand or to indite a letter. Such an accomplishment entitled a man to be called a *munshi*. Buchanan Hamilton mentions the fact that the chief Hindu zamīndār could read both Persian and Hindī, as if this was an unusual degree of learning; and adds that by far the greater part of the landholders consisted of mere peasants, half of whom could not read, though the chief of each family generally acquired the art of being able to make a mark resembling the characters which composed his name. He estimated the total number of persons in the six police circles which have been taken to represent the present district of Gayā, who were fit to act as writers, at 8,930 persons. In other words, taking his estimate of the total population of these circles (1,500,500), only 0·6 per cent. of the total population, including those who had come from other districts to seek employment, were fit to act as writers.

During the first half of the 19th century the State left the care of education to private enterprise; the only schools in the district were the *maktabs* and *pindās*, as the schools teaching Persian and Hindī were called; and nothing was done to supplement the indigenous system of education. It was not till 1845 that a Government English school was established, and this remained the only Government school for ten years. In 1854 the famous educational despatch was issued, in which the Court of Directors laid down that Government should afford assistance to "the more extended and systematic promotion of general education in India," and sketched a complete scheme of public education, controlled and aided, and in part directly managed, by the State. As a result of these orders, 15 Government vernacular schools were opened in 1855 and 1856, and at the end of the latter year 574 pupils were receiving instruction. A start was thus made in the education of the people, but very little progress was made, and 14 years afterwards the number of public educational institutions was only 28, viz., the Government schools mentioned above, one normal school, 5 aided English schools, and 6 aided vernacular schools: the number of pupils was still only 1,367. In 1872, however, Sir George Campbell's scheme of educational reform was introduced, under which grants were given in aid of the schools hitherto unaided, and many of the indigenous rural schools called *pāthshālas* were absorbed into the departmental system. The prejudice against the aided schools was, however, very great, and the Government scheme was received with extraordinary distrust. The ignorant masses of the population, for whose special benefit these aided *pāthshālas* were established, had persuaded themselves that Government had some deep design on their lives or liberties. The paid teachers (*gurus*) were looked upon as Government spies; and it was thought that the pupils who were foolish enough to attend their schools were to be forced to emigrate, or possibly to be sold as slaves to the King of Burma. This strange but widely-spread feeling gradually disappeared, and the subsequent advance of education was phenomenal, the number of schools rising to 1,729 in 1884-85 and the number of pupils under instruction to 26,346. This extraordinary rate of progress was not sustained, and in the next decade the number of educational institutions fell to 1,019 (1894-95) with an attendance of 24,698 pupils. This decline is, however, largely due to the fact that primary schools attended by less than 10 pupils were excludeb from the departmental returns.

In the last ten years the number of schools has been practically stationary, amounting to 1,011 in 1904-05, but on the other hand the number of pupils has increased to 33,221.• Besides these, there are 470 schools, with 4,547 pupils, which do not conform to any departmental standard and are outside the Education Department system. During the last decade, therefore, the number of public schools has decreased by 8, but on the other hand the attendance has increased by one-third; and there are now 19·4 children at school to every 1,000 of the population, and one school to every 3 square miles. The supervision of these schools rests with a Deputy Inspector of Schools assisted by 5 Sub-Inspectors and 14 Inspecting Pandits, the whole of this inspecting staff being under the Inspector of Schools, Patna Division. The census of 1901 confirms the evidence of general progress furnished by the educational statistics, as the number of males entered as literate, *i.e.*, as able to read and write, has increased from 67 to 72 per mille since 1891. Altogether, there are 72,380 male literates out of the male population of 1,011,271, and of these 3,247 are able to read and write English.

SECONDARY EDUCATION.

High English schools.

There are no colleges in the district, but secondary education is imparted to 1,123 pupils at 4 high English schools, *i.e.*, schools teaching up to the Entrance examination of the Calcutta University. There was one such school in 1872-73, at which 191 pupils received instruction, and 5 schools in 1894-95 with a total of 1,320 students. Of the 4 schools now existing, three, viz., the Zila school, the Town school and the Sāhibganj school, are situated at Gayā, and the fourth, which is maintained by the Tekāri Rāj, is situated at Tekāri. With the exception of the Gayā Zila school, they are all private institutions unaided by Government. The annual cost of education is reported to be Rs. 20-12, and the cost of each pupil to Government is Rs. 2-2.

Middle English schools.

The district contains 9 Middle English schools, *i.e.*, schools teaching up to the Middle Scholarship examination, in which English forms part of the recognized course of studies; and the number of pupils is 531. The number of these schools was 14 in 1884-85, and the attendance was 733; but owing to want of support from the local inhabitants, there were only 6 schools of this class in 1894-95 with 381 pupils. Of the 9 schools now established, 2 at Gayā and Dāūdnagar are aided by Government, 5 at Arwal, Aurangābād, Deo, Jahānābād and Nawāda are aided by the District Board, and 2 at Bhadaiya and Fakīrpur are unaided.

Middle Vernacular schools.

The third class of secondary schools consists of the Middle Vernacular schools, which read up to the Middle Scholarship, but in which the vernacular is the only recognized course of studies. Here, as elsewhere, the popularity of these schools appears to be on the wane, as parents of the class for whom they are intended prefer an English education for their children. The number of these schools has accordingly fallen from 16 in 1884-85 to 8 in 1894-95 and to 7 in 1904-05, while the attendance has declined during the last decade from 410 to 364.

PRIMARY EDUCATION. The advance of primary education is in striking contrast to the slow growth of secondary education. In 1872-73 there were only 367 primary schools with 6,442 pupils, but in 1884-85 the number of children receiving instruction had risen to 23,468 and the number of schools to 1,685. There was a falling off during the next decade, and in 1894-95 the number of pupils was reduced to 22,148 and the number of primary schools to 983,—a result due in a large measure to the exclusion of petty schools with less than 10 pupils from the class of public institutions. During the last ten years the number of these schools has fallen still further, and in 1904-05 they numbered 966; but on the other hand the number of pupils under instruction has risen to 30,536, of whom 27,616 are Hindus and 2,920 are Muhammadans, the average yearly cost of educating each pupil being Rs. 2-14, of which Re. 1-2 is paid from public funds. The attendance is now 8,388 more than in 1894-95, and the decrease in the number of schools during the last 20 years merely shows that ephemeral institutions disappeared under the presence of competition, and that when these small and inefficient institutions closed their doors, the pupils transferred themselves to larger and more efficient schools.

On the other hand, the number of pupils has only increased by 7,000 during the last 20 years, but several causes have contributed to the slow growth of primary instruction. When the Education Department began to devote its attention to the extension and improvement of primary instruction, it had in the first place to deal with a portion of the population living in the more populous and accessible parts of the district, which was well-to-do and alive to the value of education. Their efforts were aided by the existing system of indigenous schools, and in such circumstances progress was comparatively easy. These favourable circumstances have now been to a great extent exhausted, and the portion of the problem which remains to be dealt with is far harder, as the benefits of education have now to be conveyed to the poorer ryots and the lower castes, who have from time immemorial lived without instruction and are altogether indifferent to it.

SPECIAL SCHOOLS. The number of special schools increased from 1 in 1872-73 to 3 in 1894-95 and to 15 in 1904-05, the number of pupils rising from 13 to 118 and 411, respectively. These schools consist of 4

Guru-training schools, one in each subdivision, at which Primary school teachers are trained, and of 11 *tols*, which impart instruction in Sanskrit and send pupils up to the examination of the Bihār Sanskrit Sanjivan. Besides these schools, a Lower Primary night school has recently been opened at Gayā, which is maintained by the municipality.

Female education. In Gayā, as in other parts of Bihār, female education is still in a very backward state, and the rate of progress has been much slower than in the case of the male population. Considering, however, how strong and paralyzing is the influence of the *pardā* system, there has been on the whole a noticeable advance. The number able to read and write has doubled during the last ten years, though it is still only 2 per 1,000 females; there are now 10 schools for girls reading up to the Lower Primary standard with an attendance of 256; and, besides these, there are 2,439 girls reading in boys' schools.

CHAPTER XIX.

GAZETTEER.

Aphsanr.—A village in the extreme north of the Nawāda subdivision, situated some three miles to the south of Dariyāpur Pārbatī in 25° 4′ N. and 86° 40′ E. Population (1901) 1,022. The village contains one of the most interesting remains in the district, a large statue of the Varāha Avatāra or boar incarnation of Vishnu. The figure shows the earth, represented as a female grasping one of the boar's tusks in order to mount its neck; and the whole body of the boar is covered with *rishis*, in the act of worship, nestling in its bristles. The style in which this work has been executed, as well as the material used, grey sandstone, indicates that it belongs to the Gupta period. This statue stands in front of a high brick mound, which marks the remains of a temple of Vishnu, which, according to an inscription found here, was built about the year 600 A.D. by Adityasena, one of a later Guptas of Magadha. This inscription contained an important record of the Gupta dynasty, but was unfortunately lost over 50 years ago. The structural remains of the temple are now buried below the mound, and it is probable that excavation would be rewarded by disclosing considerable portions of the original building. Close to the mound are other statues of later date; they are all Brahmanical, and from the absence of any mention of Aphsanr by the Chinese pilgrims, it may be concluded that it was an important Brahmanical site, and not a large Buddhist settlement. *See* also Reports of Arch. Surv. Ind., Vol. I, p. 40, Vol. VIII, p. 114-115, Vol. IX, p. 27, Vol. XV, pp. 10-11, and Vol. XVI, p. 79; also Report Arch. Surv. Bengal Circle, 1901-02.

Arwal.—A village situated on the eastern bank of the Son in the north-west of the Jahānābād subdivision, 22 miles due west of Jahānābād. The original village of Arwal has long since been swept away by the Son, but a group of villages close by the old site now goes by the name. The place was once the centre of a paper-making industry, and still focuses the local trade, which is served by the Patna-Gayā canal passing through the village. It contains a police-station, dispensary, telegraph- and post-office, an inspection bungalow maintained by the District Board, and a staging bungalow belonging to the Irrigation Department. It is also the head-quarters of the Solano family, who hold extensive property in the neighbourhood. They are a Spanish family of Malaga, and have resided here for about half a century, the foundations of their fortunes being laid by Don Raphael Solano, who purchased the indigo factories of Tarai, Pura and Baghoi in 1840. Close by is the village of Sipāh, formerly inhabited by pensioned soldiers, who received grants of land in lieu of pensions.

Aurangābād subdivision.—The south-western subdivision of the district, lying between 24° 29′ and 25° 7′ N., and between 84° 0′ and 84° 44′ E., and extending over 1,246 square miles. Its population was 472,507 in 1891, but fell in 1901 to 467,675; of these Hindus number 421,127 and Muhammadans 46,519. It contains two towns—Aurangābād, its head-quarters, and Dāūdnagar, besides 2,042 villages, the number of occupied houses being 90,396. The density of population is 375 per square mile, and is greatest in the north-west, where the land is irrigated by the Son canal system. The subdivision comprises the three police circles of Aurangābād, Dāūdnagar, and Nabīnagar, and the *parganas* or fiscal division of Charkānwān, Manorah, Siris, Anchhā, Goh, Dādar and Kutumbā. Of the total area (797,440 acres), 523,000 acres are cultivated and 241,000 are irrigated, 33,000 acres being irrigated from Government canals. Rice is the staple crop, being grown on 232,000 acres, and next in importance come gram (70,000 acres), wheat (50,000 acres) and maize (27,000 acres), while barley, *maruā* and linseed each occupy about 20,000 acres.

Aurangābād town.—Head-quarters town of the subdivision of the same name, situated 9 miles from the Jamhor railway station in 24° 45′ N. and 84° 23′ E. The population in 1901 was 4,685. Aurangābād is a long straggling town on the Grand Trunk Road, and contains no buildings of any interest. Besides the usual court-houses, public offices and sub-jail, there is a dispensary and inspection bungalow. The trade of the place is not important, consisting mainly of food-grains, oil-seeds, leather and piece-goods.

Bakraur.—A village in the head-quarters subdivision, situated half a mile to the east of Bodh Gayā on the narrow neck of land between the Nilājan and Mohāna rivers. Immediately to the south of the village are the remains of a large brick stūpa, still standing 25 feet above the ground and 150 feet in diameter; and at a short distance from it is the stump of a sandstone pillar, the shaft of which was set up in Gayā (*q. v.*) in 1789. This stūpa and pillar commemorate the legendary incident of the Gandha-hasti or perfume elephant. According to Hiuen Tsiang, who visited the place in the 7th century, Buddha in a former existence was the offspring of a perfume-elephant and wandered in the woods round this place, gathering food to support a blind mother. He was captured by the king and placed in the royal stables, but there he refused to eat or drink. When the king enquired the reason, he replied that he could not, as his mother was blind and had been without food or drink for many days, while he himself remained bound in a dreary dungeon. Thereupon the king released him in pity for his feelings and admiration for his resolution. About 500 yards to the south-east of the stūpa there is a sacred place of pilgrimage called Mātangi, which contains the remains of a large tank marked by ancient embankments, called Mātanga-Vāpi, and a modern temple with a lingam called Matangeswar. Mātanga in Sanskrit means elephant, and it seems clear that these names preserve a reminiscence of the ancient Buddhist legend. Bakraur also contains a small Hindu *math* or monastery, and a tank sacred to the sun, where an annual fair is held, during which thousands come to bathe in its holy water. *See* also Reports Arch. Surv. Ind., Vol. I, pp. 12-13, and Report Arch. Surv. Bengal Circle, 1901-02.

Barābar Hills.—A group of hills on the northern boundary of the head-quarters subdivision, lying between 25° 0′ and 25° 3′ N., and 85° 1′ and 85° 5′ E., and stretching 6 to 8 miles east of the Belā railway station. They are composed of gneissose granite weathering into huge boulders, and contain several distinct peaks, of which the most conspicuous are the Murli peak to the north, the Sandagiri peak to the south, and the Siddheswar peak, which they both join, on the east. A small temple on the latter peak contains a lingam called Siddheswarnāth, which from an inscription in one of the neighbouring caves is known to be as old as the 6th or 7th century; and close by on the top of the hill are some curious caves used occasionally by wandering ascetics. It has been identified with the lofty hill from which Buddha contemplated the kingdom of Magadha; and it is still the object of an extensive pilgrimage from the neighbouring tracts. Immediately to the south at its foot lies a small valley or basin entirely surrounded by hills, except on the north-east and south-east, where walls have been built to complete the enclosure. Towards the southern corner of the basin are two small sheets of water, which find an outlet underground to the south-east and reappear in the sacred spring called Pātālganga, where a bathing festival is held once a year in the month of Bhādo (August-September). On this side is the principal entrance to the valley, which lies over large rounded masses of granite, now worn smooth and slippery by the feet of numerous pilgrims.

Barābar caves.

In the southern corner of the valley there is a low ridge of granite rock, about 500 feet long, from 100 to 120 feet thick, and 30 to 35 feet in height, in which some remarkable caves have been cut in the solid rock. On the northern side lies a large cave called Karna-Chaupar or the hut of Karna, at the western end of which there is a raised platform, which was probably the pedestal of a statue. The whole of the interior has been chiselled to a wonderful polish, which shows the proficiency with which the Indian masons of the third century (B.C.) were able to deal with such intractable material as the hard granite of the Barābar Hills. That the cave dates back to this early age is proved by an inscription on a sunken tablet at the western corner of the entrance recording the dedication of the cave by Asoka himself. To the east of the doorway the rock has been cut away, and some rude sculptures, representing a lingam and some Brahmanical figures, have been carved.

On the opposite side of the ridge is the Sudāma cave, consisting of two chambers. The inner one is nearly circular; and the antechamber contains a shallow recess, which may have been intended as a niche for a statue, or as an entrance to another projected chamber. But the work was abandoned soon after its commencement, and remains rough and unfinished, while all the rest of the cave is highly polished. On the eastern side of the doorway there is an inscription of ancient Pālī character, recording the dedication of the cave by Asoka.

The Lomāsrishi cave, on the same side of the ridge, is similar to the Sudāma cave, both in the size and arrangement of its two chambers, but the whole of the interior of the circular room has been left rough, and both the floor and the roof of the outer apartment remain unfinished. The chisel marks are still visible on the floor, while on the roof, which has been only partially hewn, the cuts of the chisel are still sharp and distinct. The excavation of the roof would appear to have been abandoned owing to the work having reached a deep fissure which forms one of the natural lines of cleavage of the rock. The doorway of this cave is of the same size and of the same Egyptian form as that of the Sudāma cave, but the entrance has been sculptured to represent the ornamental entrance of a wooden building. The ends of the roofing beams and the bamboo lattice-work of the gable can be seen distinctly, and below there is a frieze of elephants surrounding the doorway. In the space between this frieze and the doorway there is an inscription of the same character as those of the later princes of the Gupta Dynasty. General Cunningham therefore assigns the date of this sculptured façade to the 3rd or 4th century A. D.; but the cave itself corresponds so exactly with the Sudāma cave that it must have been excavated at the same time, the doorway being enlarged and ornamented later.

The fourth cave of the Barābar group is excavated in a large block of granite to the eastward of the main ridge. It is known as Viswājhoprī or the hut of Viswāmitra, and consists of two rooms, an inner apartment, which is rough and unpolished, and an ante-chamber, which is polished throughout, and contains an inscription recording the dedication of the cave by Asoka.

Nagarjuni caves.

About half a mile to the east of the Siddheswarnāth peak are the Nagarjuni Hills, consisting of two narrow ridges of granite, running nearly parallel, about half a mile distant from each other. The southern ridge contains three more caves, of which two are situated in a small spur on the northern side, while the third and largest cave, known as the Gopī cave, is excavated in the southern side of the ridge at a height of 50 feet above the plain. It is approached by a flight of rude stone steps, but the entrance is concealed by a tree and partly by the wall of an *idgāh* built by some former Muhammadan occupants. On the outside, immediately over the doorway, a small sunken tablet contains an inscription stating that the Gopī's cave was bestowed by Dasaratha, immediately after his accession, on the venerable Ajīvikas to be a dwelling place for them as long as the sun and moon endure.

The other two caves, which are situated in a low rocky ridge on the northern side of the hill, have inscriptions recording their dedication in the same terms. To the south there are two raised terraces, the upper of which is believed by General Cunningham to have been the site of a Buddhist *vihārā* or monastery. There are several squared stones and granite pillars near the top, which in the opinion of the same authority, were added by the Muhammadans, who occupied the caves in later years. The platform is covered with their tombs; and all around there are heaps of bricks and fragments of carved stones, which show that several buildings must once have existed here.

The westward cave is situated in a gap or natural cleft of the rock, and is entered by a narrow passage, only 2 feet 10 inches in width. In an inscription on the right-hand jamb of the doorway this cave is called the Vadathika cave, which General Cunningham suggests may mean the cave of the secluded mendicants. This meaning is appropriate to the position of the cave, for it is entirely separated from the cave to the east, is encompassed by the bluff rocks of the gap in which it is situated, and is effectually screened from view. The cave next to it has a small porch or antechamber, from which a narrow doorway leads to the principal room. The roof is vaulted and all the walls are highly polished. From an inscription on the left-hand side of the porch we learn that the cave was called Vāpika—a term which probably refers to the well (*vāpi*) in front of it.

From the account given above it will be seen that the two groups of caves are separated by date as well as position, the Barābar caves having been excavated in the reign of Asoka, while those of Nagarjuni were excavated in the 1st year of the reign of his grandson Dasaratha, *i. e.*, about the year 231 B. C. They were all dedicated to the Ajīvikas, who were either a set of Brahmanical ascetics devoted to Narāyan, a form of Vishnu, or a penitential order closely associated with the Jains, the members of which went about naked and were noted for ascetic practices of the most rigorous kind. From inscriptions of later date we learn that the caves were for ages occupied by Brahmanical ascetics. About the 3rd or 4th century A. D., the kings Sardula Varman and Ananta Varman placed Brahmanical images in three of the caves; and in the 6th or 7th century the teacher Yogananda left a record of his adoration of the Siddheswar lingam in the Vāpika cave. This occupation by Brāhmans in the 7th century may account for the silence of the Chinese pilgrim Hiuen Tsiang regarding the caves, which would otherwise have certainly attracted his attention. At a still later date, somewhere about the 12th century, we find a *yogi* and a pilgrim visiting the caves and inscribing their names; and it appears probable that neither of the two groups of caves were ever appropriated by the Buddhists.

The Barābar caves are known locally as the Satgharwa, and it has been suggested that the name is a corruption of *sapta-garbhà* or the seven caves, or is simply *sāt ghar* or the seven houses. These explanations do not appear very satisfactory, as the Barābar caves are only four in number, and the term would therefore have to include the three Nagarjuni caves. It appears a more plausible hypothesis that the true name is *sant-ghar* or the dwelling places of the saints or ascetics. The Nagarjuni Hills derive their name from the tradition that Nagārjuna, the famous Buddhist teacher, lived in one of their caves; and the name Barābar is apparently a corruption of *bara awara*, the great enclosure, a designation applied to the valley in which the caves are situated. This is naturally a strong defensive position, as it possesses plenty of water and is only accessible at two points—on the north-east and south-east. Both these points were closed by walls; and as there are also traces of walls on the surrounding hills, it seems certain that the place was once used as a stronghold. The term may however have been applied to the larger valley enclosed on the west by the Barābar Hills, on the north and south by the parallel ridges of the Nagarjuni Hills, and on the east by the Phalgu, where the numerous heaps of brick and stone scattered over the plain seem to mark the site of a large town. Buchanan Hamilton calls this plain Rām Gayā, and states that the people of the neighbourhood claimed that it was once a centre of pilgrimage, which fell into decline, because the Gayāwāls set up a new pilgrim city at Gayā. For further particulars, *see* Rep. Arch. Surv. Ind, Vol. I, p. 40, and Vol. VIII, p. 30; also List of Ancient Monuments in Bengal, 1895.

Bārun.—A village in the Aurangābād subdivision, situated on the eastern bank of the Son in 24° 55′ N. and 84° 11′ E. Here the Grand Trunk Road crosses the broad sandy bed of the Son by a stone causeway 2½ miles long, and the Main Eastern canal branches off from an anicut across the river. Just below this, the river is spanned by a huge railway bridge, which is not only the largest bridge in India, but is surpassed in length only by the Tay bridge. The latter is 10,527 feet in length with a waterway of 9,400 feet, and the bridge at Bārun is 10,052 feet with a waterway of 9,300 feet. It is made of iron girders laid on stone-built pillars, and comprises 93 spans of 100 feet each, the piers running in apparently interminable succession over a wide flat river-bed, which in the hot weather is nothing more than a vast expanse of sand. The bridge was commenced on February 1897 and was opened in February 1900, the total expense of the work being 34 lakhs of rupees, or £24 per lineal foot of waterway. The cost of the bridge was as low as the rate of construction was rapid, owing to the comparatively easy conditions of the work, a firm clay being found at a short distance below the river-bed, which gave an excellent foundation for the piers. Bārun contains a police outpost, and is served by the Son East Bank station on the Mughalsarai-Gayā Railway.

Bishunpur Tanrwā.—*See* HASRA HILL.

Bodh Gayā.—Village in the head-quarters subdivision, situated 6 miles south of Gayā on the west bank of the Nilājan.—*See* Chapter III.

Brahmajuni Hill.—*See* GAYA TOWN.

Dariyāpur Pārbatī.—A village in the Nawâda subdivision, situated 6 miles north of Wārisalīganj, on the northern boundary of the district. This village has been identified by General Cunningham as the site of the Buddhist monastery, called the Kapotikā or Pigeon monastery, which was built to commemorate an incident in the life of Buddha. According to the legend, Buddha was once preaching at this spot, and close by a fowler was spreading his snares. Having caught nothing all day, the fowler attributed his ill-luck to Buddha's preaching, and coming to him, loudly reproached him, and asked how he was to feed his hungry children. Buddha promised that they should not remain hungry, if he would light a fire, and this having been done, a large pigeon fell from the sky into the flames. The monastery built at this spot was visited by Hiuen Tsiang, who describes it as being close to a steep isolated hill, laid out in terraces and covered with holy buildings. This corresponds with the position of the village, which lies by a hill called Pārbatī, or *ghar pārāvat;* and this name appears to be a corruption of Pārāvata, the Sanskrit for pigeon. The foot of the hill is washed by the river Sakrī on the west, and on three sides it rises precipitously, but in the middle of its northern face it shelves down to the village by gentle stages. The whole surface is strewn with ruins, the remains of the "multitude of *vihārās* and temples" seen by the Chinese pilgrim in the 7th century; and the level terraces still remain quite distinct, though nothing is left of the temples but a number of mounds. In the centre stood a famous temple of Avalokiteswara; and this spot is now covered by the *dargāh* of Hājī Chandar or Chānd Saudāgar, "the Musalmān cuckoo having," in General Cunningham's words, "as usual, occupied the Hindu nest." It stands on a small eminence and is built in the midst of a level terrace, where Mr. Beglar traced rows of cells, as of a monastery, which are traditionally said to be the remains of the palace of Bāwan Suba. On the highest part of the hill, 500 feet to the south-west of this spot, there are the remains of a brick building; 50 yards further to the west a conical-shaped peak marks the remains of a stūpa; and in another high mound, 100 yards to the south, the basement of a building and the stumps of 16 granite pillars have been laid bare. A mound on the plain to the west of the village is believed to represent the remains of the Pigeon monastery which gave its name to the village, but like many other mounds near the place, it has been used as a quarry by the villagers. The ruins all round have been largely dug into for bricks, as well as for treasure, which has been found more than once; and the result is that very little is left of the original buildings which once crowded the site. See Reports Arch. Surv. Ind., Vol. VIII, pp. 108—114, and Vol. XV, pp. 6—10.

Dāūdnagar.—A town in the Aurangābād subdivision, situated on the eastern bank of the river Son and on the western bank of the Patna-Gayā canal, in 25° 3′ N., and 84° 24′ E. Population (1901) 9,744. The town was founded by Dāūd Khān, the Governor of Bihār under Aurangzeb, some of whose descendants still live there. Tradition relates that, when he was on his way back from the conquest of Palāmau (1660 A.D.), he encamped on the spot where the town now stands. Finding it a place infested by robbers and wild beasts, he had the jungle cleared, built the town, which was named after him, and erected a palace for himself. According to Colonel Dalton* this palace contained (1871) the great gates of the Palāmau Fort, known as the Singh Darwāza, and the pride of the Cheros, which Dāūd Khān carried off when he left Palāmau. His grandson, Ahmad Khān, still further strengthened the town by building a fort called Ghauspur, and added the portion which still contains his tomb and is called Ahmadganj after him.

The trade of Dāūdnagar was once very considerable, and in Buchanan Hamilton's time it contained a cloth factory dependent on the Commercial Resident at Patna and a factor of the Opium Agent at that city. Its prosperity is on the wane, water communication having brought the area it used to tap into close proximity to the two main centres—Patna and Gayā; but it has still some trade in tusser cloth, brass utensils, carpets, blankets, linseed and molasses. A sugar refinery is at work, and the manufacture of coarse blankets, country cloth and carpets is carried on. It is a centre of some local importance, with a municipal organization, a Bench of Honorary Magistrates, a dispensary and police-station. It also contains the offices of an Assistant Engineer and a Circle Officer of the Irrigation Department. The principal building is the *sarai* or fortified inn, erected by Dāūd Khān. It was intended to protect travellers from robbery on the road along the banks of the Son to Patna, and was surrounded by a moat and rampart of brick, with battlements and loop-holes, strengthened at the corners by bastions.

Deo.—A village in the Aurangābād subdivision, situated 6 miles south-east of Aurangābād in 24° 39′ N. and 84° 26′ E. It contains a temple dedicated to the sun, called Suraj Mandir, which local tradition ascribes to a fabulous age, but which probably

* J. A. S. B., Vol. XL, Part I, 1871.

dates back only to 1450 A. D. It is beautifully built of blocks of cut stone without cement, and has a tower, about 100 feet high, ornamented with carved scrolls and surmounted by a carved umbrella-like top. The roof is of solid stone supported by stone pillars with plain but handsome capitals. Theae is a remarkable resemblance in the style of this temple and of those at Konch and Umgā, which points to their having been built about the same time. Fairs are held here in the months of Kārtik (October-November) and Chait (March-April), which are largely attended for the purposes of trade, for the fulfilment of vows and for religious worship. One of the ceremonies consists in fastening a number of cords to a hook in the roof of the temple, which are extended to represent the rays of the sun. To the south-east of the village is a tank also sacred to the sun, and close by is another, celebrated for its lotuses.

Deo Rāj.—Deo is the seat of the Deo Rājās, one of the oldest families in Bihār, who trace back their descent to the Rānās or Udaipur. According to the family tradition, Mahārānā Rai Bhān Singh, a younger brother of the Rānā of Udaipur, encamped at Umgā on his way to the shrine of Jagannāth in the 15th century. There was a hill-fort there, the chief of which had recently died, leaving an old and helpless widow, who was unable to keep order over her mutinous subjects. On hearing of Bhān Singh's arrival, she put herself under his protection, adopting him as her son. He soon made himself master of the Umgā fort, and quelled the incipient rebellion. After his death two of his descendants ruled there, but the fort was subsequently deserted in favour of the present seat of the family. Rājā Chhatarpati, from whom the present Rājā is seventh in descent, was the first to espouse the cause of the English. In the contest between Warren Hastings and Chait Singh, the Rājā of Benares, the Deo Rājā being too old to take the field in person, his son, Fateh Narāyan Singh, joined the forces under Major Crawford, and afterwards aided the English in the war with the Pindārīs. For the former service the young Rājā was given a *nānkār*, or rent-free tenure, of eleven villages; and his subsequent services were rewarded with the Rāj of Palāmau, which was afterwards exchanged for certain villages in the district of Gayā, yielding an income of Rs. 3,000 per annum. The successor of Fateh Narāyan Singh was Ghanshām Singh, who also took the field with the British forces against the mutineers in Surgujā, and received in recompense, a second time, the Rāj of Palāmau. His son, Rājā Mitra Bhān Singh, rendered good service in quelling the Kol insurrection in Chotā Nāgpur, and was rewarded with the remission of Rs. 1,000 from the Government revenue accruing from the Deo estate. The services of the present Rājā's grandfather, Jai Prakāsh Singh, during the Mutiny of 1857, and the aid he afforded in quelling the insurrection in Chotā Nāgpur, were rewarded by the title of Mahārājā Bahādur, a knighthood of the Star of India, and the grant of a *jāgīr* or rent-free tenure. The present representative of the family is a minor, and the estate is under the management of the Court of Wards. The estate owned by him extends over 92 square miles, and was brought under survey and settlement between 1901 and 1903.

Dharāwat.—A village in the extreme south of the Jahānābād subdivision, about 5 miles north-west of the Barābar Hills, which has been identified as the site of the Buddhist monastery of Gunamati. Gunamati was a learned Buddhist of Southern India, who heard of the fame of Mādhava, a Brāhman heretic of these parts, who had a deep knowledge of the most difficult and abstruse questions. Determined to engage him in controversy, Gunamati sent him a challenge, and warned him that he was coming to humble him. In alarm at this threat, Mādhava gave orders that Gunamati was not to be admitted to the town, which he held in fief; and when he appeared before the gates, the Brāhmans jeered at his shaven head and singular dress, and turned him back. Gunamati then appealed to the king, who commanded that Mādhava should meet him. The discussion lasted six days, and at the end of that time Mādhava was completely defeated in the argument, vomited blood and died. The king then built a great monastery to celebrate the victory of Gunamati. This monastery was visited in the 7th century A. D., by Hiuen Tsiang, who described it as being on the declivity of a hill and flanked by a precipice, with lofty walls and towers standing up between the rocks.

Not only does the position of Dharāwat correspond with the account of his itinerary given by the Chinese pilgrim, but the site of the ruins still extant agrees with Hiuen Tsiang's description; and it has been suggested that the name of the Kunwa Hill to the south of the village is a survival of the old name of Gunamati or Gunmat. On the northern slope of this hill there are the ruins of a great monastery, out of which numerous Buddhist statues have been dug up, and on the top there are several other Buddhist ruins of an early age. Near the foot of the hill a terrace, 60 feet long, has been traced; and 200 yards to the westward is another terrace, some 250 feet long, on which several Buddhist figures formerly stood. The villagers have unfortunately ransacked these remains, leaving in places only a number of trenches to mark the position of the walls; and most of the statues have been carried off to the Brahmanical temples in the neighbourhood. The excavations made by General Cunningham show however that the lower platform was covered with a great building with its back wall against the hill, as described by Hiuen Tsiang; against this wall some Buddhist statues of granite were found; the outline of two large quadrangles was disclosed; and the remains of several cells were also laid bare. The remains on the top of the hill consist of a stūpa and two small temples, besides three masonry platforms or basements. General Cunningham was of opinion that these temples were built in 9th or 10th century; that the date of the stūpa cannot be placed much later than the 4th century A. D.; and that in all probability it was coeval with the foundation of the monastery on the slopes below.

At the foot of the hills which shut in Dharāwat on the south, stretches a large tank 2,000 feet in length and 800 feet broad, the name of which, Chandokhar, an abbreviation of Chandra Pokhar, perpetuates the legend (mentioned in the account of Lāth) that it was made by Rājā Chandra Sena. Two modern temples at its north-eastern corner and a small shrine at some distance to the east contain a large collection of ancient statues, of which the most remarkable is a statue of Karttikayini, the female energy of the war-god, inscribed with the Buddhist creed—a curious example of the way in which Buddhism coalesced with Brahmanism in the days of its decline. Between the two temples lies another colossal image, representing the Bodhisat Avalokita, which is called Bhairo by the people. It shows a life-size figure standing under an arch formed by a thick lotus stem, from which numerous offshoots strike off, ending in flowers which support tiny figures of men, women and animals. The figure has 12 arms, and in the head dress is a small figure of Buddha seated with both hands in his lap. Round the head is inscribed the Buddhist creed and on either side are the figures of two female votaries.

Dharāwat probably offers the most fertile field for exploration in the whole district. The village itself contains a large number of mounds, which probably mark the site of the old town of Dharāwat; and ruins of mounds and brick terraces are scattered over the hills to the south. Vast quantities of bricks have been dug out by the villagers from this great collection of ruins, and a number of Buddhist statues have been unearthed; but there has as yet been no systematic excavation, and there can be little doubt that valuable archæological results would reward a thorough exploration. Much however has been destroyed by the excavations of the villagers, which are likely, unless checked, to efface the last traces of the lofty terraces and buildings which once occupied the picturesque hill-side down to the edge of the water. *See* also Report Arch. Surv. Ind., Vol. I, pp. 53—55, Vol. VIII, pp. 36—39, and Vol. XVI, pp. 39—46.

Gayā subdivision.—The head-quarters subdivision of the district, lying between 24° 17′ and 25° 5′ N. and 84° 17′ and 85° 24′ E., and extending over 1,905 square miles. Its population was 751,855 in 1901 as against 832,442 in 1891, the decrease in the number of inhabitants being due to the plague raging at the time of the census. Of the total number enumerated 662,536 are Hindus, 88,976 are Muhammadans, and the remainder are members of other religions. The density of population for the whole subdivision is only 395 persons to the square mile, but the population is very sparse to the south, which includes a portion of the northern fringe of the Chotā Nāgpur plateau. It contains 3 towns, Gayā, the head-quarters, Tekāri and Sherghāti, and 2,999 villages, the proportion of villages per square mile being 1·5 and of houses 80·2, while the average number of inhabitants in each village is 224. The subdivision comprises 6 thānas or police circles, including Gayā town, which forms an independent police division under a separate Inspector. The other thānas are Mofussil Gayā, Atrī, Bārāchatti, Sherghāti, and Tekāri. For the purposes of revenue administration it is divided into the 8 *parganas* or fiscal divisions of Gayā, Dakhner, Maher, Pahrā, Sanaut, Atrī, Sherghāti and Kābar. Out of the total area (1,219,200 acres) only 671,682 acres are cultivated and 467,626 acres are irrigated. The large proportion of uncultivated land is due to the fact that in the Sherghāti and Bārāchatti thānas, adjoining the hilly range to the south, the area of waste land exceeds that under cultivation. The principal crop is rice, which is grown on 296,700 acres, and next in importance come gram (90,800 acres), wheat (65,000 acres), maize (35,000 acres) and linseed (26,000 acres).

Gayā Town.—The chief town and administrative head-quarters of the district situated on the western bank of the Phalgu in 24° 49′ N. and 85° 1′ E. For purposes of municipal administration, the town also includes the suburbs of Mānpur and Buniādganj on the eastern bank of the Phalgu, but these villages are practically distinct from the remainder of the town. The population, which was 66,843 in 1872, rose to 76,415 in 1881, and to 80,383 in 1891, but fell in 1901 to 71,288, the decrease in the number of inhabitants being due to the plague which was raging at the time of the census. Of the total number enumerated, 54,223 or 76 per cent. are Hindus, 16,778 or 23½ per cent. are Muhammadans, while among the remainder are 156 Christians and 121 Jains. The town is bounded on the north by the Murli and Rāmsilā Hills, on the south by the Brahmajuni Hill, on the east by the river Phalgu, and on the west by open country broken by the small low ridge known as the Katāri Hill. The eastern portion stretches along a rocky ridge between the Brahmajuni Hill and the river, and the western portion slopes gradually to a plain skirted by hills to the north and south. The greater part of Gayā may, therefore, be said to lie in a valley, and its situation renders it an extremely hot and dusty station, owing to the reflection of the sun's rays from the rocks by which it is encompassed and from the parched sands of the Phalgu.

Sāhibganj. It is locally divided into two parts—the old town of Gayā and the new town known as Sāhibganj. There is a marked distinction between these two adjoining portions. The former contains the residence of the priests who preside over the Gayā pilgrimage, and is regarded by all Hindus as a place of peculiar sanctity. The latter is the trading quarter and also the seat of administration, where the civil offices and the dwelling places of the European residents are situated. Sāhibganj is principally inhabited by business men of all classes, merchants, traders, artizans, money-lenders and professional men. It is a modern town with many straight, broad streets and numerous cross roads, such as are seldom seen in other parts of Bihār. It was laid out by Mr. Law, a Collector at the end of the 18th century, after whom it was called Ilāhabad or Law's city; and it contains few buildings of any interest. Stretching along the river bank in the portion of the town between old Gayā and Rāmsilā Hill, are the old houses formerly occupied by the European residents, from whom the name Sāhibganj is apparently derived; they are situated in a quarter called Ramnā, the name of which shows that it was formerly the site of a deer park. Further to the north at the foot of Rāmsilā Hill is the old European cemetery adjoining the Muhammadan Imāmbāra. This cemetery, which is now no longer used, contains graves dating back to the early part of last century; the most interesting of these are the monument erected in 1821 in memory of Francis Gillanders, Collector of taxes on pilgrims at Gayā, the tomb of Ricketts, the founder of the Doveton College in Calcutta, who died at Gayā in 1835, and a large grave and memorial tablet erected over the remains of a number of seamen of the Naval Brigade who "died of disease while serving at Gayā during the year of sorrow, 1857-58." A large pillared archway stands close to the Jama] Masjid, which was built by a Collector of Gayā at the end of the 18th century, and was apparently intended to guard the entrance of a *sarai*. Not far off, in front of the Pilgrim Hospital, is a large sandstone pillar, over 16 feet high, which was brought here from Bakraur, where it formed the shaft of a pillar said to have been erected by Asoka; a Persian inscription shows that it was set up in its present position in 1789.

To the south-west of Sāhibganj are the public offices, revenue, magisterial, civil, opium, police, etc.; to the west are the European residences grouped in the neighbourhood of a large *maidān;* and beyond these again lie the jail, the race-course and the golf links. The latter have been laid out on the rocky flanks of the Brahmajuni Hill at a place known locally as Gaibachhwā, and so called from a stone image of a cow suckling its calf which stands there. Close to the jail, under the northern side of the Brahmajuni Hill, are the cemetery and the police lines, and further to the north-east, on the side of the *maidān*, are the Church and an excellent Public Library called the Halliday Library, which was founded in 1857 in commemoration of the visit of Sir Frederic Halliday, then Lieutenant-Governor of Bengal. It has a funded capital of Rs. 12,000 in Government securities, and possesses nearly 3,000 volumes, besides a poor collection of local art-ware and manufactures. Between this portion of the town and the railway station are the quarters of the railway staff. Gayā, which was previously an unimportant terminus of the Patna-Gayā line, has become a large railway centre with a resident District Traffic Superintendent, a District Engineer, an Assistant Engineer and a Railway Doctor, besides a large floating construction staff and a numerous population of lesser railway officials and employés. Large areas of land have been acquired by the Railway Company in this part of the town, which is now covered with the quarters constructed for the staff. The railway station itself is situated close to some small red granite hills, the spurs of Rāmsila Hill; and to the west a large railway bridge spans the Phalgu, passing a small rocky island crowned with a Hindu temple. To the south a large wooden bridge spans the river and connects Sāhibganj with the suburbs of Mānpur and Buniādganj, and a short distance up the river is a small hill, called Rām Gayā, which forms one of the sacred places of pilgrimage.

Old Gayā.

The old town of Gayā opposite this hill on the western bank of the Phalgu presents a complete contrast to the modern town. Many of the buildings are situated on rocky points and the spires, of the temples, the lofty houses and the numerous *ghāts* leading down to the Phalgu, with the crest of the Brahmajuni Hill in the background, form a very picturesque view from the opposite bank of the river. It is a town of narrow streets and crooked alleys, shut in by high masonry houses; in place of the broad thoroughfares and busy bazars found in the modern quarter of Sāhibganj, the visitor to Gayā proper meets a labyrinth of narrow streets and lanes flanked by high masonry houses with overhanging balconies or frontages of carved woodwork black with smoke and age. Many of these are loopholed for defence against raids, and the existence of small forts on high escarpments and, until recently, of great city gates shows that the town was built with the object of preserving the sacred shrines and the treasures of its priests from rapine. "Old Gayā," says Buchanan Hamilton, "has been often attacked and sometimes plundered. The sanctity of the place would have been no security against Mahrattas' rapacity; and when these invaded the district, the priests boldly formed themselves into 14 companies, to each of which was entrusted the defence of an entrance into the town. Except at these entrances the houses and a few walls formed a continued barrier, and the projecting angles and small windows of the houses formed a strong defence, so that the Mahrattas were on all occasions repulsed."

The Vishnupad.

The great interest of old Gayā lies however in the sacred shrines which attract pilgrims from all parts of India. None of them are very ancient, but most have been erected on old sites, or have been built with old materials; and a large number of ancient statues, mostly Brahmanical, are found in all parts of the town and more especially about the temples, where they are fixed in the walls or in small recesses forming separate shrines. The latter cluster most thickly round the Vishnupad, the great temple which is the centre of the Gayā pilgrimage. This temple, which derives its name from the footprints of Vishnu enshrined within it, is a solid structure of grey granite, which was built in the 18th century by the Marāthā princess Ahalyā Bai. The main building is an open hall or *mandapa*, 58 feet square, supported on eight rows of pillars clustered in groups of four and disposed in two storeys, one above the other, which gives a massive but somewhat heavy appearance to the exterior. The centre is covered by a gracefully shaped dome, formed in the usual Indian manner by overlapping stones. The sanctum of the temple is an octagonal tower with a lofty pyramidal roof, the total height of the tower being about 100 feet. The sides of the octagon are alternately plain and indented, each angle as it reaches the pyramidal roof finishing in a series of small pinnacles one above the other, until they all culminate in a single tall and rather graceful pinnacle crowned by a large gilded flag. The sanctum, which has folding doors plated with silver, enshrines an identation also encased with solid silver, supposed to be the foot-print of Vishnu himself, which is simply a long shallow hole in the rock somewhat resembling a man's footmark in shape but much larger. Immediately in front hangs a bell presented by Rānajīt Pānde, the minister of the Rājā of Nepāl, and at the entrance to the sanctum there is a second bell bearing the following inscription:—"A gift to the Bishnupad by Mr. Francis Gillanders. Gayā, 15th January, 1790." Gillanders, as we know from the inscription on his tomb, was Collector of the old pilgrim tax, and his epitaph bears witness to the kindly feelings which he felt towards the pilgrims and which he has exhibited in this unusual manner. The temple stands in a courtyard, irregular in shape and much contracted in size by several other buildings, of which the most interesting is an open hall, called Solahvedi, with pillars of solid granite resting on the bare rock, where the pilgrims assemble before beginning the round of holy places. In another courtyard close by stands a small granite temple dedicated to Vishnu as Gadādhar or the mace-bearer, and near its north-western corner there is a small rough pillar, and a rude carving of an elephant, called Gaj, from which the five *kos* forming the circuit of pilgrimage are measured. In the passage near the gate there is a fine statue of Indra seated on a throne supported by two elephants, and to the north-west of it stands the temple of Gayāsurī Devī, containing a statue of the eight-armed Durgā slaying the buffalo or Maheshāsura. There are a number of other minor shrines grouped round the Vishnupad, and in the precincts of the temple itself and near the *ghāts* leading to the river-bed are numerous lingams and statues. The latter are nearly all of the time of the Pāla kings (800—1200 A. D.), but in a small shrine on the way to the Vishnupad there is a figure of an elephant in the act of plucking flowers or fruit from a tree, which dates back to at least the beginning of the Christian era.

A little to the north of the Vishnupad, and by the side of the road leading to it, is a temple sacred to the Sun, in which is enshrined a fine statue of the Sun-god, with his seven horses driven by Arun on the pedestal. It stands to the west of the sacred Surajkund, a large tank of pea-green water lying deep below the surface, which is said to resemble the famous Swetganga tank at Purī. Another large statue of the same god is enshrined in the temple of Sūrya, close by the Vishnupad, at the Bāhmani Ghāt, where there are a number of small temples of much repute but poor appearance. About half a mile to the south-west of the Vishnupad, and immediately under the

Brahmajuni Hill, is the famous Akshayabat, or undying banyan tree, at which the pilgrims make their offerings to the Gayāwāls and conclude their pilgrimage. Close to it is the temple of Prapitāmaheswar, built entirely of granite blocks, the remains of former buildings, and to the westward is a large tank called Rukminikund. The only other temple calling for separate mention is the temple of Krishna Dwārika, containing a statue of Krishna which is said to have been discovered during the excavation of a well at a date later than the Muhammadan invasion.

Brahmajuni Hill. The hills in the immediate neighbourhood of Gayā also partake of the sanctity of the city, and are accordingly crowned with temples. The highest of these to the south of the town is called Brahmajuni, or the female energy of Brahmā, a name which is derived from a small natural fissure in the rocks at the top of the hill, through which a person can just manage to crawl. This is looked upon as a symbol of the *yoni* or womb, and it is believed that by crawling through it the pilgrim escapes rebirth from a human womb. Close by, on the summit of the hill, is a small temple containing a statue, said to be a representation of Brahmā, though it properly belongs to Siva, as the figure has five and not four heads, as in regular statues of Brahmā. This figure is placed on an old pedestal, which is said to have been inscribed with a verse recording the erection of the statue in 1633; and on the left there is a small figure with a horse on the pedestal, which General Cunningham believed to be most probably a statue of Sambhunāth, the third of the 24 Jain hierarchs, whose cognizance is a horse. The hill rises almost precipitously from the plain to the height of 450 feet; and the ascent most commonly used is to the south-east, where there is a long flight of stone steps erected some 40 years ago for the convenience of pilgrims by the Marāthā Deva Rao Bhao Sāhib, but the hill can also be approached by a rugged path near the Police lines. To the right of this path, overlooking the gorge which separates the central peak from its northern flank, is a gigantic rock, which presents a remarkable resemblance to the head of a man in a full-bottomed wig.

Rāmsilā Hill. To the north of the town the granite hill of Rāmsilā rises to a height of 372 feet. Like Brahmajuni, it is approached by a flight of stone steps leading up to a small temple perched on its crest. The temple contains a lingam, called Pātāleswara Mahādeo, as well as small figures of Siva and Pārvatī. The upper portion of the building is modern, being composed of various ancient fragments, but the lower part of the temple is undoubtedly old, and the date of 1071 Samvat or A.D. 1014, found on one of the blocks of granite may record the actual time of the erection of the temple.

See also Reports Arch. Surv. Ind., Vol. 1, pp. 1—4, and Vol. III, pp. 107—139; also Report Arch. Surv., Bengal Circle, for 1901-02.

Gayāwāls.—The pilgrim priests of Gayā who preside over the *srāddha* ceremonies performed by the pilgrims. The legend of their origin has been given in Chapter IV, from which it will be seen that they have special claims to sanctity, as without them the Gayā *srāddha* would be impossible. At the end of the pilgrimage it is indispensably necessary to worship the Gayāwāl's feet and receive his blessing, when he pronounces the word "*Suphal*" and thereby certifies that the offerings have been fruitful and the souls of the ancestors are saved. They alone have the right to officiate as priests and receive offerings, and no *srāddha* is efficacious without their patronage. Their position is therefore a high one, and a committee of Hindu gentlemen, appointed by the Magistrate of Gayā during the last census to determine the classification of castes, held them to be a high class of Brāhmans as "the Hindus of the whole of India, including Brāhmans of all the countries who come to Gayā, worship the Gayāwāls in the same way as if they were worshipping Sri Vishnu himself." They accordingly classed the Gayāwāls with the Pāncha Gaur, Pāncha Drāvida and Sākadwīpi Brāhmans. At present there appears to be a danger of their total extinction. The number of their houses is said to have been originally 1,484; in Dr. Buchanan Hamilton's time they numbered about 1,000 families; in 1893 a prominent Gayāwāl counted the number on the occasion of a visit of the Lieutenant-Governor of Bengal and found there were only 128 families; while the census of 1901 shows there were of pure Gayāwāls only 168 males and 153 females. The cause of this rapid diminution must be sought partly in the life they lead, which is indolent and sedentary, but the chief cause of their gradual decrease is the marriage difficulty. A peculiar class of Brāhmans, able to marry and adopt only within their own ranks, marriage is a serious difficulty, as marriageable girls are few; and most of the widowers are therefore unable to marry. This has led to a mistaken view of their marriage laws, which has found expression in the quaint statement* that "Gayalese widowers are barred the privilege of wiving after the death of their first wife, as Hindu widows after the death of their first husband."

* Balfour's Cyclopædia of India, 1885.

The necessity of perpetuating the race has accordingly led to a curious form of adoption, which is quasi-commercial in character. Old families are constantly dying out, and in the nature of things new houses cannot arise. To further complicate matters, the heads of many of the surviving houses are women. The Gayāwālins fifty years ago were more or less emancipated, but at the present day they are *pardānashin*. As *pardānashin* women they can receive foot-worship only from their own sex, and nowhere but in their houses, whereas strictly this should be performed at the Askhayabat or undying fig-tree, where the pilgrims' round ends. There must therefore be some delegated recipient of worship, as no pilgrimage to Gayā and no offerings made there are valid without this rite. The difficulty is met by adoption, of which there are two forms. In some cases a child under five years of age is adopted, and this adoption is final and irrevocable. The majority of adoptions, however, are of a different kind, and are really matters of business convenience. In order to remove the inconvenience caused by the Gayāwālin's inability to receive pilgrims, and to save her from the loss of income caused thereby, the practice has sprung up of adopting by deed and, in many cases, of adopting adults. Generally, according to the terms of the deed, the adopted son comes into the property on the death of the adoptrix, but the deed usually reserves her right to repudiate the adpoted son in case of misconduct.

The income of the Gayāwāls is chiefly derived from what they receive from the pilgrims in the shape of money and other gifts. Their annual income varies from Rs. 200 or Rs. 300 to perhaps Rs. 30,000 or Rs. 40,000, but only a few families have an income of more than Rs. 20,000. This easily acquired, though fluctuating, income and the sedentary habits of the Gayāwāls are not conducive to a life of moral or intellectual progress; as a class they have long been under the stigma of leading loose and dissolute lives, and their general want of education is notorious, though there are some noticeable exceptions among them.

Some of the Gayâwāls do not bear the titles of other Brāhmans, but have peculiar family designations. In some cases their names end with the *paddhati* or family designation of inferior castes such as Bārik (the makers of leaf plates), Mahto, a common name of Kurmis, &c. In other cases the family designation appears to be derived from some peculiar characteristic of an ancestor, such as Nakphopha, probably a nickname given because of some deformity of the nose, Bithal, a title derived from the name of a dog, and Chiranyan, a name apparently derived from a fondness for birds.

Ghenjan.—A village and Government estate situated on the Morhar in the south of the Jahānābād subdivision about 5 miles west of the Makhdumpur railway station. The village contains a number of ancient Buddhist and Brahmanical statues, the most interesting of which is a large seated Buddha wearing a necklace and three-pointed diadem. There is also a large statue of Avalokitesvara with an inscription on the pedestal stating that it was the gift of the Sthavira Ratna Sinha, who came from Nālanda and dedicated it for the benefit of two disciples. The ruins of an ancient brick temple exist to the north-east of the village; and in the village itself there is a modern temple containing a large standing figure of Tāra, now worshipped as Bhagavatī and carefully hidden by a yellow cloth. Many minor images are collected at this temple; and at some distance in the open fields there are a large statue of Buddha and an image of Vishnu.—See Report Arch. Surv., Bengal Circle, 1901-02.

Gurpā Hill.—A hill in the head-quarters subdivision, situated to the south-east of Gayā, at a distance of one mile to the north of Gurpā station on the railway from Gayā to Katrāsgarh. It extends for some distance from south-west to north-east and has three peaks, the highest of which rises to a height of nearly 1,000 feet. The hill is very steep and difficult to climb, being composed of polished slippery boulders, but a rough track leads across it to the south-western side, ultimately losing itself in a rough upward incline at the base of the highest or north-eastern peak. Here there is a small rude shrine, consisting merely of six small mounds of earth, sacred to Duārpāla or the door-keeper of Gurpāsinmāi, the god of the hill. By its side, concealed by jungle growth, there is the mouth of a tunnel or cave, which branches into two at a short distance from the entrance. One passage leading downwards is choked with debris, while the other leads upwards till it becomes a mere fissure in the rocks. At this point another passage branches off to the north-east up a staircase of 28 stone steps, at the end of which it turns sharply to the right and ends in a platform formed by a huge boulder. At the edge of this platform is a small pool formed by a natural depression in the rock, which is an object of worship in the neighbourhood. After this, the tract leads up a steep incline over boulders polished by the action of rain water to the smoothness of marble, until another platform is reached. From this point a second tunnel or cave runs across the top of the hill. It is formed by huge rocks leaning against one another and thus forming a natural archway, and it ends in a precipice about 500 feet high. The track to the top of the peak continues from the platform at the entrance of this cave by means of a steep stairway of steps or niches cut in the stone and leading to the summit. On a small boulder at the side of the cave there are some Buddhist sculptures; and on the top of the peak itself there are two miniature shrines made of huge bricks, sculpture and statuary, loosely piled together without mortar or cement, which enclose a pair of foot-prints on stone slabs, a number of Buddhist statues, and some small votive stūpas. On the western peak there is another square basement of bricks, and on the southern peak there are more fragments of statuary, sculptures and stūpas.

It has been suggested that Gurpā Hill is the Kukkutapādagiri of the Buddhist legend related in the next article on Hasrā Hill. In the legend, as told by Hiuen Tsiang, it is stated that the hill was also called Gurupādagiri, or the mountain of the venerable master, because the people did not dare to alter the name of Kāsyapa, and therefore spoke of him as Gurupāda, or the venerable master. Hiuen Tsiang also relates that Kāsyapa ascended the north side of the mountain and proceeded along the winding path till he came to the south-western ridge. Here the crags and precipices barred his further advance, but forcing his way through the tangled brushwood, he struck the rock with his staff and thus opened a way. He then passed on till he was again stopped in his ascent by the rocks interlacing one another, but once again he opened up a passage and came out on the peaks on the north-eastern side. It has been pointed out in favour of the identification of the Gurpā Hill with the sacred Kukkutapādagiri that the name Gurpā is an exact Prākritic development of the Sanskrit Gurupāda; that the large tunnel running through the hill and forming a passage leading to the top corresponds with the cleft through it which was made by Kāsyapa, and that its distance from Bodh Gayā and the three peaks on the summit agree closely with the account given by Hiuen Tsiang.

See An account of the Gurpā Hill, by Bābu Rākhāl Dās Banerji, J. A. S. B., Vol. II, No. 4, April 1906.

Hasrā Hill —A hill 4 miles S.S.W. of Wazīrganj, which has been identified by Dr. Stein as the Kukkutapādagiri Hill of Fa Hian and Hiuen Tsiang, where Kāsyapa, the earliest and greatest of Buddha's disciples, lies buried, the mountain having burst asunder to receive him. According to Hiuen Tsiang, when Buddha was on the point of attaining Nirvāna, Kāsyapa, his chief disciple, received from him a commission to preserve the law, and for this purpose he summoned a great convocation, the first great Council of the Buddhist Church, which was held in the Sattapanna cave at Rājgīr. Twenty years afterwards, in disgust at the impermanence of the world, he resolved to die, and set out for Kukkutapādagiri or the Cock's foot mountain. On arriving at the middle point of the three peaks, he took out the garment of Buddha, and expressed an ardent vow, whereupon the three peaks covered him over. Here he lies buried, awaiting the advent of Maitreya, the future Buddha, on whose coming Kāsyapa will issue forth, and, after delivering to him the garment of Buddha, enter into Nirvāna.

Hasrā is the name given to a low ridge about 200 feet high at the northern extremity of a higher range of hills rising abruptly from the level plain. A small defile, about a quarter of a mile long, which is known as the Hasrā Kol, separates the ridge from the hill on the south. The whole of this little valley is strewn with ancient building materials extracted from numerous ruined mounds, and it is clear that it must once have been occupied by an important Buddhist religious establishment. One of these mounds near the western entrance of the valley evidently marks the position of a building of some dimensions, and a large circular brick mound close to the south of the southern face of the ridge represents the remains of a large stūpa; in spite of its having been used as a quarry by the villagers, it still stands 25 feet high and measures 75 by 92 feet.

Much ancient sculpture is said to have been found in the course of the excavation for bricks carried on by the neighbouring villagers, and those in a good state of preservation have been removed to the rustic shrines in the vicinity, but many broken pieces of relievos and ornamented bases of statues may still be seen in several places. One such relievo, which shows a Buddha (now headless) seated in meditation, has the Buddhist formula engraved on it in characters of about the 10h century.

Immediately to the south of the Hasrā Kol is a high hill, some 1,000 feet high, with jungle-covered slopes, which is connected at the highest point on the east with two other spurs of about equal height, all three radiating from one central eminence covered, like the rest, with dense jungle. The central summit of the three peaks, which is known to the people by the name of Sobhnāth, is surmounted by a square parapet, 9 to 10 feet high, built of rough walls and forming a platform or terrace measuring 75 feet on each side. On the top is a mound composed of large bricks, which evidently marks the remains of the stūpa which Hiuen Tsiang mentions on the summit of the Cock's foot mountain. According to his account, "the sides of this mountain are high and rugged, the valleys and gorges are impenetrable. Tumultuous torrents rush down its sides, thick forests envelope the valleys, whilst tangled shrubs grow along its cavernous heights. Soaring upwards into the air are three sharp peaks; their tops are surrounded by the vapours of heaven, and their shapes lost in the clouds. Behind these hills the venerable Mahā-Kāsyapa dwells wrapped in a condition of Nirvāna." Dr. Stein has shewn that the distances and bearings given by Hiuen Tsiang are in full agreement with the position of the Hasrā Hill, and that its natural features strikingly illustrate the origin of the legend as to Kāsyapa's ascent. "The position of the spurs," he says, "corresponds closely to his account, which mentions, besides the northern side of the mountain, ranges to the south-west and north-east. In the confused masses of rocks heaped up all along the crest lines of the three spurs we can look for the passages which Kāsyapa was supposed to have opened with his staff. The tangled brushwood, which surrounded the hill in the days of both pilgrims, still covers it in remarkable thickness, and in the narrow gorges which lead down between the spurs, the rainy season must indeed produce tumultuous torrents. That the name (Kukkutapādagiri) is likely to have been derived from the three spurs resembling in relative position the foot of a cock has already been noticed by Hiuen Tsiang's translators. It is impossible to look down from the top of the central peak, or even to examine the shape of the hill on the map, without being struck with the appropriateness of the simile."

In the village of Bishunpur Tanrwā, about 1½ mile to the west of the Hasrā Hill, a ruined shrine, called the Bhairavasthān, contains a series of fine sculptures of highly finished workmanship, which are said to have been excavated in the Hasrā Kol valley some 25 or 30 years ago. The largest and best preserved of these is a large statue of Buddha with an attendant figure on either side, the whole having evidently formed one group originally. The height of the central figure is 5 feet from the base, and that of the attendant figures 3½ feet each. The characters of the Buddhist formula inscribed on the pedestal point to the 9th or 10th century as the probable date of these fine sculptures. *See* Notes on an Archæological Tour in South Bihār and Hazāribāgh by M. A. Stein, Ph. D., Indian Antiquary, Vol. XXX, 1901, pp. 84—90; also Reports Arch. Surv. Ind., Vol. VIII, pp. 104—106.

Hasuā—Town and police outpost in the Nawāda subdivision, situated on the right bank of the river Tilaiyā on the Gayā-Nawāda road, 9 miles from Nawāda and 27 miles from Gayā town, in 24° 30′ N. and 85° 25′ E. Population (1901) 6,704. It has a considerable reputation for the manufacture of ornamental pottery, contains the residence of several wealthy zamīndārs, and has recently gained some commercial importance, as it has a railway station, called Tilaiyā, on the South Bihār Railway. The place is also of some historical interest as having been the head-quarters of Nāmdār Khān and Kāmgār Khān, military adventurers of the 18th century. Previous to the Permanent Settlement, Nāmdār Khān, and his brother, Kāmgār Khān, were *āmils* of the Muhammadan Subāhdārs. The former owned 14 *parganas* and 84 *ghātwāli gadis* or rent-free tenures, which extended beyond the confines of the district into Patna and Hazāribāgh. The latter was little better than a freebooter, and his forts are found in every part of the subdivision.

Jahānābād subdivision.—Northern subdivision of the district, lying between 24° 59′ and 25° 19′ N. and 84° 27′ and 85° 13′ E., and extending over 606 square miles. The population was 386,535 in 1901 against 393,817 in 1891; of these 350,282 are Hindus and 36,248 are Muhammadans. The surface is generally flat and well irrigated, and the soil supports a larger population than any other part of the district, the density being 638 to the square mile and the average number of houses to the square mile 123·8. The subdivision contains one town, Jahānābād, its head-quarters, and 1,078 villages, and the average number of inhabitants per village is 352. Of the total area (387,840 acres), no less than 314,579 acres are irrigated. The staple crop is rice, which is grown on 139,000 acres or nearly half the cultivated area, and next in importance come gram (42,000 acres) and wheat (30,000 acres). The subdivision comprises 2 police circles, Jahānābād and Arwal, and is divided for fiscal purposes into the four *parganas* of Arwal, Bhalāwar, Ekil and Okri.

Jahānābād town.—Head-quarters town of the subdivision of the same name situated at the confluence of the Morhar and Jamunā rivers in 25° 13′ N. and 85° 0′ E. Population (1901) 7,018. The town is divided into two portions—the residential and trading quarter, with the dispensary and post-office, being situated on the north of the right branch of the Morhar, while the public offices, Subdivisional Officer's residence and the dāk bungalow are on the south of the river. For the convenience of the public there is a small way-side railway station, called Irki, near the latter portion of the town, and the main station of Jahānābād is a short distance to the north. The town was once famous for its weaving industry, and in 1760 it formed one of the eight minor branches connected with the central cloth factory of the East India Company at Patna. In the early years of the last century the town contained about 700 houses, a cloth factory and a native agency for the manufacture of saltpetre. Soon after this the factory began to languish, and eventually it was abolished; local tradition asserts that the Company's connection with the factory came to an end about 1820. But the local industry did not cease in consequence, and a considerable export trade in cotton was carried on in the neighbourhood, till Manchester entered into the competition after the time of the Mutiny. The weaver then found it cheaper to buy English thread, and the consumer began to prefer Manchester piece-goods to the produce of the Indian hand-looms. The manufacture of cotton cloths consequently declined and was displaced by imported goods, but large numbers of the Jolāhā or Muhammadan weaver class still live in the neighbourhood. Lying, however, as it does, on the railway midway between Patna and Gayā, Jahānābād has continued to increase in size and importance; its trade has only been diverted into other channels, and now consists chiefly of food-grains, oil-seeds, piece-goods and fancy articles of European manufacture.

There are no buildings of any interest, and no trace is left of the old brick house said to have been built by the Dutch as a cloth depôt, which is mentioned in the Statistical Account of Bengal as existing 30 years ago.

Jethian.—A village in the head-quarters subdivision, situated some 10 miles north-west of Tetwa Khās (Atrī police-station) at the western side of the valley enclosed by two ranges of hills running south-west from Rājgīr. Jethian is a place of great archæological interest as having been identified with the ancient Buddhist site of Yashtivana or the forest of the staff, so called from a bamboo staff which was used to measure the body of Buddha and then miraculously took root. Hiuen Tsiang has left a detailed account of Yashtivana and the holy Buddhist sites in its neighbourhood. According to his account, Yashtivana was a place surrounded by bamboos, where Buddha for seven days worked miracles for the sake of the Devas and preached the mysterious and excellent law; and in the midst of the bamboo forest was a stūpa built by Asoka. About 10 *li* to the south-west on the south side of a mountain were two hot springs, which Buddha himself caused to appear and in which he bathed, and at the side of them was a stupa marking the spot where he walked for exercise. To the south-east there was another stūpa before the transverse ridge of a mountain, where Buddha expounded the law during three months of rain, and here King Bimbisāra, wishing to come and hear him, cut away the mountain and piled up stones to form steps for the ascent. To the north was a solitary hill in a cave in which the *rishi* Vyāsa lived, and a little distance to the north-east on the side of a small hill there was a stone chamber, large enough to seat 1,000 persons, where Buddha expounded the law for three months. Overhanging this chamber was a large rock, on which Sakra, king of the Devas, and Brahma-rājā pounded some sandal-wood, with the dust of which they sprinkled the body of Buddha; at its south-west angle there was a lofty cavern, which, according to popular legend led to the city of the Asuras. By the side of the cave the pilgrim noticed a remarkable road ascribed to Bimbisāra, who in order to reach the spot where Buddha was, had cut a passage through the rocks, opened up the valleys, levelled the precipices, made a path across the river-courses, built up walls of stone, and bored through the opposing crags.

The researches of Dr. Stein have led to the identification of all the sites mentioned by Hiuen Tsiang. At the western foot of the hill, about ¾ of a mile to the east of the village of Jethian, there is a small undulating plateau, where there are traces of old buildings. This spot is called Jeshtiban, an almost perfect preservation of the ancient name Yashtivana. About two miles to the south-west of Jethian on the other side of the ridge the four hot springs of Tapoban issue at the rocky foot of the hill side, the name being a corruption of *tapta pānī* or hot water, or, more probably, meaning the grove of penances. Only two of these have a large flow; and from the existence of a large mound by the side of the largest, it appears that here are still to be found the two springs mentioned by Hiuen Tsiang and the remains of the stūpa by their side. The springs are visited by pilgrims and by the sick of the neighbourhood seeking relief; and a large fair takes place once a year, when, in the words of the Chinese traveller, "Men from far and near flock here to bathe, after which those who have suffered from disease or chronic affections are often healed."

The site where Buddha expounded the law during the three rainy months has been identified with the place of worship known as Sahudrasthān at the end of a small spur 1½ mile S. E. of Jethian near the gap in the hill range called the Saffi Ghāt. Here there is a shrine resting on a square platform of old bricks, and the slopes below on all sides of the projecting end of the spur are covered with fragments of ancient bricks, which have obviously been removed from the structure to which the platform once belonged. Further evidence in favour of the identification of this structure with the stūpa mentioned by Hiuen Tsiang is supplied by an ancient road carried over a walled foundation, which begins immediately below the Sahudrasthān and can be traced very distinctly for about 600 yards along the hillside to the west. This road can clearly be recognized as that mentioned by Hiuen Tsiang as having been built by Bimbisāra. The rock-dwelling of Vyāsa can also perhaps be identified with a rocky recess at the southern foot of the isolated hill of Bhaluāhi, which forms the south-western end of the range ½ a mile from Saffi Ghāt.

On the northern face of a rocky hill called Chandu, which rises in the eastern range about 2 miles from Jethian and 1½ mile south-east of Khiri, lies the great cave of Rājpind, which is clearly the same as that mentioned by Hiuen Tsiang as containing the lofty cavern called the palace of the Asuras. It is about 90 feet deep in its open part and 20 to 25 feet high, with a breadth of from 20 to 37 feet. In one corner a high fissure runs upwards, which the people believe runs far into the mountain; and above the entrance is a large perpendicular mass of solid rock, which in the days of Hiuen Tsiang was supposed to have had sandal-wood pounded on it for the perfuming of the body of Buddha. A striking confirmation of this identification is found in the existence of an old paved road, supported by walls of massive masonry, which runs along the hillside westwards from Khiri in the direction of the cave. It is between 6 and 12 feet wide, and rises with an easy gradient until after 500 yards it reaches a platform, partly walled up, which gives a fine view over the valley below. The road, cut out in places from the rocky hillside, then descends towards the cave, the entrance of which is reached at about 150 yards from the platform, and here the road widens out into a terrace, 16 feet broad, resting on a massive wall. This road with its walls and platforms fully bears out the more general points in Hiuen Tsiang's account of Bimbisāra's road-making.

Another road of great interest exists on the opposite side of the valley north of Khiri. Here there are the remains of an old paved road, flanked by parallel walls, which leads over the Chakra Ghāt, as the defile through the hills is called. There can be no doubt that the walls were intended for defensive purposes, to protect those using this route from attacks, for which the steep hills on either side would offer great advantages. Protecting walls in exactly similar positions have, Dr. Stein says, been traced in the Swāt Valley, where the prevalence of such elaborate ancient defences is easily accounted for, and it is curious to meet their counterpart in the centre of old Magadha, apparently so peaceful and centralized.

See Notes on an Archæologcial Tour in South Bihār and Hazāribāgh, by M. A. Stein, Ph. D., Indian Antiquary, Vol. XXX, 1901, pp. 61—63 and 81—83.

Kakolat.—*See* Nawāda subdivision.

Kauwādol Hill.—A hill 6 miles to the east of Belā railway station in the extreme north of the head-quarters subdivision, and nearly one mile to the south-west of the Barābar Hills. It is a detached hill rising abruptly from the plains to the height of about 500 feet; it is formed entirely of huge masses of granite piled precipitously one above the other, and is crowned by a gigantic block of stone, which is quite inaccessible. It is said that this pinnacle was formerly topped by another block, which was so perfectly balanced that it used to rock even when a crow alighted on it, and from this circumstance the hill acquired the name of Kauwā-dol or the crow's swing or rocking stone. There is a rough track on the eastern side leading to the foot of the topmost pinnacle, the last portion of which passes over an extremely steep slope of smooth slippery rock, which can only be climbed with bare feet or rubber shoes. Kauwādol has been identified as the site of the ancient monastery of Sīlabhadra. Sīlabhadra was a learned Buddhist of the royal family of Samatata (Lower Bengal), who overcame a learned heretic in a public disputation. As a reward for this victory, the king gave him the revenues of a town, with which he built a magnificent monastery. This was visited by Hiuen Tsiang in the 7th century. He mentions it as being situated about 20 *li* (3¼ miles) to the south-west of the Gunamati monastery by the side of a solitary hill, which he describes as being a single sharp crag like a stūpa. The position of the Kauwādol Hill with respect to the Gunamati monastery at Dharāwat leaves no doubt as to the accuracy of its identification with the Sīlabhadra monastery, which is confirmed by the resemblance of the lofty peak shaped like a stūpa with the peak of Kauwādol, which from a distance looks like a ruined stūpa without its pinnacle.

The remains of the monastery still extant consist of the ruins of an ancient Buddhist temple at the foot of the eastern flank of the hill. The temple enshrines a colossal statue of Buddha, seated in the act of invoking the earth when he was attacked by Māra and his host of evil powers. This is one of the largest statues of Buddha extant, and is in fair preservation, except that a portion of the halo has been broken; the figure is about 8 feet high, with a breadth of 4 feet across the shoulders and of six feet across the knees. It is still *in situ* inside a small brick-built cell, but the temple is otherwise in ruins, only parts of its original brick walls and some 13 granite pillars being traceable; these pillars probably supported an open hall in front of the temple. Among the rocks at the foot of the northern face of the hill there are numerous figures carved in high relief on many of the larger masses of granite. They are much worn, and some have become very faint, as the stone has not withstood the influences of the climate. Most of them represent Brahmanical figures, and by far the most numerous are sculptures of the four-armed Durgā slaying the buffalo demon Maheshāsura. There are, however, three Buddhist figures—one a seated Buddha, the other Vajrasatva, and the third Prajnaparamita. The row in which these figures have been carved contains a number of sculptured Hindu deities, and is a striking example of the fusion of Buddhism and Brahmanism in the period (800—1200 A. D.) to which these carvings belong. *See* also Reports, Arch. Surv. Ind., Vol. I, pp. 40-41, Vol. VIII, pp. 40-41, and Vol. XVI, pp. 46—50; also Report, Arch. Surv., Bengal Circle, for 1901-02.

Konch.—A village, 4 miles west of Tekāri, in the head-quarters subdivision, containing an ancient brick temple. The temple, which now contains a lingam of Siva Kochesvara, is lighted by a tall opening in front, formed by overlapping courses of bricks after the fashion of the original great temple at Bodh Gayā. Externally, however, it differs from that temple in having its sides curved instead of being in straight lines from top to bottom, and in having no external niches with figures enshrined in them. It originally had a flat-roofed pillared hall in front, but this has now fallen in, and the stone pillars supporting it are lying in front of the temple. Inside the shrine the most remarkable piece of sculpture is a slab representing the *avatāras* or incarnations of Vishnu, which differs from other such representations by dividing the Vāmana Avatāra into two scenes, by leaving out the ninth or Buddha Avatāra, and by representing Vishnu in his tenth or Kalki Avatāra in the company of a female deity with a small horse standing in front of them. General Cunningham was of opinion that the date of this temple should be ascribed to the 8th century A. D., but as tradition points to Bhairavendra, who lived about 1450 A. D., as its builder, and as it closely resembles in style the temples at Deo and Umgā which date back to his time, it has been held that the date ascribed to the Konch temple should be put forward some seven centuries. The village also contains a large number of other statues, Buddhistic images and remains of minor temples. *See* Reports, Arch. Surv. Ind., Vol. VIII, pp. 54—61, and Vol. XVI, pp. 52—59; also Report, Arch. Surv., Bengal Circle, 1901-02.

Kurkihār.—A village about 3 miles north-east of Wazīrganj in the head-quarters subdivision. The village is of large size, and must evidently have been a place of considerable importance in former ages, judging from the extent of its ruined mounds and the remarkable amount of old sculpture, carved building stones and ancient bricks, which have been and are still being extracted from them. Kurkihār was identified by General Cunningham with the site of the ancient Kukkutapādagiri or Cock's foot mountain visited by Hiuen Tsiang in the 7th century, but the arguments adduced by Dr. Stein in favour of Hasrā (*q. v.*) being the true site appear conclusive. Though Kurkihār must be denied any claim to distinction as making the site of Kāsyapa's legendary resting place, it still deserves special mention on account of the remarkable abundance of ancient remains which it contains. Carved slabs of large size and architectural fragments of all kinds are found in plenty, often built into the walls of the houses; votive stūpas of different sizes are seen in numbers on the edge of the large tank adjoining the village on the south, where they now serve as washerman's stones, as well as in other places; and great quantities of large bricks of ancient make are still being dug out of the great mound south of the village. Some well-preserved sculptures have been removed by the local zamīndār to his bungalow in the village, the most interesting of which is a relievo representing a teaching Bodhisatwa seated in a niche of rocks between two female attendants. In the frieze above are worshippers approaching a stūpa with offerings, and the top of the relievo shows five Bodhisatwas each enshrined in a small niche. The moulding below the lotus seat contains the usual Buddhist formula inscribed in characters of the 9th or 10th century A. D., and the composition of the whole relievo shows a curious resemblance to many of the products of Græco-Buddhist art in Gandhāra. There is another collection of ancient sculptures in the court-yard of the temple of Bhagavatī, among which is a singularly beautiful figure of Buddha in meditation, which probably dates back to the 10th century A. D. At Punāwān, 3 miles to the south-west, are more Buddhist remains; but much has been destroyed by the villagers digging for bricks, and the remains of an ancient temple of Triloknāth, which once stood here, have now been all carried away.

See also Notes on an Archæological tour in South Bihār and Hazāribāgh, by M. A. Stein, Ph. D., Indian Antiquary, Vol. XXX, 1901, pp. 84—90, and Reports, Arch. Surv. Ind., Vol. I, pp. 13—16, and Vol. XV, pp. 4—6.

Lāth.—A village on the south-eastern boundary of the Jahānābād subdivision situated 2 miles north of Dapthu. Here an extraordinary monolith lies in the open fields. It consists of a granite column, measuring 53¼ feet in length by an average of

3 feet in diameter. This immense column is lying horizontally on the ground, pointing north and south, and about half of it is below the surface of the field. Local tradition asserts that it was intended to be placed in the Chandokhar tank at Dharāwat, 8 miles to the east, and accounts for its present position by the following legend :—

Dharāwat was ruled over by Rājā Chandra Sena, who had a fight with his sister's son, whom he slew; but after the battle, he found that he could not release from his hand the dagger with which he had done the deed. One day, a thirsty calf came towards him, when the Rājā placed a *lotā* of water before it, which it drank up greedily, and the dagger at once became loose in his grasp. In remembrance of this event, he determined to make a lake, which should extend as far as his horse when let loose should circle round. The minister, apprehensive of the horse making a longer circuit than convenient, selected the present north-east corner of the tank at Dharāwat (where there is a now small ruined temple) as the starting point of the horse, turning his head southwards, so that the hills on the south would be the limit of the size of the tank in that direction. The ground thus marked out forms the Chandokhar Tāl. The next morning the Rājā himself dug out five baskets of earth, and his followers did the same, except one Rājput soldier, who sat with his sword in his hand. When the Rājā asked him why he did not dig out five baskets of earth like the rest, he replied that he was a soldier, and only used to carry arms. On hearing this the Rājā gave him a letter to Bhīkham, king of Lankā or Ceylon, and ordered him to bring back a *lāth* or monolith, to place in the middle of the lake. Bhīkham accordingly gave up the pillar, which the soldier carried off; but as he got near Dharāwat the cock crew, and he was therefore obliged to drop it at once at the place where it still lies.

Another legend related by the villagers states that the *devas*, who were carrying the pillar by night to Janakpur in Nepāl, dropped it, hearing a noise in the village and thinking that the villagers were stirring with the on-coming of dawn. The noise they heard was merely a potter working at night; and since then the potters have been cursed, and no potter will live in the village. It may be added that the mineralogical character of the pillar clearly shows that it came from the Barābar Hills, and no one would think of taking it to the Chandokhar Tāl *viā* Lāth.

Mānda Hills.—A group of hills in the south-west of the head-quarters subdivision near Madanpur on the Grand Trunk Road. The quantities of pottery and bricks scattered round these hills show that they once overlooked a large town, and traces of

Buddhist and Saivite shrines are still traceable among the rocks. Burha, 2 miles to the east, contains several sites in which *chaitya* and a large *vihārā* or Buddhist monastery once stood, and there are some hot mineral springs, to which the place probably owed its former importance. Guneri, 3 miles to the south-east, was also the site of a large town and of a *vihārā*, the name of which appears from inscriptions to have been Srī Gunacharita. The village still contains a fine statue of Buddha, round which are grouped numerous smaller Buddhist and Saivite figures; to the north of the village are the remains of several temples round a large tank.

Nabīnagar.—A village and police-station situated on the left bank of the Pūnpūn, 18 miles south of Aurangābād in the subdivision of the same name. Nabīnagar is the centre of a considerable trade in blankets and brass vessels, and contains a tiled hut, known as the temple of Sokhā Bābā, to which persons suffering from snake-bite are brought as a last resource. If the person bitten recovers, clarified butter and molasses are offered to Sokhā Bābā.

Close to Nabīnagar is Chandragarh, the residence of a family of Chauhān Rājputs, who came originally from Mewār. Three members of the family were each granted the title of Rai Bahādur, a sword and a *lākhirāj* grant for good services rendered during the Mutiny. The village contains an old fort built in 1694 A. D.

Nagarjuni Hills.—*See* Barābar Hills.

Nawāda Subdivision.—Eastern subdivision of the district, lying between 24° 31′ and 25° 7′ N., and 85° 17′ and 86° 3′ E., and extending over 955 square miles. Its population was 453,868 in 1901 against 439,565 in 1891. The south of the subdivision, which includes a portion of the northern fringe of the Chotā Nāgpur plateau, is very sparsely populated; and the density for the whole subdivision is 475 persons to the square mile. It contains 2 towns—Nawāda (population 5,908), its head-quarters, and Hasuā (6,704), and 1,752 villages. The number of inhabitants per village is 251, and the average number of houses per square mile is 91·6. The subdivision contains 3 police-stations, viz., Nawāda, Pakrībarāwān and Rajaulī; and for revenue purposes it is divided into the *parganas* or fiscal divisions of Jarra, Narhat, Pachrukhi, Roh and Samai. Of the total area (611,200 acres), 318,800 acres are under cultivation, of which 241,000 acres are irrigated. The staple crop is rice, which is grown on 141,000 acres, and next in importance come gram (43,000 acres) and wheat (30,700 acres). Wārisalīganj to the north of Nawāda town is an important mart, founded by Wāris Alī Khān, a member of the family of Kāmgār Khān; the name is sometimes spelt Worseleyganj from an erroneous belief that it was named after

Mr. Worseley, a former Deputy Magistrate of Nawāda. Some 15 miles south-east of Nawāda are the falls of Kakolat, in the northern face of the range in which the Mahābar Hill (1,832 feet high) is situated. Akbarpur, 10 miles south of the same town, is a large village containing a monastery of the Nānakpanthi sect ; and at Budhauli in the jurisdiction of the Pakrībarāwān police station there is a wealthy Hindu monastery or *math* under an abbot or *mahanth* of the *Purī* sub-order of *Dasnami* ascetics. About 14 miles south-east of Pakrībarāwān lies the pretty valley of Kauwākol with some of the most picturesque scenery in the district, and close by iron ore exists at Pachambā. There are also several mica mines in the south of the subdivision situated at Basauni, Belam, Chatkarī, Dubaur, Sapahī and Singar.

Nawāda town.—Head-quarters town of the subdivision of the same name, lying on both sides of the river Khuri in 24° 53′ N. and 85° 33′ E. Population (1901) 5,908. The name is a corruption of Nau-ābād or the new town. It is divided into two blocks by the river, the portion on the left bank being the older, while that on the right bank is modern and contains the public offices, sub-jail, dispensary and school. Since the opening of the South Bihār Railway, on which it is a station, Nawāda has been growing into an important trade centre. Two miles to the north there is a handsome Jain temple standing in the middle of a large tank to the west of the public road, but the town itself contains no important buildings and has but little historical interest. Before its acquisition by the East India Company, it was ruled by the nearly independent Rājās of Hasuā, and after its acquisition it was the centre of great disorder till 1845, when it became the head-quarters of the newly-created subdivision. The elements of disorder came to the front again during the Mutiny, when Nawāda was overrun by marauding parties. The local offices were destroyed, but the Government records were saved by the native officials, who hid them in a cave in a neighbouring hill. These are the only public records dating beyond 1857 which still exist in the district.

Pachār Hill.—A hill near the eastern boundary of the Aurangābād subdivision, about 2 miles to the south-east of Rafiganj. The principal object of interest is a cave half way up the southern face of the hill, a natural fissure in the rocks, the opening of which has been closed by a brick wall giving access to the cave through a small stone-faced door. In front of it stands a portico resting on stone pillars, and inside the cave is a large statue of Parsvanāth and other minor images, which are evidently all Jain. There are no traces of Buddhist remains, and the cave clearly belongs to the Jains; the existence of a Jain sanctuary in this locality is of some interest on account of its isolation. Cheon, a village near about ¼ mile from the foot of the hill, contains the ruins of an old Brahmanical temple built of square granite blocks without cement, and there are several ruins in a cluster of hills at Deokuli, one mile to the south.

Prāgbodhi Mountain.—In Hiuen Tsiang's account of his travels in Magadha, he says:—"To the east of the place where Gayā Kāsyapa sacrificed to fire, crossing a river, we come to a mountain called Prāgbodhi (Po-ko-li-pot), *i. e.*, the mountain leading to (before) perfect intelligence, as Buddha, when about to attain enlightenment, first ascended this mountain. Ascending the north-east slope and coming to the top, the earth shook and the mountain quaked, whilst the mountain Deva in terror thus spoke to Bodhisattva:—"This mountain is not the fortunate spot for attaining supreme wisdom. If here you stop and engage in the *Samādhi* of diamond (*i.e.*, *Vajra-samādhi*), the earth will quake and gape, and the mountain be overthrown upon you." Then Bodhisattva descended, and half way down the south-west slope he halted. There backed by the crag and facing a torrent is a great stone chamber. Here he sat down cross-legged. Again the earth quaked and the mountain shook, and Deva cried out in space, "This is not the place for a Tathāgata to perfect supreme wisdom." From this, south-west, 14 or 15 *li*, not far from the place of penance, there is the *Pīpala* (*Pi-po-lo*) tree, under which is a diamond throne (*Vajrāsana*, an imperishable throne, supposed to be the centre of the earth, and the spot where all Buddhas arrived to complete wisdom)."

On the eastern side of the Nilājan, or Phalgu, river opposite Bodh Gayā, is a narrow range of hills extending in a north-easterly direction from the Mora lake to the village of Ganjās. This range is sometimes called the Mora and sometimes the Ganjās Hills, but the middle portion of it is locally known as Dhongra Hill. The slope on the south-eastern side is abrupt, while that on the north-west is more broken. About half way down the latter slope, quite hidden from below by a wall of rock, is a cave at the base of a precipitous cliff. The entrance is small, and has been fitted during comparatively recent years by some ascetic with a frame-work of wood to hold a door, if door it can be called, the aperture of which is little more than 2 feet square. Within, the cave is of an irregular oval shape, measuring about 16 feet 5 inches from north-east to south-west, and 10 feet 9 inches from north-west to south-east. The roof is vaulted, and about 9½ feet high at the highest point. The roof had apparently been roughly hewn; but centuries of weathering have obliterated any distinct traces of cutting. A broken stone image of an eight-armed goddess, with a few letters of the Buddhist formula in Kuthila character of perhaps the 9th or 10th century, lies in the cave. Below the cave on the slope of the hill is a large artificially levelled terrace, about 70 yards square, with traces of the foundations of stone buildings; while round about are other remains of smaller dimensions. Above the cave along the summit of the hill are the remains of some seven stūpas of different sizes, the largest being about 40 feet in diameter. Hiuen Tsiang says: "When Asoka Rājā came into power, he signalized each spot up and down this mountain, which Bodhisattva had passed, by erecting distinguishing posts and stūpas." Again, speaking of Buddha leaving the Prāgbodhi mountain, he says:—"Half way down the south-west slope he halted: there backed by the crag and facing a torrent is a great stone chamber." The cave as described above is undoubtedly backed by a crag, and on the right hand front below is a steep valley, down which the rain water rushes in the rainy season. The distance from Bodh-Gayā corresponds with that given by Hiuen Tsiang (14 or 15 *li*). Though the line of hills runs north-east and south-east, and therefore the slope in which the cave is, faces the north-west, more or less, it must be remembered that Buddha ascended the range at the north-eastern end and proceeded in a south-westerly direction towards Bodh Gayā. He would probably descend the hill in the same direction, *i. e.*, taking a slanting course, the direct descent being too steep. It is quite intelligible therefore that Hiuen Tsiang describes the spot as half way down the south-western slope. It would seem not impossible that the stūpas, the remains of which still exist on the top of the hill, may be those which the Chinese pilgrim tells us were erected by Asoka.

The cave described above must not be confused with that described by General Cunningham, which is evidently a natural fissure and quite distinct.*

Pretsilā Hill.—A hill 540 feet in height, situated 5 miles north-west of Gayā. The meaning of the name is the hill of ghosts, and it is sacred to Yama, the Hindu god of hell, and forms one of the sacred places of pilgrimage. On the top of the

---

* The account of the Prāgbodhi mountain has been contributed by Mr. C. A. Oldham, Director of Agriculture, Bengal, formerly Collector of Gaya. The cave described by Mr. Oldham is somewhat difficult to find, being completely hidden from below, and it is clear that it escaped the notice of General Cunningham. The cave mentioned by him in Reports Arch. Surv. Ind., pp. 105—107 is evidently one of the many fissures further to the south.

hill is a small temple appropriately dedicated to Yama, as it is the belief of the pilgrims that by the due observance of the *srāddha* or funeral rites and by offering the balls of flour and rice called *pindas* they will ensure the deliverance of the souls of their ancestors from the realm of Yama and secure their admittance to the paradise of Vishnu. A long flight of stone steps, built by a pious resident of Calcutta in 1774, leads to the shrine, which contains a rude piece of rock marked with a golden line, before which the pilgrims place the *pindas* for the repose of the spirits of their ancestors. At the foot of the hill are three tanks named Sati, Nigra and Sukha, and there is a fourth tank called Rāmkund on the summit near the temple of Yama, in which it is said that Rām himself bathed. Whoever bathes in this tank is cleansed from his sins, and whoever recites the proper *mantras* or spells with the usual offerings of *srāddha* and *pindas* is freed from pain.

Rajaulī.—A village in the south of the Nawāda subdivision, situated on the left bank of the Dhanārjī river in 24° 39′ N., and 85° 30′ E. Population (1901) 1,509. It is connected by a metalled road with Nawāda, 18 miles due north, and is an important mart to which the produce of the neighbouring hills is brought on pack-bullocks or on low solid-wheeled carts. The village is situated in the bend of the river, and possesses an excellent system of drainage, which dates back to the time when it was a municipality. The drains are of cement, but since the abolition of the municipality they have been neglected and have become silted up. Rajaulī contains a police-station, a branch establishment of the Nānakpanthi monastery at Akbarpur (8 miles to the north), and a Muhammadan charitable endowment, in which there is a sacred fire said to have been lit 300 years ago by fire brought from Mecca.

The hills south of Rajaulī present some of the most picturesque scenery in the district. They are said to have sheltered the seven *rishis*, and particular peaks are named after one or more of them. At Lomāsgiri, 4 miles to the north east, there is a cave in which Lomāsa lived. Durvāsārhi (2,202 feet high) derives its name from the holy but irascible Durvāsa, whose curses are famous in Hindu mythology. Sringirikh again was the home of the saint Sringa, and is perhaps the most interesting of all the peaks near Rajaulī. It rises to a great height, and from the summit a wonderful view can be obtained of hill after hill, clothed with rich vegetation, rolling on in almost endless confusion as far as the eye can reach. There is a rough stone platform on the top with some shapeless boulders which are objects of worship;

a fair is held annually at the foot, and devotees toil up the steep ascent to pay their devotions at these rocks.

In the neighbourhood of Rajaulī are several mica mines, the largest of which is situated a short distance up among the hills at Singar, the name of which (Sringagiri) perpetuates the legend that it was the home of the *rishi* Sringa. Dubaur, 7 miles south-east of Rajaulī, is another centre of the mica-mining interest, but among the people it is better known on account of the legends which cling round it. It was once the residence of Durvāsa, and the full name is said to be Durvāsapura; but it is even more celebrated as the birthplace of the cowherd hero Lorik, whose life makes the whole neighbourhood the home of legend. He was married to a girl in the village of Bauri (others say Agauri near Rajaulī), 3 miles south-east of Rajaulī, where to this day there are shown a large hollowed stone in which he used to mix *bhāng* and a huge rock which he cleft in two with his sword. He is said to have ruled over the country with justice and to have turned the barren land round Rajaulī into a plain cultivated like a garden, so that birds, beasts and even insects could find no place in it. His exploits are famous all over Northern India and form the subject of a popular folk song of portentous length which the Ahīrs regularly recite.

Rāmsilā Hill.—*See* Gayā town.

Sherghāti.—Town in the head-quarters subdivision of the Gayā district, Bengal, situated 21 miles south of Gayā town on the right bank of the river Morhar in 24° 33′ N. and 84° 48′ E. Population (1901) 2,641. It formerly formed part of the district of Rāmgarh; and the surrounding country was notorious for crimes of violence, which led to a Special Joint-Magistrate being stationed here in 1814. Sherghāti continued to be the head-quarters of a subdivision till 1871, and its position on the Grand Trunk Road rendered it a place of some importance. It contained a small resident European population, and the town still contains the remains of some fine bungalows surrounded by large compounds with magnificent avenues of trees. The town has declined since the subdivision was broken up, and, the railway having taken the traffic which passed along the Grand Trunk Road, it has now become a typical "sleepy hollow." The cemetery contains a number of massive monuments dating back to an early period of the British occupation; and there is an interesting old fort, containing pillars of polished granite, which is said to have been built by the Kol Rājās. The Grand Trunk Road passes through the town and crosses the Morhar, which here bifurcates into two branches, by two large brick bridges.

Sītāmarhi.—A name given to a curious isolated boulder lying 1½ mile south of the Gayā-Nawāda road and six miles south-west of Hasuā in the Nawāda subdivision. In the boulder has been excavated a small chamber about 16 feet long by 11 feet wide, and tradition relates that it was in this cave that Sīta lived during her exile and gave birth to Lava. The interior has been chiselled to a smooth polish, which is equal to that of the Barābar caves, and contains several sculptures, including a statue said to represent Sīta and her two sons. The main figure is however that of a male, and it has been suggested that it may be a figure of Buddha with two attendants. The neighbourhood is also hallowed in Hindu mythology, as Lava and Kusa are said to have fought with Rām's army on the wide uplands near this boulder. About a mile to the east is a group of bare and rocky but picturesque hills, which are covered with ruins. On one of these, near the village of Rasūlpura, is the tomb of a local saint named Sheikh Muhammad. Judging from the style of the dome, the building dates from a very early period, and it no doubt occupies the site of some older Hindu shrine. A mile to the north-east of Sītāmarhi is the village of Bārat, where the poet and saint Vālmīki is said to have lived when Sīta was sent into exile. It was at his order that Viswākarmā, the architect of the gods, constructed the rock cave for her. At present the only object of interest at this place is an old mud fort standing on a high mound.

Tekāri Rāj.—A large estate belonging to a family of Bābhans, which rose into importance after the invasion of Nādir Shāh in 1739 and the dismemberment of the Mughal Government. Their earliest known ancestor was one Dhīr Singh, a petty landed proprietor of Utren, 4 miles south of Tekāri, who settled at Tekāri. His son, Sundar Singh, who was as unscrupulous as he was bold, soon found means to increase his estate in the anarchy and confusion which prevailed, and obtained possession of no less than 9 whole *parganas* and portions of several others. He was given the title of Rājā by the Emperor of Delhi as a reward for the support which he gave to Alī Vardi Khān in resisting the invasion of the Marāthās, and in the Sair-ul-Mutākharin he is referred to as the chief zamīndār of Mug (Magadha), who not only had large possessions in Gayā, but also held a great extent of territory at the foot of the hills and had connections with the semi-independent hill chieftains. He invited the Imperial Prince, later known as Shāh Alam, to invade Bihār, and was ready to join him with a large force, when he was treacherously assassinated by the captain of his guard (1758). He was succeeded by his nephew, Buniād Singh, who appears to have been a man of peace. He refused to side with the Emperor Shāh Alam, in whose counsels Kāmgār Khān, an old enemy of Sundār Singh, now played a prominent part. The Rājā's lands were ravaged, while he shut himself up in his fort at Tekāri; and as soon as he left it, he was captured by Kāmgār Khān and confined in the Emperor's camp. Soon after his release, he wrote to the English promising allegiance, but his letter fell into the hands of Kāsim Alī, who summoned him to Patna, and put him and his brothers to death in 1762. Shortly before this event, Buniād's wife gave birth to a son, named Mitrājit, and Kāsim Alī sent a party to kill the infant, but the mother having intelligence of their approach, concealed her child in a basket of dried cowdung, and sent him in charge of a poor old woman to Dalīl Singh, her husband's chief officer, who kept him in safety till after the battle of Buxar, and then made him over to the officer commanding the fort. Under the administration of Shitāb Rai, Mitrājit Singh was deprived of nearly all his possessions. He was subsequently restored to his estates and became a staunch friend to the British, assisted in quelling the Kolhān rebellion, and was honoured with the title of Mahārājā. He died in 1840, and the Rāj was divided between his two sons - the elder, Hit Narāyan, getting a 9 annas share, and the younger, Mod Narāyan, the remainder.

Five years later Hit Narāyan was made a Mahārājā; but, being a man of a religious turn of mind, he became an ascetic and left his vast property in the hands of his wife, Mahārānī Indrājit Kunr, who, with her husband's consent, adopted Mahārājā Rām Narāyan Krishna Singh as her son, and on his dying without male issue, left the property to his widow, Mahārānī Rājrūp Kunr. The latter appointed as her successor her daughter, Rādheswarī Kunr, who died in 1886, leaving a minor son, Gopāl Saran Narāyan Singh. The latter being only 3 years old, the 9 annas share of the Tekāri estate was brought under the management of the Court of Wards on his behalf, and remained under its charge till 1904. During this period, much was done for the development of the resources of the property. Prior to the assumption of the charge of the estate by the Court of Wards, eight-ninths of the villages were in the hands of *thīkādārs* or *mukararidārs* to whom large sums of *zarpeshgī* were due; and at its release in October 1904 more than half of the estate was held in direct possession, four-ninths of the property having been recovered at a cost aggregating Rs. 2,90,000 for refund of *zarpeshgī*. The means of irrigation have been steadily maintained and improved at a cost of over 6 lakhs, or over 4 per cent. of the rents received;

the estate has gone through a survey and settlement at a cost of nearly 3 lakhs; and in spite of these and other heavy calls on the assets of the estate, its income has increased by about one-fifth, viz., by Rs. 1,17,000. The total area of the estate in this district is 388$\frac{3}{4}$ square miles, but it also includes property in Muzaffarpur, Sāran and Champāran. In addition to the landed property, the estate has a considerable number of houses in Tekāri, Gayā, Patna and Bankipore, and also maintains temples at Brindāban, Ajodhyā, Patna and Tekāri. The rent-roll is about 7$\frac{1}{3}$ lakhs, but it fluctuates greatly from year to year, as 70 per cent. of the cultivation is held on the *bhāoli* system of cash rents; the *bhāoli* income has however progressively improved to the extent of 1$\frac{1}{4}$ lakh under the management of the Court of Wards. The total current demand of land revenue and cesses is a little over 2$\frac{1}{2}$ lakhs. The present proprietor, Gopāl Saran Narāyan Singh, was born in October 1883, and was married in 1902 to a daughter of Rājā Satrujīt Pratāp Sahi of Tamkohi, in the district of Gorakhpur.

The 7 annas share of the estate which, as already stated, was held by Mod Narāyan Singh, passed on his death to his two widows, who transferred the property in 1870 to a nephew of their late husband, Bābu Ran Bahādur Singh. The latter was granted the title of Rājā in 1888, but died before being invested with the *khilat*, and was succeeded by a granddaughter. On her death, six years later, the estate devolved on her daughter, Rājkumāri Bhubanesvar Kunr, who is still in possession of it, though being a minor, she is under the guardianship of her grandmother. The 7 annas share contains 715 villages, and comprises an area of 523 square miles; the rental is about 6 lakhs of rupees.

Tekāri town.—Town in the head-quarters subdivision situated on the left bank of the river Morhar 16 miles north-west of Gayā town in 24° 56′ N., and 84° 50′ E. The population fell from 11,532 in 1891 to 6,437 in 1901, owing to a furious outbreak of plague at the time of the census and the consequent general exodus of the inhabitants. The chief interest attaching to this town centres round the fort of the Rājās of Tekāri, an irregular pile of buildings, surrounded by a strong earthen rampart with bastions and a large moat.

Umgā.—A village in the south-east of the Aurangābād subdivision, situated 8 miles east of Deo and close to Madanpur. The village, which is also called Mungā, was originally the seat of the Deo Rāj; for it was here, as related in the article on the Deo Rāj, that its founder came to the rescue of the local ruling family. After making himself master of the hill fort, and subduing its rebellious subjects, he married the widow of the local chieftain, Bhairavendra; and his descendants remained here for 150 years before leaving the place for Deo. The chief object of interest at the present time is an ancient stone temple, picturesquely situated on the western slope of the hill and overlooking the country for many miles. The height of the temple is about 60 feet, and it is built entirely of square granite blocks without cement, while the columns supporting the roof are massive monoliths. A remarkable feature of the temple is the presence of some short Arabic inscriptions over the entrance doorway, on the faces of the pillars and on the jambs of the doorway, the latter being limited to the name of Allah. They were engraved by the Muhammadans, who once used the shrine as a mosque, and to their presence may be attributed its preservation from the destructive hands of Musalmān fanatics. They are now much defaced, some of the letters having been deliberately chiselled off by later Hindu devotees. Outside the temple a large slab of dark blue chlorite records the dedication of the temple by Bhairavendra, in 1439 A. D., to Jagannāth, his brother Balabhadra and his sister Subhadrā:—the shrine contained wooden images of these deities 30 years ago, which have since decayed and have not been replaced by new ones. This inscription states that the city of Umangā flourished on the top of a high mountain under the rule of 12 of his ancestors, who probably ruled over an extensive tract of country. Captain Kittoe states that an inscription found on a stone in the hills of Surgujā mentions a Rājā Lachhman Deva, who fell in battle against some hill chief he had gone to attack, and identifies him with Lachhman Pāl, the 3rd of the line. Near Fatehpur, some 45 miles to the east, there is an old temple of Siva, called Sadheshvara Mahādeo, with an ancient tank and ruins close by; and there is another shrine of the same name in Sandhail about 4 miles north-west of Umgā. There is every probability that these shrines were erected by the 6th of the line, Rājā Sandh Pāl. Besides this, the ancient temple of Konch 30 miles to the north-east, which closely resembles that at Umgā, is attributed to Bhairavendra. It would seem, therefore, that the dominion of these chiefs extended over a large area in Gayā and Hazāribāgh. The descendants of Janārdan, a pandit of the court of Bhairavendra, who is mentioned as the composer of the inscription, are still living in Purnādih, a hamlet of Umgā; and one of them, a Sanskrit scholar of some renown, is the chief pandit of the Rāj Kumār of Deo.

To the south of the temple there is a fine large tank with a flight of stone steps, on the north and south of which part of the old fort is still standing. Higher up the hill are the ruins of another temple in the same style as that already mentioned; and close by is a curious little altar with a huge boulder alongside of it under which goats and other animals are still sacrificed. Numerous other ruins of shrines are scattered over the hills, and legend relates that there were 52 temples there at one time. [*See* also an article by Captain Kittoe in J. A. S. B., Part II, Vol. XVI, 1847; Records Arch. Surv. Ind., Vol. XI, pp. 140-141; and The Umgā Hill Inscriptions, by Bābu Parameshwar Dayāl, J. A. S. B., Vol. II, No. 3, 1906.]

INDEX.

A.

B.

C.

D.

E.

F.

G.

H.

I.

J.

K.

R.

S.

Y.

B. S. Press—10304—522—12-10-1906—W. M. D'C.

9